The Memorykeepers: Gendered Knowledges, Empires, and Indonesian
American History

I0121080

Gendering the Trans-Pacific World

DIASPORA, EMPIRE, AND RACE

The titles published in this series are listed at *brill.com/gtpw*

The Memorykeepers:
Gendered Knowledges, Empires, and Indonesian American History

By

Dorothy B. Fujita-Rony

BRILL

LEIDEN | BOSTON

The author would like to thank the UCI Humanities Center for supporting publication of the book with a subvention grant for the paperback edition.

Originally published in hardback in 2020.

Cover illustration: H.L. Tobing, ca. 1964. Mark Family Collection. Photograph by Demak Tobing Mark.

The Library of Congress has cataloged the hardcover edition as follows:

Library of Congress Cataloging-in-Publication Data

Names: Fujita-Rony, Dorothy B., 1964- author.
Title: The memorykeepers : gendered knowledges, empires, and Indonesian American history / by Dorothy B. Fujita-Rony.
Other titles: Gendered knowledges, empires, and Indonesian American history
Description: Leiden ; Boston : Brill, [2021] | Series: Gendering the Trans-Pacific world: diaspora, empire, and race, 2352-7897 ; volume 4 | Includes bibliographical references and index.
Identifiers: LCCN 2020026816 (print) | LCCN 2020026817 (ebook) | ISBN 9789004431980 (hardback) | ISBN 9789004436237 (e-book)
Subjects: LCSH: Indonesian Americans—History. | Archives—Personal Archives—Indonesian Americans. | Women, Toba-Batak—Personal Narratives. | Tobing, H. L., 1911-1994.| Women, Toba-Batak—Autobiography.| Rony, Minar T., 1932- . | Toba-Batak (Indonesian people)—United States]—History. | Sumatra (Indonesia)]—Emigration and immigration]—History—20th century. | Asian diaspora.
Classification: LCC DS632.T62 F84 2021 (print) | LCC DS632.T62 (ebook) | DDC 305.48/899224620730922 [B]—dc23
LC record available at https://lccn.loc.gov/2020026816
LC ebook record available at https://lccn.loc.gov/2020026817

Typeface for the Latin, Greek, and Cyrillic scripts: "Brill". See and download: brill.com/brill-typeface.

ISSN 2352-7897
ISBN 978-90-04-46506-0 (paperback, 2022)
ISBN 978-90-04-43198-0 (hardback)
ISBN 978-90-04-43623-7 (e-book)

This book is printed on acid-free paper and produced in a sustainable manner.

This book is dedicated in loving memory to
R. Gerhard L. Tobing and H.L. Tobing

∵

Contents

Acknowledgments   XI
List of Figures and Maps   XIII
Note on Orthography and Names   XVII

Introduction
Daughter of a Daughter: The Labor of Memorykeeping   1
1   Questions   3
2   The 'Indonesian American' Context   8
3   'Return' and 'Belonging'   13

PART 1
Empire and Gender

1   **Empires**
Interimperialism, Migration, and the United States   19
1   Introduction   19
2   When Empires Came to You: The Toba Batak   21
3   Multilingualism and Interimperial Temporality   39
4   The United States Cold War   44
5   Conclusion   55

2   **Gendered Knowledges**
Patriarchies and the Politics of Belonging   59
1   Introduction   59
2   The Toba Batak Culture as Political Location   60
3   Colonial Domesticity   65
4   Converging Gender Hierarchies   72
5   Negotiation and Challenge   81
6   Conclusion   88

PART 2
Curating Time

3   Stories and Silences
    Telling the Past   91
    1   Introduction   91
    2   Searching for Archives   94
    3   What Is Said   99
    4   And What Is Not Said   107
    5   Two Pictures   111
    6   Conclusion   114

4   Artifacts and Memories
    Representing Meaning   116
    1   Introduction   116
    2   Knowledge as Legacy   117
    3   Memorykeeping as Response to Precarity   118
    4   The Labor of Artifacts   122
    5   Conclusion   140

PART 3
Memorykeeping

    Prologue to Part 3
    A Journey and a Path   145

5   Across Empires
    The Narrative of H.L. Tobing   151
    1   Raja Pontas   151
    2   The Old Times   152
    3   Family   153
    4   The *Adat*   155
    5   Christianity   157
    6   Tarutung   159
    7   Living in the Village   161
    8   Dutch Rule   163
    9   Elementary School   164
    10   Salatiga   167
    11   Early Marriage   169

12   Semarang   173
13   Magetan   175
14   Pearaja   177
15   Bengkalis   180
16   Japanese Occupation and World War II   182
17   Kisaran   187
18   Medan   189
19   Progress   190
20   Opportunities   191
21   United States   192
22   Homecoming   196

6 For Those Who Follow
The Autobiography of Minar T. Rony   198
1   Beginnings   198
2   Bengkalis   203
3   Siantar   207
4   Return to Bengkalis   208
5   Bukit Batu   212
6   Pearaja   215
7   Jakarta   222
8   Return to Siantar   226
9   Medan   229
10   Teacher and Guide   230
11   The United States   232

Conclusion
The Urgency of Time   244

Timeline   249
Glossary   251
Bibliography   257
Index   268

Acknowledgments

In the course of developing this book, I have incurred many debts. First, I want to thank H.L. Tobing and Minar T. Rony for making this book possible through their devoted memorykeeping and generous gift of family history. I also want to remember the family members who played a part in this history I have described, and whose memory we honor: R. Gerhard L. Tobing, R. Apoel P. Loembantobing, A. Kohar Rony, Demak Tobing Mark, and William R. Mark. I want to thank all the different branches of the family who feature in this history: Bonur Pardede Loembantobing; Elice Loembantobing Barry, Brittneyuli Marion Dameria Barry, and Elliot Matthew Tobing Barry; Rayendra L. Tobing, Hanna Carolina L. Tobing, and Jayden L. Tobing; Tota Melani Loembantobing and Alexandra Siahaan; Fatimah Tobing Rony, and Saenah Boch; Billy Mark, Shandon Mark, and Daniel Mark; Malcolm Mark, Eileen Mark, Duncan Alexander Mark, Meredith Tobing Mark, and Evan Crawford Mark; Bistok P.L. Tobing and Artauli R.M. Panggabean Tobing, and Natalia Tobing. I also thank Sahat Tobing, Donda Tobing, and Inang Uda Tao, as well as the extended Tobing and Simorangkir families for their help in this process. I want to give additional thanks to Bistok P.L. Tobing and Artauli R.M. Panggabean Tobing for their indispensable and wise research help as we traveled across the Pacific and the Atlantic.

I thank the Brill series editors of the Gender and the Transpacific series, Judy Wu and Catherine Choy, for their encouragement of this project and seeing it through all phases of development. In addition, I want to acknowledge Jason Prevost, Gerda Danielson Coe, Debbie de Wit, and Thalien Colenbrander at Brill Publishers for their guidance of my project, and Elizabeth Stone for her careful copy-editing. I thank the reviewers for this manuscript whose insights made it a better book. I further thank Peter Keppy for his help in our research on World War II. I also thank the staff at the Archiv- und Museumsstiftung der VEM, especially Julia Besten, Wolfgang Apelt, and Christoph Schwab. I thank Matthijs Holwerda, Marije Plomp, and the staff at Special Collections at Leiden University Libraries as well. At University of California, Irvine (UCI), I thank Long Bui, Isabela Quintana, Judy Wu, Claire J. Kim, Julia Lee, James Lee, Linda Vo, Thuy Vo Dang, Madelynn Dickerson, Jennifer Choy, Robert Escalante, Robert Moeller, Lynn Mally, Kai Evers, and Vicki Ruiz. In addition, I thank the Asian American Women Historians writing group for reading multiple drafts of different sections, especially Judy Wu, Valerie Matsumoto, Constance Chen, Jane Hong, Susie Woo, Isabela Quintana, and Kelly Fong. I am thankful too for the UCI School of Humanities grants which enabled me to travel to different archives in order to conduct research. Next, I want to thank Gregory Robinson, Teresa Bill, Gary Y. Okihiro, Franklin Odo, K. Scott Wong, Judy Yung, Madeline Hsu, Davianna McGregor, John Kuo Wei Tchen, Charles Lai, Dorothy Cordova, Fred Cordova, Anne Frank, Jack Herzig, Aiko Yoshinaga-Herzig, Michelle Caswell, Emily Porcincula Lawsin, Judy Patacsil, Joan May Cordova, and Terese Guinsatao Monberg for all the help they have given me over the years in helping me to understand the importance of archives and the role of history. I also would like to acknowledge Dr. N. Lavada Austin, Dr. Kristen Iverson, and Kathleen O'Connell for their help and wise counsel during these past few years. I thank Francesca Polletta and Edwin Amenta, and Jennifer and Luis Martinez as well. There are many others to be thanked and acknowledged too who have made this book such an important journey for us.

Finally, my mother Minar T. Rony would like to thank Sameha Kotb and Oemi Schmidgall-Tellings for their wonderful friendship over these past decades. I also would like to acknowledge my son Theodore Fujita-Rony for the gifts he has brought to our lives. Last but not least, my deepest thanks to my husband Thomas Y. Fujita-Rony, for his love and support over the decades, without whom this project would not have been possible.

Figures and Maps

Figures

1   "Batak Dorf" [Batak Village], Archiv- und Museumsstiftung der VEM (Archives and Museum Foundation of the UEM) referred to henceforth as AMS der VEM. Archives number: 203–140   25

2   "Gemeenschapsgebouw (sopo) van de Batak in de Silindoengvallei bij Taroetoeng," [Building structure (*sopo*) of the Batak in the Silindung Valley near Tarutung] Structure used to store rice, also a meeting place. Special Collections, Leiden University Libraries, Collection Royal Netherlands Institute of Southeast Asian and Caribbean Studies, referred to hence as KITLV, KITLV 101156, part of KITLV A703, ca. 1910   25

3   A view of Lake Toba from Balige in the present day. Photograph by author   26

4   "Raja Pontas," AMS der VEM. Archives number: 203–209   27

5   "Cornelia Frau Van Obaja" [Cornelia, Wife of Obaja (Raja Pontas)], AMS der VEM. Archives number: 203–509   28

6   "Foto Ephorus Dr. Nommensen" [Photo of Ephorus Dr. Nommensen], AMS der VEM. Archives number: 203–201   28

7   "Tauffest Singamangaraja" [Christening [Si] Singamangaraja], AMS der VEM. Archives number: 203–383   30

8   "Pearaja Kirche und Schulgebäude, Pearadja, Sumatra" [Pearaja Church and School Building, Pearaja, Sumatra], AMS der VEM. Archives number: 203–426   31

9   "[Area below] Pearaja," AMS der VEM. Archives number: 203–767   31

10 "Heidnische Opferfeste, Sumatra" [Pagan Sacrificial Rites, Sumatra]. Ritual performance in Batak culture banned by the missionaries that actually was part of a funerary rite. AMS der VEM. Archives number: 203–154   33

11 "Het dorp Pea Radja bij Silindoeng in de Bataklanden," [Pearaja Village in Silindung in the Batak Region] Special Collections, Leiden University Libraries, part of KITLV a38, KITLV 12140, ca. 1890   62

12 "Pastoren und Lehrerfrauen der Gemeinde Pearadja, Sumatra" [Pastors and Teachers' Wives in the Pearaja Local Community, Sumatra], AMS der VEM. Archives number: 203–436   67

13 "Krankenpflegerinnen Pearaja" [Pearaja Caregivers], AMS der VEM. Archives number: 203–98   67

14 Inscription from H.L. Tobing's [Hermina Simorangkir] 1928–1930 schoolbook, when she was a student in Salatiga, Tobing Family Collection   69

15   Minar T. Rony and Apoel Loembantobing in their cribs, c.1933. Their beds show
      the introduction of new kinds of spatialities in domestic arrangements. Tobing
      Family Collection   73

16   H.L. Tobing and Minar T. Rony, c.1934. Minar T. Rony Collection   74

17   The back of the previous photo, with the inscription in Minar T. Rony's adult
      handwriting, "With Mama." Minar T. Rony Collection   74

18   Minar T. Rony at 35 Cave Street in New Haven, 1959. Minar T. Rony
      Collection   86

19   Writing on back of previous image. The note in Batak reads, "This is how cold it
      is during the winter. [Signed] Minar. New Haven, Dec. 1959"   86

20   Minar T. Rony as a toddler, ca. 1933–1934. Tobing Family Collection   92

21   H.L. Tobing and Minar T. Rony, ca. 1935. Tobing Family Collection   92

22   Apoel Loembantobing and Minar T. Rony, ca. 1935. Tobing Family
      Collection   93

23   H.L. Tobing with Fatimah Tobing Rony and Dorothy Fujita-Rony, ca. 1965.
      This picture and the next seem to be taken on the same outing. Minar T. Rony
      Collection   96

24   Minar T. Rony with Fatimah Tobing Rony and Dorothy Fujita-Rony, ca. 1965.
      Minar T. Rony Collection   96

25   Gerhard L. Tobing in his medical office, ca. 1930. The cabinet is filled with
      medical supplies and equipment, and a Batak *ulos*, a woven Batak spiritual
      cloth, is hung on the wall by his desk. Tobing Family Collection   106

26   In this photograph, Gerhard L. Tobing stands alongside his children on a
      carousel, c.1935. Tobing Family Collection   107

27   "Vrouw en kinderen van Radja Pontas uit het dorp Pea Radja bij Silindoeng
      in de Bataklanden," [Wife and children of Raja Pontas from Pearaja Village in
      Silindung, Batak region] Special Collections, Leiden University Libraries, part
      of KITLV A38, KITLV 12145, ca. 1890   112

28   Minar T. Rony at Gerhard L. Tobing's grave. Photograph by author   115

29   H.L. Tobing's notes on Gerhard L. Tobing's life. Tobing Family Collection   121

30   Beer mugs collected by Minar T. Rony that represent memories of her father,
      Gerhard L. Tobing. Photograph by author   126

31   Betel nut set kept by Minar T. Rony. Photograph by author   127

32   Porcelain and other souvenirs collected by Minar T. Rony that remind her of
      childhood. Photograph by author   128

33   Crocheting was a skill passed down by the women in my family, and I continue
      to practice it today. This blanket was made by my grandmother, who taught me
      how to crochet when I was a little girl. Photograph by author   130

34   "Adatdansen door Toba-Batakkers, vermoedelijk in de Silindoengvallei bij
      Taroetoeng," [Ritual dance of the Toba Batak in Silindung Valley, Tarutung]

Special Collections, Leiden University Libraries, KITLV 101167, ca. 1910.
This photograph located in Special Collections, Leiden University Libraries,
appears to be in the same sequence as the next photograph, which is located in
the AMS der VEM   132

35   "Heidnisches Fest, Sumatra" [Pagan Festival, Sumatra], AMS der VEM. Archives
      number: 203–156. Ritual dance   133

36   Minar T. Rony and Bistok P.L. Tobing researching documents and
      newspapers at Special Collections, Leiden University Libraries.
      Photograph by author   134

37   Artauli R.M. Panggabean Tobing and Minar T. Rony reading documents at
      Special Collections, Leiden University Libraries. Photograph by author   134

38   Bistok P.L. Tobing examining Gerhard L. Tobing's school records at Special
      Collections, Leiden University Libraries. Photograph by author   135

39   Archivist Julia Besten showing Minar T. Rony the same image of her ancestors
      from Figure 27 at the Archiv- und Museumsstiftung der VEM in Wuppertal,
      Germany. Photograph by author   137

40   "Hinterblibenen—Sisingamangaraja" [Bereaved—Sisingamangaraja], AMS der
      VEM. Archives number: 203–423   138

41   Detail of Photograph 40, "Hinterblibenen—Sisingamangaraja" [Bereaved—
      Sisingamangaraja], AMS der VEM. Archives number: 203–423   138

42   The author learning weaving in Pearaja in 1985. Dorothy B. Fujita-Rony
      collection   145

43   "Simorangkir mission stasion" [Simorangkir Mission Station], AMS der VEM.
      Archives number: 203–583   154

44   Ulos in Minar T. Rony's personal collection. Ulos are given at ceremonies or on
      special occasions, and represent both spirituality and connection. Photograph
      by author   162

45   "[Area below] Pearaja", AMS der VEM. Archives number: 203–766   165

46   Gerhard L. Tobing, ca. 1930. Tobing Family Collection   170

47   Family photographs in the early years show the family engaged in leisure
      pursuits. Here, Apoel Loembantobing and Minar T. Rony are visiting Borobudur
      with their family, ca. 1935. Tobing Family Collection   175

48   H.L. Tobing, Minar T. Rony, and Apoel Loembantobing waving goodbye,
      ca. 1935. Minar T. Rony Collection   176

49   Demak Tobing Mark and Apoel Loembantobing in New Haven, shortly after
      Demak's arrival in the United States, 1960. Tobing Family Collection   192

50   H.L. Tobing at Minar T. Rony's home, ca. 1964. Mark Family Collection   194

51   Demak Tobing Mark and H.L. Tobing at same visit, ca. 1964. Mark Family
      Collection   194

52   The ancestral home in Pearaja, with the burial site of our ancestor Raja Pontas
      and the Huria Kristen Batak Protestan [HKBP, the Batak Christian Protestant
      Church] in the background. Photograph by author   196

53   Minar T. Rony, ca. 1935. Minar T. Rony Collection   198

54   Gerhard L. Tobing with Minar T. Rony and Apoel Loembantobing, ca. 1935.
      Minar T. Rony Collection   200

55   Minar T. Rony and Apoel Loembantobing, ca. 1935. Minar T. Rony
      Collection   201

56   "Schule in Pematang Siantar" [School in Pematang Siantar], AMS der VEM.
      Archives number: 203–483. School from the complex where Minar T. Rony
      taught in Siantar, 1952–1955   227

57   Apoel Loembantobing at 35 Cave Street, New Haven, ca. 1960. Minar T. Rony
      Collection   234

58   A. Kohar Rony, Minar T. Rony, and daughters, 1967. Minar T. Rony
      Collection   238

59   Fatimah Tobing Rony and Dorothy B. Fujita-Rony at American University,
      Washington, D.C., 1966. Minar T. Rony Collection   239

60   Minar T. Rony and daughters, ca. 1969. Minar T. Rony Collection   240

61   H.L. Tobing and granddaughters, ca. 1969. Minar T. Rony Collection   240

62   A. Kohar Rony in Annapolis, ca. 1977. Minar T. Rony Collection   242

Maps

1   Transpacific and transatlantic views from Los Angeles: Minar T. Rony's
      geographical knowledge   2

2   Indonesia, with the islands of Sumatra, Java, and Kalimantan (formerly Borneo)
      marked   20

3   Sumatra, featuring the sites of Medan, Pematang Siantar, and Tarutung   22

4   Java, showing Jakarta, Semarang, Salatiga, and Magetan   23

5   Lake Toba region with part of the Sumatra coast, with sites of Pematang Siantar
      (also known as Siantar), Bakara (also spelled Bakkara), Lintong Nihuta, and
      Tarutung marked   26

6   Medan and Pematang Siantar Region, featuring the locations of Pancur Batu,
      Medan, Tanjung Morawa, Tebing Tinggi, Pematang Siantar, and Kisaran   38

7   Kalimantan (formerly Borneo), with site of Amuntai noted   172

8   Island of Bengkalis (where the town of Bengkalis also is located), Bukit Batu
      (on Sumatra), and Singapore   180

9   The United States, showing Los Angeles, California; Washington, DC; Ithaca,
      New York; and New Haven, Connecticut   193

Note on Orthography and Names

The Indonesian language went through two stages of orthographic change in 1947 and 1972. In 1947, the following changes were implemented: oe to u, tj to c, dj to j, é to e, j to y, nj to ny, sj to sy, ch to kh. In 1972, new changes included the addition of f, v, z, q, and x.

For the sake of consistency, unless the older spelling still is in use, such as in some people's names, the new orthography will be utilized.

On a related matter, individuals in this book have different preferences regarding how to state their names, including their compound last names. I have tried to adhere to their choices as much as possible.

Introduction

Daughter of a Daughter: The Labor of Memorykeeping

In the summer of 2018, I accompanied my then eighty-five-year-old mother, Minar T. Rony (whom I will refer to as Rony), from Los Angeles first to her father's ancestral village of Pearaja in Sumatra, Indonesia, and then a month later to visit archives in Leiden, Netherlands and Wuppertal, Germany. Although she lives in Los Angeles, Rony has a global outlook based on her transpacific and transatlantic knowledges, as is clear from her narrative in Chapter 6. Like others in her generation who grew up in the then Dutch East Indies before World War II and remained in Indonesia during the Cold War, Rony had direct experience with multiple empires. In Rony's case, Rony encountered the Dutch, German, Japanese, and American empires firsthand. In this trip, we followed a journey reflecting the geographical knowledges demonstrated in Rony's autobiographical narrative. Not only did we visit our ancestral village in North Sumatra, but we also went to other sites that were pivotal to family history. For example, one site was Bakara (also spelled Bakkara) near Lake Toba, because Rony remembered being taken there by her mother in 1942 to visit the descendants of my paternal great grandmother's relative Raja Si Singamangaraja. We also journeyed to Lintong Nihuta, because Rony recalled evacuating to that site with her mother and her brother during the Japanese invasion of World War II, in order to find shelter with her great uncle. Later in the summer, from our home in Southern California, we travelled in the other direction across the Atlantic Ocean to Europe, to travel to archival sites in Leiden, Netherlands, and Wuppertal, Germany. In Leiden, we studied documents at the Special Collections at Leiden University, which was important not only as a holding for the colonial records from the early 20th century of the Toba Batak, Rony's ethnic group, but also because Leiden University was where her father, Gerhard L. Tobing, attended school for twenty months from 1937 to 1939 for advanced medical training. After Leiden, we conducted research at the Archiv- und Museumsstiftung der VEM (Archives and Museum Foundation of the UEM, referred to henceforth as AMS der VEM) in Wuppertal, Germany, as Ludwig Ingwer Nommensen and other German missionaries had travelled to Rony's ancestral region to convert the Toba Batak to Lutheranism in the late 19th century.[1]

---

1 VEM is the Vereinte Evangelische Mission, also known as the UEM (United Evangelical Mission) in English.

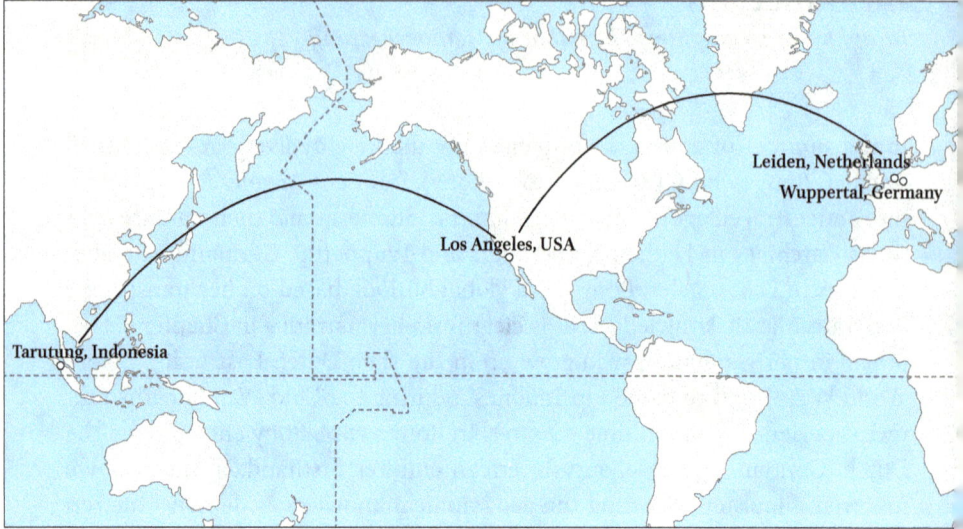

MAP 1   Transpacific and transatlantic views from Los Angeles: Minar T. Rony's
                    geographical knowledge

This transpacific looping to Indonesia, along with the further transatlantic
looping to Europe underscores an important premise of my project. Focusing
on H.L. Tobing's (my grandmother) and Rony's gendered labor as family memorykeepers through their personal narratives, this book explores how women's
memorykeeping forges integrative possibility, not only physically across islands, oceans, and continents, but also temporally, across decades, empires, and
generations. Despite the many ruptures they experienced, whether through
militarism or migration, both Tobing and Rony utilized memorykeeping as political space. Their labor demonstrates how gendered knowledges can produce
alternate cartographies of memory, especially within the diaspora, as well as
chart alternative mappings of belonging. As Tony Ballantyne and Antoinette
Burton argue, "European empires created a kind of 'cartographic imagination'
that was central in the emergence of how the domain of 'the global' was understood during the nineteenth and twentieth centuries."[2] Tobing's and Rony's
memories and archival collections reflect how colonials and postcolonials create a kind of "cartographic imagination" in response.[3]

---

2   Tony Ballantyne and Antoinette Burton, *Empires and the Reach of the Global: 1870–1845*
     (Cambridge, MA: Belknap Press, An Imprint of Harvard University Press, 2014), 2.
3   Daniel E. Bender and Jana K. Lipman, "Introduction: Through the Looking Glass: U.S. Empire
     through the Lens of U.S. History," in *Making the Empire Work: Labor & United States*

This project will focus on how Tobing and Rony organized personal archival collections, and what this tells us about gendered knowledges that cross multiple empires. Their labor was not only about traveling backwards in time to preserve the family's past, but also about connecting sites and knowledges across space—namely, Asia, the United States, and Europe—and consolidating these knowledges for future generations, in a gendered reclamation and reconciliation of these global processes. While their direct memories collectively span the second decade of the 20th century up to the present, they also carry memories from others in the past that reach back even further in time to the late 19th century. In addition, they experienced the impact of Dutch rule, the influence of German Lutheran missionaries, the militarism of the Japanese empire, and the economic and scholarly ambitions of Americans who travelled around the world to Sumatra in the mid-20th century. Furthermore, in the course of their lives, Tobing and Rony participated in different family, educational, and professional migrations that would take them to sites across Indonesia, and especially to places in Sumatra and Java. These routes expanded across the Pacific to the United States during the Cold War—Rony in 1958 and Tobing in 1964. While Rony decided to make the United States her permanent home, Tobing chose to return to the family village in 1979, which became her primary residence for the rest of her life. Through the different parts of their lives, Tobing and Rony collected family photographs, letters, and other artifacts documenting their expanded journeys and the family history.

1   Questions

I am interested in exploring how very local, familiar, and intimate explorations of the course of women's lives can open very large questions about interimperialism as well as how gendered knowledge is passed from one generation to the next.[4] Tobing and Rony both lived in a period in Indonesia where they experienced the impact of rule from multiple empires. This interimperiality was particularly apparent in the tumultuous events happening from the 1930s to the 1940s, when different imperial powers contested for control, even as

---

Imperialism, ed. Daniel E. Bender and Jana K. Lipman (New York: New York University Press, 2015), 5; Ballantyne and Burton, ibid.

4   Ann Laura Stoler, *Duress: Imperial Durabilities in Our Times* (Durham, NC: Duke University Press, 2016), 141; Ballantyne and Burton, *Empires and the Reach of the Global*, 21–23; Andrew Herod, *Labor Geographies: Workers and the Landscapes of Capitalism* (New York: The Guilford Press, 2001), 38; Augusto Espiritu, "Inter-Imperial Relations, the Pacific, and Asian American History," *Pacific Historical Review*, 83/2 (May 2014): 238–254.

Indonesia underwent decolonization and became an independent nation.[5] Empire was always 'here'—in their home spaces, as well as 'there'—overseas. As a result, Tobing and Rony developed sophisticated mappings of the location of 'empire.' Both of them grew up with the knowledge of the simultaneous and overlapping nature of empires, especially as various empires competed for raw materials, economic and political resources, and strategic advantage in the world around them.[6] As Tobing's and Rony's narratives amply demonstrate, empire had a profound impact on all aspects of life, including racial categorization, economic labor systems, transportation infrastructure, and family formation. Ideas about the Netherlands and Germany—and Japan as well in World War II—shaped even the most everyday places of their lives, such as home and school.

This project investigates how women's memorykeeping, as well as the details of their lives, give us another view to consider the impact of empire, especially in the intimate realms of women's private thoughts. I became interested in how the narratives of Tobing and Rony offer us a way of considering the multiple spaces that women inhabited, spaces which I had access to not just because of my position as a daughter and granddaughter, but also because I had deep knowledge about how these issues developed for them over multiple historical eras. In doing so, I want to signal my awareness that despite the sharp distinctions made between the position of women and men in Toba Batak culture, in fact there is great fluidity in how people approach gender, and there are multiple ways that people negotiate ideas about femininity and masculinity. If anything, my research on Toba Batak culture has underscored the social construction of a gendered binary, which distributes rights and privileges based on perceived gender identities. In this book, I examine what Tobing's and Rony's narratives might reveal to us not just as historical testimony in this regard, but also as a lens on knowledge production under the hierarchies of empire and gender.

In focusing on their memorykeeping, I am referring to the specific gendered nature of how Tobing and Rony made it an important part of their family labor

---

5 Jane Burbank and Frederick Cooper, *Empires in World History: Power and the Politics of Difference* (Princeton, NJ: Princeton University Press, 2010), 3.

6 Keith L. Camacho, for example, has documented how the Mariana Islands were under Spanish dominion at the turn of the 20th century, followed by control by the United States and Germany, and subsequently Japan as well. Keith L. Camacho, *Cultures of Commemoration: The Politics of War, Memory, and History in the Mariana Islands* (Honolulu: University of Hawai'i Press, 2011), 23. See also Frances Gouda and Julia Clancy-Smith, "Introduction," in *Domesticating the Empire: Race, Gender, and Family Life in French and Dutch Colonialism*, ed. Julia Clancy-Smith and Frances Gouda (Charlottesville: University Press of Virginia, 1988), 4–5.

to amass knowledge about the family, as seen through their narratives. Even as they navigated the major changes resulting from multiple regimes moving through their lives, Tobing and Rony collected stories and artifacts as part of the family collection. I have heard their stories and learned about their artifacts all my life, ever since I was a young child, and these issues profoundly have shaped me as an individual and as a scholar. I see their memorykeeping as a gendered space of autonomy that they created for themselves in the middle of their busy schedules, justified as being for the family, and therefore family labor. In part, this memorykeeping was a response to the constraints in which they found themselves as women, as well as a reaction to the impositions and disruptions of colonialism, war, changes in language and livelihood, and regular migration. As a strategy to address these issues, this memorykeeping built ties over time and space, processes especially important for communities who have suffered loss through migration and war.[7] Tobing and Rony were both motivated by the knowledge that the history needed to be documented or otherwise forever lost, a knowledge that obliged them to perform this labor for the family as well as for themselves. Hence, archiving and documenting family history became a priority, both to ensure that a rapidly disappearing way of life would be remembered, as well as to make it possible for future generations to know how the past was lived by family members.

By creating these personal archives, Tobing and Rony were developing repositories of memory in the private spaces of their homes, knowledges and interpretations that often were quite different from those in established institutional archives.[8] Michel-Rolph Trouillot argues that archival sites shape the creation of historical narratives, as collections are amassed in "an active act of production that prepares facts for historical intelligibility."[9] From that perspective then, how might personal archival collections that exist outside of institutions or even a singular national space give us a different perspective on these issues? And how are these issues gendered? How might the local and everyday function as a site of meaning, such as the reminiscences being told, the food that is prepared, or the jewelry being worn?[10] What are the affective

7   Khatharya Um, "Exiled Memory: History, Identity, and Remembering in Southeast Asia and Southeast Asian Diaspora," *Positions*, 20/3 (2012): 842–844, https://doi 10.1215/10679847-1593564.

8   Terry Cook, "Evidence, Memory, Identity, and Community: Four Shifting Archival Paradigms," *Archival Science*, 13/2 (2013): 104. DOI 10.1007/s10502-012-9180-7.

9   Michel-Rolph Trouillot, *Silencing the Past: Power and the Production of History* (Boston, MA: Beacon Press, 1995), 51–52.

10   Vernadette Vicuña Gonzalez, "Making Aloha: Lei and the Cultural Labor of Hospitality," in *Making the Empire Work: Labor & United States Imperialism*, ed. Daniel E. Bender and

meanings they might suggest, especially in the context of regular loss in an interimperial context?

Challenged by these kinds of question, in this book I explore how stories and artifacts can convey memory and take on specific function in terms of their intergenerational nature and intergenerational purpose. Although these practices might seem quotidian, my aim is to see how they can provide us with an important lens through which to interrogate culture. For both Tobing and Rony, memorykeeping was a critical political arena that could incorporate loss, difference, and return. Photographs and other artifacts could provide space for connection, even when family members could not physically be together, a key issue for families undergoing regular migration. This is one of the reasons why family reunions, as well pictures that depict travelers about to set off on a journey, form crucial subsets of Tobing's and Rony's photograph collections. This is work that Rony and I also did deliberately in the past few years, as we sought to bring photographs together that had been spread across different sites, in a physical effort of reconciliation.

Through these processes, photographs and other artifacts emerge as important because of the affective qualities by which we encounter and produce memories. Marianne Hirsch's discussion of postmemory, the profound connection that younger generations might feel to earlier events, so much so that they feel they have experienced them, is a way to explain the crucial emotional tie that binds younger generations in the diaspora to long ago stories of their families' homes.[11] Another kind of emotional relationship is the haunting that younger generations might feel about these previous histories, which as Avery Gordon writes "draws us affectively ... into the structure of feeling of a reality we come to experience ... as a transformative recognition."[12] Memorykeeping thus helps to provide temporal stability, by providing a space through which the past can be encountered, and its meanings recognized by younger generations.

Although this book features Tobing's and Rony's personal narratives as its archival base and conducts a granular analysis of their lives, it is not intended

      Jana K. Lipman (New York: New York University Press, 2015), 161–182; Micaela di Leonardo, "The Female World of Cards and Holidays: Women, Families, and the Work of Kinship," *Signs*, 12/3 (Spring 1987): 440–453; Valerie Matsumoto, *City Girls: The Nisei Social World in Los Angeles, 1920–1950* (Oxford: Oxford University Press, 2014), 227–228.

11   Marianne Hirsch, *The Generation of Postmemory: Writing and Visual Culture after the Holocaust*, Kindle ebook edn (New York: Columbia University Press, 2012), 4.

12   Avery F. Gordon, *Ghostly Matters: Haunting and the Sociological Imagination*, 2nd ed., Kindle ebook (Minneapolis: University of Minnesota Press, 2008), 7–8; Grace M. Cho, *Haunting the Korean Diaspora: Shame, Secrecy, and the Forgotten War*, Kindle ebook edn (Minneapolis: University of Minnesota Press, 2008), 4–5, 12.

just as a family memoir or biography as such. Instead, I am utilizing Tobing's and Rony's narratives to see what insights can be produced, especially from the stories not regularly told in public settings.[13] Feminist analysis insists on different ways of seeing and listening, even in the space of visible absences and silences. It teaches us to question how institutional structures are gendered, as well as what those structures might occlude, and the violence and omissions that might have happened. It thus draws our attention to alternate perspectives, and other ways of imagining possibility, to see what is not there and to hear what is not said.[14] Furthermore, it pushes us to think creatively about spaces, locations, and scales, in the process forging new sets of questions concerning power and resistance.[15] For example, if we do attend to different spaces of political location in intimate spaces, then familial frames emerge as critical spaces of interrogation and take on other kinds of political import, even as we need to always be aware of the narratives constructed about 'family.'[16]

Memorykeeping also is linked to temporality. Tied as it is to the family project, memorykeeping is not just for the memorykeeper herself, but for others too, not only in the present, but for those in the past and future as well. This project has shown me that memorykeeping requires a consciousness that stories and items from the past are being kept for the future, for generations who might not even exist yet, in places where the family has not even imagined that they might reside. I have come to realize that this concern for intergenerational culture is especially significant for the Toba Batak, whose lives are so defined by generation in relation to the originary ancestor, as well as in connection to each other. The importance of generation among the Toba Batak challenges how we typically think of Asian American temporality on very fundamental levels. Unlike conventional ways of marking time in US Ethnic Studies narratives based on arrival to the United States, Rony identifies as the sixteenth

---

13   Eric Tang, *Unsettled: Cambodian Refugees in the NYC Hyperghetto* (Philadelphia, PA: Temple University Press, 2015), 18, 21.

14   Aisha K. Finch, *Rethinking Slave Rebellion in Cuba: La Escalera and the Insurgencies of 1841–1844*, Kindle ebook edn (Chapel Hill: The University of North Carolina Press, 2015), 11–12.

15   Lan P. Duong, *Treacherous Subjects: Gender, Culture, and Trans-Vietnamese Feminism*, Kindle ebook edn (Philadelphia, PA: Temple University Press, 2012), 250; Catherine Ceniza Choy and Judy Tzu-Chun Wu, "Gendering the Trans-Pacific World," in *Gendering the Trans-Pacific World*, ed. Catherine Ceniza Choy and Judy Tzu-Chun Wu (Leiden: Brill, 2017), 4.

16   Erin Khue Ninh, *Ingratitude: The Debt-Bound Daughter in Asian American Literature* (New York: New York University Press, 2011), 5–6; Cathy J. Schlund-Vials, *War, Genocide, and Justice: Cambodian American Memory Work*, (Minneapolis: University of Minnesota Press, 2012), 131–138.

generation from her family's originary ancestor. And, in our family stories, relatives remember the entrance of the European colonizers and settlers to their region of the world. As I discuss in Chapter 1, these relatives did not travel to find empire. Instead, empire came to them. These imperial arrivals are one reason why family photographs and documents are located in our family's private collections on both sides of the Pacific, as well as across the Atlantic in the archives of Leiden University in the Netherlands and the AMS der VEM in Wuppertal, Germany.

2   The 'Indonesian American' Context

For many readers from outside my fields of Asian American Studies and US history, this might seem an unusual book because of the nature of its focus. As a result, let me say a few words about the disciplinary context of this book. Grounded in Asian American Studies, this book heeds the call by scholars to destabilize cultural narratives about the United States and question received truths, and to think comparatively across different fields and objects of study in order to illuminate new kinds of analyses.[17] Its production literally and conceptually spans two political moments: first, the emphasis in the early 1980s to reclaim community-based history through oral history and archival development, and secondly, the interrogation of women's history, knowledge production, and the transpacific US empire instigated by the disciplines of American Studies, Southeast Asian American Studies, and Critical Refugee Studies.[18]

My hope is that even though I have written this project from my location within the fields of Asian American Studies and US History, it will be of use

---

17   Yến Lê Espiritu, *Body Counts: The Vietnam War and Militarized Refuge(es)* (Berkeley: University of California Press, 2014), 11; Jodi Kim, *Ends of Empire: Asian American Critique and the Cold War*, Kindle ebook, (Minneapolis: University of Minnesota Press, 2010), "Introduction: Unsettling Hermenutics and Global Nonalignments," under section "The Cold War's Imperialist Gendered Racial Political Unconscious," 293 of 4138; Catherine Ceniza Choy, *Empire of Care: Nursing and Migration in Filipino American History*, Kindle ebook (Durham, NC: Duke University Press, 2003), under "Introduction: The Contours of a Filipino American History," 199–288 of 4679.

18   For community-based works from this period, see for example, Fred Cordova, *Filipinos, Forgotten Asian Americans: A Pictorial Essay, 1763–circa 1963* (Dubuque, IA: Kendall/Hunt, 1983); Arnold Genthe and John Kuo Wei Tchen, *Genthe's Photographs of San Francisco's Old Chinatown* (New York: Dover Publications, 1984); Michiko Tanaka and Akemi Kikumura, *Through Harsh Winters: The Life of a Japanese Immigrant Woman* (Novato, CA: Chandler & Sharp, 1981).

to practitioners in other disciplines, and will help generate more interest in Indonesian American history. In writing this project, I was keenly aware of the lack of documentation regarding Indonesian American history within the United States, especially for the Cold War era. Furthermore, as our research deepened, I also became more cognizant of the intervention that this book would make in our understanding of the 20th-century history of Toba Batak women in an interimperial context that included the United States. Finally, because of the book's focus on women's memorykeeping, I recognized that this book would help to provide greater insight into the gendered ways that women created repositories of memory in the diasporic context.

I wanted to note that while this book is primarily monolingual in English, in fact, its subject matter occupies complex multilingual terrain. Indeed, throughout the entire research process, I was well aware of the need to navigate through different languages and cultural sensibilities, especially those represented in Batak, Indonesian, Dutch, German, and American realms. Translation was a constant part of the environment in which I operated as a researcher, both linguistic and cultural. For example, as a scholar trained in American Studies, I am aware that my focus on English-language secondary sources frames my argument from a particular US perspective. I acknowledge that while this perspective might convey a different way of seeing, it has its limitations and represents other hierarchies as well. My hope is that this book can be seen as a contribution to a wider scholarly conversation, that will join others in developing these areas of study. In conducting this research with my family, who shared their knowledge of four primary languages in addition to their familiarity with additional languages as well, I was privileged to be the recipient of constant translation and explanation.

Given the fact that this is the first book written in Asian American Studies about Indonesian Americans, I want to include a brief discussion about the relationship of this book to the nascent field of Indonesian American history. I wrote this book because of its potential to demonstrate an alternative cartography of memory, a central point of this project. Throughout my life, the events of this family history have not been in accord with standard migration narratives of Asian Americans, Southeast Asian Americans, or even other Indonesian Americans. In fact, several years ago, when I tried to submit an essay about H.L. Tobing to an Asian American women's history anthology, I was turned away on the grounds that it 'just didn't fit.' In writing this book then, my hope is that it will contribute to the development of the field of Indonesian American history in its own right. Following Lisa Lowe's discussion of "the politics of our lack of knowledge," this book project thus attends to the forces which make it more difficult to read the histories of those of us who 'don't fit,' and to offer a model as well as an immediate archival resource to suggest how we can undertake these kinds of history.[19]

How might Indonesian American history offer us new ways of seeing as well as conceptualizing Asian American history? In many ways, Indonesian American history occupies a positionality that is betwixt and between, which contributes to its lack of conventional legibility. Despite Indonesia's enormous importance on the global stage as the fourth largest country in the world, Indonesian migration to the United States, the third largest country in the world, has always been relatively small compared to other Asian groups. Most Americans do not know that Indonesia is approximately the same size as the United States in terms of geographical length, or of its dominance in the Southeast Asian region with demographic numbers that are roughly equal to those of the Philippines, Vietnam, and Thailand combined.[20]

Within the United States, where questions of an ethnic group's political legitimacy are often structured around issues of numbers and representation, Indonesian Americans do not have the same kind of political clout, especially because our community is considered smaller as well as relatively recent in regard to arrival. In terms of domestic population numbers according to United States government statistics, Indonesian Americans number about 100,000 in the United States, rendering them about fifteenth in size in terms of Asian American groups.[21] Even in the smaller category 'Southeast Asian American,'

---

19   Lisa Lowe, *The Intimacies of Four Continents* (Durham, NC: Duke University Press, 2015), 39.

20   United Nations, World Population Prospects, vol. 1, 2017 Revision. Available at: https://population.un.org/wpp/Publications/Files/WPP2017_Volume-I_Comprehensive-Tables.pdf.

21   While Indonesian Americans numbered 63,000 in 2000 according to official statistics, their numbers increased by 50 percent to 95,000 in 2010, and 113,000 in 2015. The Los Angeles area is the largest site for the Indonesian American population by far with 14,000 community members, followed by Riverside with 7,000, and New York and Washington, DC each numbering 5,000 members. San Francisco and Seattle follow next with 3,000 each, then Houston, Atlanta, and Boston with 2,000, and Philadelphia with 1,000 community members. The median age of foreign-born Indonesian Americans, who comprise roughly three-quarters of the population, is 41, while the median age of US-born Indonesian Americans, who comprise the other quarter of the population, is 12. These statistics are revealing, because they help us to see that a third of the entire Indonesian American community is concentrated in Southern California in Los Angeles and Riverside, while almost 20 percent of the population is located in New York, Washington, DC, and Philadelphia, with the final two population centers in the south in the major cities of Houston and Atlanta. These official statistics though, tell only part of the story, in part because official statistics tend to capture only the stable sector of the population, and reveal less about the transient segments, like the many students who attend US colleges and other schools, or those Indonesians without papers who might not be documented. "Indonesians in the U.S. Fact Sheet," Pew Research Center, Social and

Indonesian Americans regularly fall out of the picture, as 'Southeast Asian American' in the United States often refers to those who originate in mainland Southeast Asian countries such as Vietnam, Laos, and Cambodia, due to the United States' long engagement in the Vietnam War. Southeast Asian Studies is another discipline where Indonesian American history is perceived as second-ary, as the main focus is on Southeast Asia itself. Indonesian American history thus may be perceived as a story of 'overseas Indonesians' who have migrated away from the 'homeland.'[22]

This lack of political recognition is compounded by our diversity in ethnic-ity and originating region, which also results in a varied range of languages, religions, and home cultures. This makes a difference in our ability to be 'seen' and recognized as 'Indonesian.' For example, there are sizeable numbers of Chinese Indonesian Americans in the United States, who might identify as 'Chinese American' not only because of the centrality of Chinese Americans to Asian American political representation, but also because of cultural and linguistic affinities and the circumstances of their migration, especially given the historical discrimination against Chinese communities in Indonesia.[23] Perhaps it is more accurate to characterize Indonesian American community formation through its varied strands of migration. My family's migration thus represents a particular strand, as both my parents migrated to the United States during the 1950s and were language teachers and foreign students. There also were maritime workers who jumped ship in the 1940s, 'Indos' of Indonesian and Dutch ancestry who moved to the United States during the US Cold War era through refugee legislation, Chinese Indonesians who fled the violence and economic turmoil of the mid- and late 20th century, and more recent immi-grants who won the ability to migrate through changes in US immigration law in the 1990s. Hence, as opposed to looking for a single form of migration to be representative of the whole, it is crucial to acknowledge the multiple forms

---

Demographic Trends. Available at: http://www.pewsocialtrends.org/fact-sheet/asian -americans-indonesians-in-the-u-s/ (accessed January 3, 2019).

22   Junyoung Verónica Kim, "Asia—Latin America as Method: The Global South Project and the Dislocation of the West," *Verge: Studies in Global Asia*, 3/2 (Fall 2017): 101–102, DOI: 10.5749/vergstudglobasia.3.2.0097; Khatharya Um, *From the Land of Shadows: War, Revolution, and the Making of the Cambodian Diaspora* (New York: New York University Press, 2015), 258; Viet Thanh Nguyen and Janet Hoskins, "Introduction: Transpacific Studies: Critical Perspectives on an Emerging Field," in Janet Hoskins and Viet Thanh Nguyen, *Transpacific Studies: Framing an Emerging Field*, Kindle ebook (Honolulu: University of Hawai'i Press, 2014), under Section "Toward a Transpacific Studies".

23   See, for example, Li-Young Lee's family's history in Indonesia, as discussed in Li-Young Lee, *Breaking the Alabaster Jar: Conversations with Li-Young Lee*, Kindle ebook, American Reader Series, No. 7 (Rochester, NY: BOA Editions, Ltd., 2006), and Li-Young Lee, *The Winged Seed: A Remembrance* (Rochester, NY: BOA Editions, Ltd., 2013).

of migration that contribute to the processes of Indonesian migration to the United States overall.

As a reflection of these phenomena, although I have used the phrase 'Indonesian American history' in the subtitle of this book to signal that I am discussing Indonesian migration to the United States, in fact the base of my inquiry is of two Toba Batak women who have a specific ethnic community formation and language. Their ethnic identity has great impact upon how they understand their lives in the context of the Indonesian diaspora, especially due to the sheer vastness of the Indonesian archipelago and the differences in ethnic experiences.[24] I register these issues because they are both fundamental to this project, as well as suggest the kinds of scholarship that still need to be undertaken. I recognize that the history I am writing here represents just one trajectory in the multifaceted formation of Indonesian America, part of a larger historical picture that remains to be more fully documented.

Indonesian migration, of course, is a global complex phenomenon that stretches back several centuries due to patterns of trade and its maritime economy. Certainly, especially as an archipelago, Indonesia has been a space for multiple kinds of migration whether by land or sea, or by forced or free means.[25] For example, in the late 19th century, Indonesians left as indentured contract laborers to places throughout the Pacific, including other parts of Southeast Asia and sites in the German Pacific empire. Indonesians migrated to Australia because of the late 19th-century sugar industry or because of the pearl-shell industry that recruited these workers up to the middle of the 20th century.[26] In addition to the search for work, education has been another important impetus for migration, as well as political persecution, such as in the case of those who became exiles because of the 1965–66 targeting of leftists.[27] Today, Indonesian overseas communities are spread out in different regions of the world, including nearby Australia as well as Singapore, Malaysia, and other

---

24   Antje Missbach, "Moral Comforts from Remaining in Exile: Snapshots from Conflict-Driven Indonesian Exiles," in *Routledge Handbook of Diaspora Studies*, ed. Robin Cohen and Carolin Fischer, PDF e-book (New York: Routledge, 2018), 197–198, https://doi .org/10.4324/9781315209050; J. Francisco Benitez and Laurie J. Sears, Chapter 6 "Passionate Attachments to Area Studies and Asian American Studies: Subjectivity and Diaspora in the Transpacific," in Hoskins and Nguyen, *Transpacific Studies*, under Section "Critical Melancholia and Race in the Transpacific".

25   Missbach, "Moral Comforts," 198; Julia Martínez and Adrian Vickers, "Indonesians Overseas: Deep Histories and the View from Below," *Indonesia and the Malay World*, 40/117 (July 2012): 112–116. DOI: 10.1080/13639811.2012.683667.

26   Martínez and Vickers, "Indonesians Overseas," 115–116.

27   Martínez and Vickers, "Indonesians Overseas," 111–112, 115.

parts of Southeast Asia; Kuwait, Saudi Arabia, and the United Arab Emirates in the Middle East; Denmark, Sweden, and Norway in Europe; Bangladesh in South Asia; and the United States and Canada in North America.[28] Thus, while the United States is a desired destination, it is only one of many places where Indonesians have migrated.[29] Indonesian American community formation thus must be seen in the context of these larger global dynamics, especially given the specific cultural, economic, and political dimensions that result from our relationship to the US nation.

3   'Return' and 'Belonging'

This book not only represents a physical journey in which I followed Tobing's and Rony's cartographies of memory, it also has been a temporal, transgenerational journey of thirty-five years. Over the decades, my relationship and responsibility to the project changed, especially after we lost my grandmother, Tobing, in 1994, and Rony became the senior person in our immediate extended family. I myself moved in generational status as well due to the passage of time, in the process experiencing a shift of perspective and responsibility regarding the labor that I had assumed.

In many ways, the travel that we have undertaken in the past few years is highly unusual. On one level, it speaks to our privilege and mobility as Americans with English-language skills, because the processes of tourism rest on complex factors such as class, nation, and migration.[30] But on another level too, it also becomes legible within the interimperial patterns of my family's history. I understand now that when my mother gave me a ticket to spend time with Tobing in the village in 1985, I was following a pattern of return under empire that already had been undertaken by Tobing and my grandfather, and then

---

28   Missbach, "Moral Comforts," 197, 200.

29   Junyoung Verónica Kim, "Asia—Latin America as Method," 102.

30   For further critique, see Ariel Heryanto, "Can There Be Southeast Asians in Southeast Asian Studies?," in *Knowing Southeast Asian Subjects*, ed. Laurie J. Sears (Seattle: University of Washington Press, in association with Singapore: NUS Press, 2007), 77–78; Martin F. Manalansan IV and Augusto F. Espiritu, "The Field: Dialogues, Visions, Tensions, and Aspirations," in *Filipino Studies: Palimpsests of Nation and Diaspora*, ed. Martin F. Manalansan IV and Augusto F. Espiritu (New York: New York University Press, 2016), 1–11; Denise Cruz, "Notes on Trans-Pacific Archives," in *Gendering the Trans-Pacific World*, ed. Catherine Ceniza Choy and Judy Tzu-Chun Wu (Leiden: Brill, 2017), 14; Vicente L. Rafael, "Southeast Asian Studies in the Age of Asian America," in *Southeast Asian Studies: Pacific Perspectives*, ed. Anthony Reid (Tempe: Monograph Series Press, Program for Southeast Asian Studies, Arizona State University, 2003), 262–263.

my mother and her siblings. I see too that my listening to the stories of Tobing in 1985 was not a break with the past, and not just some new application of academic techniques that I had learned as an undergraduate at Yale College, but a continuation of intergenerational women's memorykeeping. Thus, just as Tobing's meticulous saving of family documents was a strategic, deliberate intervention during the colonial and postcolonial period, my learning of her history too was in line with this same kind of preservation of family history. In 1985, I used a typewriter, while today we have computers and scanners to accomplish this labor. From a view over time, we can see how these different technologies and interventions form a continuum of response to change.

I also wanted to note that the primary reason that Tobing and Rony wanted to share their knowledge was to create a historical record for younger generations in the family as well as for others interested in their understanding of the past. In relating their experiences, they both were extremely concerned about other people's reactions, and they did not intend for their words to cause negative or painful feelings for anyone. They shared their stories because they recognized that this history would be an important resource, especially for younger generations like myself who lived in the diaspora, and who might never know what it was like to live within the Indonesian culture. In addition, both were extremely aware of the unique quality of their experiences, which were not common to other Toba Batak women or even Indonesian women from their cohort, especially because of the time period in which they migrated to the United States. Thus, Tobing and Rony were very careful in how they explained their memories of the past. They regularly emphasized to me the importance of learning from other elders and seeking additional resources about Toba Batak culture, especially given its complexity. In fact, Tobing and Rony collected materials about Toba Batak culture throughout their lives, and always sought to learn more about their heritage.

One of the things that this experience taught me was not to take the stories of our elders for granted as, in fact, time is not limitless. In my memories of growing up with my family in Washington, DC and Maryland, Rony was busy working full-time, running the family household, and regularly hosting additional relatives in our home for extended periods. She did not have the luxury of time, as I did as a new college graduate in Pearaja when I could listen to Tobing's stories for hours on end. Even so, in the months when Tobing did stay at our family home, Tobing and Rony talked often about the past, usually in the kitchen after dinner when the dishes were done, as that is when there was finally a chance to have some quiet time after a long day. Today, it is the turn of my mother and I to share stories regularly as we go about our everyday lives, one of the reasons why this project evolved so organically. As Rony nears her ninth decade, it also is my role to realize the urgency of preserving her history, and to recognize the valuable gendered and interimperial knowledges that her stories represent. My knowledge of family history, like Rony's emerged not only from my personal inclination to be interested in this history, but also because of our labor within the gendered spaces of home and family. On a basic level, this book materialized because as a daughter, I wanted to support my mother in this project of preserving family memory. Hence, the book became an intergenerational discovery of history as we retraced the formation of our gendered knowledges across the Pacific to Indonesia, and across the Atlantic to the Netherlands and Germany.

Reflecting its evolution and my disciplinary training, this book is divided into three parts. Part 1 focuses on what Tobing's and Rony's narratives can tell us about empire, gender, and knowledge-making. The first chapter utilizes my family's migration to explore the role of interimperialism and US empire through my family's example. Chapter 2 then documents and discusses the importance of gendered knowledges, to set the stage for my argument in later chapters that their memorykeeping emerged as a response to the role of patriarchal culture in an interimperial context. Next, Part 2 focuses on the processes of memorykeeping itself. Chapter 3 examines how gendered knowledges shape the storytelling process. The following chapter, Chapter 4, provides a close examination of the role of artifacts in Tobing's and Rony's memorykeeping. Part 3, finally, presents Tobing and Rony's personal narratives. I begin with a section prologue as to how this memorykeeping project evolved, and then move first to Chapter 5, Tobing's narrative, and then to Chapter 6, Rony's autobiography. Finally, to close the book, I end with my reflections on what this journey of reclamation has taught me, as the role of memorykeeper is generationally passed on to me.

From my perspective, perhaps the most profound knowledge that Tobing and Rony gave me through addressing their experiences is that you can be different and still belong. This is something that they knew through their own personal experiences as Toba Batak women confronting the ruptures caused by multiple empires and gender hierarchies. They both wanted me to 'return' and supported my passage and time in Pearaja over the decades, even though they saw my connection was more tenuous as an American granddaughter and daughter. I ascribe this, too, to their cosmopolitanism, and their knowledge of the function of empire and diaspora. They had a different global understanding of the world, and knew firsthand about imperial dominance and linguistic necessity, as they navigated Batak and Dutch cultures, the Japanese occupation during World War II, the rise of Indonesia as a new nation after the revolution, and the arrival of Americans to their part of the world. As can be seen from their discussions, they grew up expecting that one might live abroad for long periods, and even undergo permanent migration to another site. In their labor as memorykeepers, however, they passed on gendered knowledges developed over empires, integrating the different parts of the family experience over time and space. By insisting that the next generation also belonged to this history, they made space for me to continue their work, even though I was born on the other side of the world from their homeland. This book is a result of our inter-generational labor over most of the twentieth century and the early decades of the twenty-first century.

PART 1

Empire and Gender

∴

Empires

Interimperialism, Migration, and the United States

1   Introduction

In discussing her 1970s dissertation research on Dutch agribusiness in North
Sumatra, Ann Laura Stoler explains how her research was "shadowed by U.S.
empire" even though the links between the United States and Dutch agricultural enterprises in Indonesia were more difficult to see at the time. As she
reflects about these connections between the United States and Indonesia:

> The history that stretches between Route I-94 outside Detroit, where
> Uniroyal's eighty-foot-high tire (a former Ferris wheel for the 1965 New
> York World's Fair) now stands, and the intimate management of race that
> pervaded North Sumatra's rubber belt in 1917, when Goodyear (then the
> largest tire producer in the United States) began to acquire its holdings, is
> severed by historiography but held taut by imperial ligaments.[1]

Scholars such as Ann Laura Stoler have accomplished instrumental work in
enabling us to see the connections that span the United States and Indonesia,
reminding us of the vital importance of establishing new frames to better
see these historical phenomena. Following Stoler's lead, this chapter utilizes
my family's history to suggest how the United States was a player in the interimperial drama that took place in Sumatra in the 19th and especially the
20th century. My story thus begins at the inverse of the familiar US migration
narrative, so populated by the tales of migrants who came to the United States
to find their 'American Dream.' In the conventional narrative trajectory, what
was happening in the home country created the causal factors for migration
to the United States: war, natural disaster, and poor economic opportunity.
Rather, from my vantage point, the migration of family members to California
and Connecticut was precipitated by the Americans who traveled around the
world to Sumatra first, not the other way around. Hence, migration to the

---

1   Ann Laura Stoler, "Intimidations of Empire: Predicaments of the Tactile and the Unseen," in
    Haunted by Empire: Geographies of Intimacy in North American History, ed. Ann Laura Stoler,
    Kindle ebook (Durham, NC: Duke University Press, 2006), under "Preface".

© KONINKLIJKE BRILL NV, LEIDEN, 2021 | DOI:10.1163/9789004436237_003

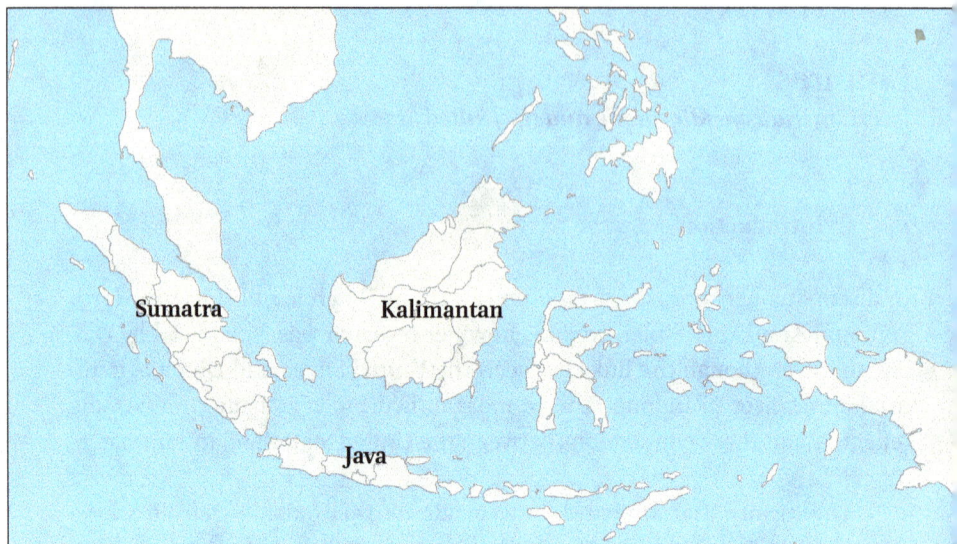

MAP 2   Indonesia, with the islands of Sumatra, Java, and Kalimantan (formerly Borneo)
           marked

United States was another part of a larger interimperial context which shaped my family's history throughout the 20th century.

As Tony Ballantyne and Antoinette Burton remind us, the imperial should be studied "both in the very real specificities of place but also from an angle of vision that captures the conditions of empire building and global connectedness."[2] To discuss these issues, I begin by establishing the interimperial circumstances that set the stage for Tobing's and Rony's narratives, particularly the Dutch, German, and Japanese empires. I then address the interimperial modalities that resulted, including migration, education, and especially multilingualism. The second half of the chapter focuses on the United States, arguing that my family's Cold War-era migration as knowledge workers emerged out of this interimperial framework. As such, their movement to the United States can be read as a result of developing US interests in Southeast Asia within the militarized context of the expanding Cold War.

---

2   Tony Ballantyne and Antoinette Burton, *Empires and the Reach of the Global: 1870–1845* (Cambridge, MA: Belknap Press, An Imprint of Harvard University Press, 2014), 21.

2   When Empires Came to You: The Toba Batak

For those who lived in sites with rich natural resources which also had populations targeted for religious conversion and political control, the reality of experiencing multiple empires was part of the everyday lived experience. One did not have to go far to find evidence of imperial domination. Rather, empires came to you: they appeared with regularity and were both omnipresent and simultaneous, an experience familiar to many sites in the Pacific. Thus, Indonesia was a target for multiple empires, especially because of its raw materials and strategic location. In the last decades of the 19th century and the first decades of the 20th century, imperial players scrambled for power, rendering nearly 85 percent of the world as territory that was formerly or presently under imperial control.[3] These regimes competed with one another, as well as built upon each other, utilizing components and strategies from concurrent and previous regimes.[4] As a result, the militarism and colonialism of multiple empires reshaped regions around the globe, not just spatially, but also in financial, administrative, economic, and political terms.

In its expansion of geographical possibility, empires conferred new modalities, ways of being that profoundly restructured the lives of those who came into their direct contact, as well as others whose lives were changed in their wake. Territorial reorganization and the imposition of new political systems had far-reaching implications for those who inhabited these spaces, drastically changing economic possibilities. People's relationship to the land, economic status, and gendered realities all were transformed through these processes. Labor and migration patterns changed in public and private spaces, consolidating differential possibilities for men and women. In short, the flow of empires imposed innovative ways of being.[5]

In these developments, empire both sent people searching for jobs in other areas of the emerging colonial export economy and also fundamentally changed people's associations with their home villages, necessitating altered relationships to the home region. H.L. Tobing, for example, was born in Arnhemia, now called Pancur Batu, because of her father's work on the railroad, which sent him away from his family in northern Sumatra. By the time she was seven, her family lived in Rampah on the east coast of Sumatra, resulting in

---

3   Ballantyne and Burton, *Empires and the Reach of the Global*, 1.
4   Jason Oliver Chang, "Four Centuries of Imperial Succession in the Comprador Pacific," *Pacific Historical Review*, 86/2 (May 2017), 194. DOI: http://dx.doi.org/10.1525/phr.2017.86.2.193.
5   Ballantyne and Burton, *Empires and the Reach of the Global*, 43–44, 50.

MAP 3   Sumatra, featuring the sites of Medan, Pematang Siantar, and Tarutung

her father's decision to send Tobing back as a young girl to the Toba Batak region to learn the home language and culture, an unusual choice as typically there was more educational investment in sons than daughters at that time.[6]

These changed spatialities reconfigured social relationships and necessitated other strategies of connection, which was why the process of sending family members back to the originating region was important. These issues are also manifested in Tobing's marriage at age eighteen to another Batak, a far distance away from the home region in northern Sumatra. At the time, Tobing was one of only two Batak young women at an elite *Meisjeskweekschool* (*MKS*) in Salatiga, Java, which was a school for educating native teachers for four years with the Dutch language as the medium of instruction.[7] Upon graduation from the teacher's training school, Tobing married Gerhard L. Tobing, my grandfather, and moved to Borneo (now Kalimantan) where Gerhard L. Tobing was posted as a doctor. Their case shows how the Dutch empire reshaped regional identities in an imperial context. The colonial educational system had

---

6   See 153, 159–160, this volume.

7   The full name that Tobing gave for the school was Meisjeskweekschool voor Inlandsche
     Onderwijzeressen.

MAP 4   Java, showing Jakarta, Semarang, Salatiga, and Magetan

transformed spatialities and migration possibilities, especially as many of the schools were located in Java. In the face of all of this social change, my grandparents' marriage outside of the home region was an indication of the importance for them of maintaining ethnic ties.[8]

The Dutch expansion of Sumatra's burgeoning export economy further inaugurated new patterns of work and migration, and in addition instituted an accompanying transportation infrastructure designed to maximize profits from Sumatra's export economy. In their narratives, both Tobing and Rony presented extremely detailed discussions of their transportation journeys to other destinations throughout their lives. Initially, having been raised decades later in the United States, I did not fully grasp the implication of the need for such specific memories of the different journeys. For example, around 1918, Tobing left her birth family to go to school back in the Batak region; she was taken there by her great uncle on a three-day journey by train, boat, and bus. Looking back now, I more fully understand how Tobing's discussion was a commentary on the massive innovation of these transportation systems. These modes of movement radically changed people's ability to migrate for work and education in an interimperial environment. For instance, Tobing had childhood memories of being taken by bicycle to school by her uncle, a Singer sewing machine salesman. As this story shows, not only was the modern machine of a bicycle altering people's sense of place within the lived environment, but also the arrival of US imports like sewing machines was a sign of how countries were being knitted together by the emerging early 20th-century global economy. The United States export economy was so far-reaching that Tobing's mother had a Singer sewing machine, even though she lived in a rural village in the northern Sumatra region. Not surprisingly, the word for sewing machine

---

8   See 169–170, this volume.

was "Singer," a sign of how US imports had become incorporated into local culture. Tobing reported that her mother had sewing lessons from the Singer Company, and "was really handy in everything." In fact, her mother was able to do embroidery on the sewing machine, which required considerable talent. This story demonstrates Tobing's awareness and pride in her mother's skill, as well as how women's household labor was being reshaped by the introduction of this industrial product.[9]

This was the global reality into which Tobing and Rony were born, even though the Toba Batak region in North Sumatra, where Rony's family originates, was considered relatively remote in the 19th century. Historically, the Dutch East Indies, as Indonesia was called during Dutch colonial times, was strategically important because of its role as a transit space between the Middle East and East Asia, which led to the development of different communities along coastal sites in Sumatra and Java.[10] However, unlike other places in Java where direct colonial rule was implemented much earlier, the Batak were of less interest to the Dutch colonizers, being located in the relative hinterland of northern areas of Sumatra. In the 19th century, however, successive incursions by different forces introduced massive change, including the Padri conflict which divided the southern Mandailang and Angkola from other Bataks in the region.[11]

The arrival of German missionaries and the Rhenish Mission in the late 19th century also brought major changes to the region in terms of spiritual conversion and education. Conversion came at great social cost to those Toba Batak who chose to accept Christianity though, because the converted would no longer be able to fulfill their *adat* [the customary law of the Toba Batak], or ritual obligations in the Toba Batak community in the same way—something which would have long-lasting consequences and effectively excommunicate them from their communities. Rajas who ruled the area decided to expel the converts to avoid the wrath of the ancestors. Nevertheless, my maternal great-great-grandfather Raja Pontas Lumbantobing became one of the converts of Nommensen, a leading German missionary, as he saw Christianity as an important route to modernity in a time of rapid change and European colonization. Raja Pontas even leased him some land for German mission work.[12]

---

9   See 160–161, this volume. Quote is on 166.
10   Julia Byl, *Antiphonal Histories: Resonant Pasts in the Toba Batak Musical Present* (Middletown, CT: Wesleyan University Press, 2014), 6.
11   Sita T. van Bemmelen, *Christianity, Colonization, and Gender Relations in North Sumatra: A Patrilineal Society in Flux* (Leiden: Koninklijke Brill NV, 2017), 11, 191.
12   van Bemmelen, *Christianity, Colonization*, 201–207, 210; see 151, this volume. Lumban Tobing is a compound surname, and also may be spelled as one word—Lumbantobing—depending on the context. In the old orthography, Lumban might be spelled Loemban.

FIGURE 1   "Batak Dorf" [Batak Village]
ARCHIV- UND MUSEUMSSTIFTUNG DER VEM (ARCHIVES AND MUSEUM
FOUNDATION OF THE UEM) REFERRED TO HENCEFORTH AS AMS DER
VEM. ARCHIVE NUMBER: 203–140

FIGURE 2   "Gemeenschapsgebouw (sopo) van de Batak in de Silindoengvallei bij
Taroetoeng," [Building structure (*sopo*) of the Batak in the Silindung Valley
near Tarutung] Structure used to store rice, also a meeting place
SPECIAL COLLECTIONS, LEIDEN UNIVERSITY LIBRARIES, COLLECTION
ROYAL NETHERLANDS INSTITUTE OF SOUTHEAST ASIAN AND
CARIBBEAN STUDIES, REFERRED TO HENCE AS KITLV, KITLV 101156,
CA. 1910

FIGURE 3   A view of Lake Toba from Balige in the present day
PHOTOGRAPH BY AUTHOR

MAP 5   Lake Toba region with part of the Sumatra coast, with sites of Pematang Siantar
(also known as Siantar), Bakara (also spelled Bakkara), Lintong Nihuta, and Tarutung marked

FIGURE 4   "Raja Pontas"
AMS DER VEM. ARCHIVE NUMBER: 203–209

During this same period, the Dutch were also in the process of consolidating their military, political, and economic power over the region, establishing control through the *Residentie van Tapanuli*—the Residency of Tapanuli. But not everyone acceded to the Dutch imperial regime. One of my paternal great-grandmother's ancestors, Si Singamangaraja XII [The Singamangaraja XII], famously led a resistance movement against the Dutch in 1878, commanding a large force of an estimated 1,000–2,000 men. He also led further attack in 1883. The Dutch continued to pursue Si Singamangaraja and his forces, eventually suppressing this Batak militarism.[13] Stories of resistance were kept alive within the community, however. My mother, Minar T. Rony recalled a great aunt whom she knew when she was a small child, Ompung Boru [Grandmother] Situmorang who was Si Singamangaraja's daughter-in-law. Rony explained:

---

13   Cunningham, *The Postwar Migration of the Toba-Bataks*, 8; van Bemmelen, *Christianity, Colonization*, 210–211, 215–216.

FIGURE 5
"Cornelia Frau Van Obaja"
[Cornelia, Wife of Obaja
(Raja Pontas)]
AMS DER VEM. ARCHIVE
NUMBER: 203–509

FIGURE 6
"Foto Ephorus Dr. Nommensen"
[Photo of Ephorus
Dr. Nommensen]
AMS DER VEM. ARCHIVE
NUMBER: 203–201

She lived next door in the *rumah ganjang* or long house when I was growing up. The long house was given by Raja Pontas when Si Singamangaraja
was taken in by the Dutch authorities in Tangsi Tarutung, and his family
kept under house arrest in Pearaja.[14]

This relative was married to Si Singamangaraja's eldest son, who died at the
hands of the Dutch. As Rony related in her autobiographical narrative,

> This *ompung* would tell stories about how Raja Si Singamangaraja [The
> King Singamangaraja] was trying to escape from the Dutch with his fam-
> ily. They were trying to avoid capture by the Dutch. So they hid in the
> woods, moving from place to place. Naturally, they had to find food in the
> forest, or rely on food from whomever was living near the forest. Because
> Raja Si Singamangaraja is the leader, other people are always ready to
> help and give whatever was available.[15]

In this way, Rony heard stories about the period before direct colonial rule as
well as Toba Batak resistance to the Dutch—stories which she remembered
throughout her life.

After its armed subjugation of the Toba Batak region, the Dutch colonial
government reorganized the area spatially to its own benefit, with soldiers stationed in Sipoholon and new roads built to facilitate the movement of troops.
The area around Silindung became a sub-district, and Tarutung emerged as
the administrative center. Pearaja, Gerhard L. Tobing's ancestral village, also
became an important focus for missionary activity. Hence, the area was transformed through militarism, especially with the new kinds of surveillance and
enforcement available through these processes. On a fundamental level, having roads that went to and through the area meant that military reinforcements
could be called upon very easily in case there was any unrest. Furthermore, it
also meant that the economy of the area was now more open to outsiders.[16]

Despite the imposition of direct control, Dutch rulers allowed German missionaries to operate among the Toba Batak, one of the first ways that Tobing
and Rony were exposed to an interimperial context in their daily lives. As a
result, the German mission dominated the first stages of colonial change for
the Toba Batak under Dutch rule. In addition to the transformations wrought
by Dutch colonization, the German religious mission also altered both the spatiality and temporality of everyday life in the village. The mission physically

---

14   See 199, this volume.
15   Ibid.
16   van Bemmelen, *Christianity, Colonization*, 211, 214, 215, 220.

FIGURE 7   "Tauffest Singamangaraja" [Christening [Si] Singamangaraja]
AMS DER VEM. ARCHIVE NUMBER: 203–383

oriented the community to the church in terms of local geography, as well as reshaped the organization of time for the work week, as Sunday became a day for church and no longer was reserved for the community marketplace.[17] Tobing remembered a pastor, Tuan [Mister] Marks, who kept close watch over the congregation and enforced the temporal rhythms of the work week which had been imposed:

> In Tarutung, if you don't go to church, one of the German missionaries, the pastor Tuan O. Marks went out to see what you are doing. If you dry rice, the pastor would tell you, "You don't do that on Sunday. Instead of the blessings from God, if you do this, you get punishment." And if he would see people gambling, playing cards on a Sunday behind a bamboo stool or wherever, he would chase them! And they were afraid of him, you see. So he would just go around and make sure that everybody did their duty, i.e. go to church. That was Tuan Marks.[18]

---

17   van Bemmelen, *Christianity, Colonization*, 209, 228, 252, 292–293, 320, 326, 512–513.
18   See 157, this volume.

FIGURE 8   "Pearaja Kirche und Schulgebäude, Pearadja, Sumatra" [Pearaja Church and School Building, Pearaja, Sumatra]
AMS DER VEM. ARCHIVE NUMBER: 203–426

FIGURE 9   "[Area below] Pearaja"
AMS DER VEM. ARCHIVE NUMBER: 203–767

As Tobing was born in 1911 and had been sent back to the region for education, she directly witnessed how the 'old ways' of Batak culture were targeted by mission workers as being antithetical to Christian ethics. In 1985, when I documented Tobing's stories, Tobing reported about the impact of colonial change at considerable length, including the banning of *gondang* [spiritual Batak music with drumming for the gods] by the missionaries. She recalled how one man disappeared for some days. She explained:

> They gave *gondang* for a week to drive away the bad spirits, to make him conscious again. But I heard this family who did it was banned by the church until they confessed their sins because they believed in the spirits.[19]

Tobing remembered that the German missionaries tried to get rid of "all kinds of dances or *tortor* [a type of dance] or music because they were afraid that we would go back to the old traditions and believe again in the spirits."[20] Tobing's comments underscore how traditional Batak culture posed a threat to the German mission, resulting in the case that she referred to, of a family's temporary excommunication from the religious congregation.

The German-run schools worked directly with the Dutch colonial system, thus demonstrating the interimperial connections between the Dutch and German empires. In 1910, the Batak Mission changed its Sigompulon primary school into a five-year Christian primary educational model funded through government subsidies. In 1914, the school's focus transformed once more into a *Hollands-Inlandsche School* (*HIS*) with a seven-year curriculum for natives, comparable to the *Europeesche Lagere School* (*ELS*) [European elementary school during the colonial period]. In 1921, the Sigompulon *HIS* also offered a new girls' dormitory, which is where Tobing lived as a young student.[21] This was an important shift, as this dormitory offered a sanctioned space where families could send their daughters for their studies, and where both families and colonial authorities were assured that the young women would be monitored with great scrutiny. Due to the extensive time spent in the dormitory, young female students also could be further inculcated with Lutheran morality. Tobing remembered a Germany missionary sister in 1922, Zuster [Sister] Frieda Lau. She recalled:

---

19   See 158, this volume.

20   Ibid.

21   Jan S. Aritonang, *Mission Schools in Batakland (Indonesia), 1861–1940*, trans. Robert R. Boehlke (Leiden: E.J. Brill, 1994), 288; see 166, this volume.

FIGURE 10   "Heidnische Opferfeste, Sumatra" [Pagan Sacrificial
Rites, Sumatra], according to the title of the photograph.
Ritual performance in Batak culture banned by the
missionaries that actually was part of a funeral ritual.
AMS DER VEM. ARCHIVE NUMBER: 203–154

She drilled us to become Christians, to do the Good Work. If we did
something wrong, or if someone lied, or someone didn't do her job, she
wouldn't talk to this girl until this girl came asking for forgiveness.[22]

Thus, the school imposed significant regulation and surveillance upon its
female students.

Gerhard L. Tobing also attended the school at Sigompulon, although at an
earlier time than his future wife, H.L. Tobing. But as a male from an elite social
class, Gerhard L. Tobing had many more options regarding his educational path
both in terms of profession and choice of school. As H.L. Tobing remembered,
her husband Gerhard L. Tobing attended the Hollandsche Bataksche School
(HBS) in Sigompulon, and then traveled to Jakarta to go to the *Europeesche
Lagere School* so that he would be eligible for the ten-year *School tot Opleiding
van Inlandsche Artsen* (STOVIA) [School for the Education of Native Doctors].
Rony recalled that her father told her that he was one of only eight out of a
class of forty students who passed exams to graduate from the STOVIA in 1928.
Eventually, in 1937, Gerhard L. Tobing would make the long ocean voyage to
study at Leiden University, considered one of the pinnacles of the educational
system for Dutch colonial students from around the world.[23]

---

22   See 166, this volume.
23   See 170, 177–178, this volume.

By the time Gerhard L. Tobing was actively building his professional career, yet another imperial regime entered the region: Japan. Although relatively brief compared to the Dutch and the German eras, the Japanese regime brought war and a dramatic restructuring of the accustomed interimperial context. Rony related the changes in political hierarchies as a result of militarism: "When World War II broke out, the Germans were interned by the Dutch. Later on, when the Japanese came, all the Dutch were taken away. The Japanese came halfway through the school year." Tobing recalled that the Japanese occupying force appeared on bicycles, and remarked about their reception, "The Indonesians didn't fight too much against the Japanese because we thought the Japanese would help us get rid of the Dutch."[24] Tobing evacuated to Lintong Nihuta with her daughter Rony and son Apoel for a month, and later moved to Bengkalis to run an agricultural enterprise. In part, she migrated to protect her son Apoel, especially as Apoel was tall for his age and Tobing was worried that he would be conscripted. Tobing recalled the tumultuous and violent times, "But it was very bad at that time. Many young boys were taken away to become Japanese soldiers, the *hei-ho*s."[25] In fact, Tobing's younger brother, Jan Henneri Hamonangan, was forcibly conscripted when he was about twenty years old, and was made a military worker against his will. Tobing remembered how "he became a *hei-ho*, a soldier of the Japanese. Every young man was just taken away, you know."[26] As underscored by this terrible story, violence and family separation became common during wartime, as well as considerable, tragic loss. In this case, young men in the community disappeared due to war.

As a schoolgirl, Rony experienced education under Japanese occupation, as she was attending school in Bengkalis. Rony related memories of how the Japanese empire restructured the school curriculum, as well as the temporality and spatiality of the educational experience, including the 7:00 AM morning ritual of expressing allegiance to Japan: "We all gathered there to sing the Japanese anthem, greet and bow towards *Tenno Heika*, the Emperor of Japan, towards the rising sun."[27] More than seven decades later, Rony still remembered how everyone was required to exercise, and even could recall the accompanying music to their physical routine. As part of this mandated orientation to imperial culture, Rony joined her classmates in learning Japanese songs and dances to entertain the soldiers, and even played the grandmother,

---

24   See 208, 182, this volume.

25   See 182–183, this volume.

26   See 154–155, this volume; Kaori Maekawa, "The *Heiho* during the Japanese Occupation of Indonesia," in *Asian Labor in the Wartime Japanese Empire: Unknown Histories*, ed. Paul K. Kratoska, Kindle ebook (London: Routledge, 2015), 188.

27   See 209, this volume.

Obasan, in the classic Japanese folk tale of the *Peach Boy* (*Momotaro-san*) in a regional competition designed to showcase the children's learning of Japanese culture.[28]

Jason Oliver Chang suggests that we consider the ways different imperial regimes built upon each other as a kind of architecture, which is a useful way to reflect on how those in Tobing's and Rony's generational cohorts negotiated interimperialism through the presence of the Dutch, German, and Japanese empires.[29] Even in relatively rural areas in the Toba Batak region, interimperialism was a constant, everyday presence, manifested in the curriculum that children learned in schools, or the kinds of religious worship in which they engaged in church, or the absence of people in the village who had left to find work in the burgeoning export economy, or—as in the tragic case of Tobing's younger brother—were taken away never to be seen again. These patterns were both instituted and normalized over different regimes.

It is within this interimperial context that my family experienced the fourth empire to have direct impact on their lives, that of the United States, which comprises most of the remainder of this chapter. Counter to standard US migration narratives which focus on how different factors propelled people to the United States, I argue that we need to pull back the scope of our view to see how the United States historically entered and participated within a pre-existing interimperial framework. In these processes, Sumatra became an important target for would-be colonizers alongside Java, especially because of the wealth of its exports and its location on strategic sea routes. Known for its spices, incense, and oil, the island of Sumatra was a major producer of tin and especially rubber, attracting American entrepreneurs and explorers in tandem with other imperial representatives seeking their fortunes in Indonesia. In 1686, for example, Elihu Yale, an East India Company merchant and later benefactor of Yale University, had a fort built at Bengkulu in 1686, a stark reminder of how slavery, capitalism, empire, and militarism forged the path of these early imperialists.[30] More than a century later, American interests continued because of spices. The pepper trade to Sumatra from Salem and Boston thrived from 1795 to 1831 and led to the first armed intervention that the United States made in Asia at a pepper port called Kuala Batu in Sumatra. Here, Sumatrans boarded the ship *Friendship*, killing three and wounding three others, and

---

28   Ibid.
29   Chang, "Four Centuries of Imperial Succession," 194–195.
30   James W. Gould, *Americans in Sumatra* (Leiden: Martinus Nijhoff, 1961), 2.

absconded with more than $40,000 worth of goods.[31] In response, a military force of 282 US soldiers went ashore on February 6, 1832 to retaliate, with fatalities estimated at between 60 and 150.[32] Even in areas considered relatively remote, such as the Toba Batak region, American missionaries arrived in the early 19th century. For example, Samuel Munson and Henry Lyman were two American Baptist ministers from New England who ventured to northern Sumatra to proselytize among the Toba Batak in 1833. The documentation of their travels through their memoirs provides a glimpse of the interimperial environment they encountered. At one point in their memoirs, they recorded a "Babelic scene" during their ship's journey in which ninety people spoke twelve languages, and noted "American, Indian, and Dutch passengers, besides soldiers, European [sic], native [sic], Bengalees and Malays" on board.[33] What this excerpt reveals is the kind of fluid patterns of movement afforded in this global economy, suggesting the many empires who were interested in the economic and political possibilities of Indonesia. Thus, American intervention in Indonesia occurred beside the incursions of other empires, even as US involvement would continue and expand over the ensuing centuries.

As opposed to sites such as Hawai'i, Guam, and the Philippines, in which the United States had large-scale and dominant colonial activity, these early traces of activity help indicate the path for what would come in terms of US interests in Indonesia during the Cold War era. Rather than being an aberration, if we begin to plot these various events in an expanded historical timeline, US interests in Indonesia emerge more clearly, suggesting a different way of analyzing my family's eventual migration during the Cold War. Indeed, US focus on the region became more pronounced after it secured control of possessions in the Pacific at the beginning of the 20th century. The United States increasingly jockeyed for power in the Pacific, emerging as a significant contender by the end of World War I not solely because of its political and military ambitions to control the region, but also because of economic and cultural rationales as well. Companies like General Motors and Sun-Maid Raisins all had stakes in the then Dutch East Indies.[34]

---

31   David F. Long, "'Martial Thunder': The First Official American Armed Intervention in Asia," *Pacific Historical Review*, 42/2 (Jan 1, 1973): 143–144, 147–148.

32   Long, "'Martial Thunder'", 152.

33   Samuel Munson, William Thompson, and Henry Lyman. *Memoirs of the Rev. Samuel Munson, and the Rev. Henry Lyman: Late Missionaries to the Indian Archipelago, with the Journal of their Exploring Tour* (New York: D. Appleton & Co., 1839), electronic reproduction. [S.l.]: HathiTrust Digital Library, 2011, 88.

34   Anne L. Foster, *Projections of Power: The United States and Europe in Colonial Southeast Asia, 1919–1941* (Durham, NC: Duke University Press, 2010), 1, 4, 90, 93. See also

Due to its expansionism, the US empire's presence would become more manifest as the 20th century continued. Although the impact of US interests in Indonesia on my family's history might seem sporadic, it is important to see how these historical connections played out over time, so that the eventual migration of family members to the United States during the Cold War era became a logical outcome of this interimperial environment. Read in this way, it is easier to discern how interimperial investment in Sumatra forms the impetus for a significant part of my family's migration history over a few generations, in which our migration to the United States became an eventual chapter. For example, Tobing's father was one of the first in the family to leave the home region in the early 20th century to look for work on the east coast of Sumatra, where the Dutch had invested in plantation agriculture. This region of Sumatra was a major site of capitalist development by the Dutch and other empires, especially for rubber and palm oil. As Tobing observed in 1985, "When the Dutch were in Indonesia, they had the plantations. Their wealth originally came from here, the east coast of Sumatra."[35] Reflecting the need to move exports and people from the interior to the coast, the plantations contracted with the railroad company, the Deli Maatschappij, to transport goods and people to and from the plantations. As a result, Tobing's father found a job working at a station on the Deli Maatschappij line, a railway located near present-day Medan, which facilitated the movement of exports out of Indonesia's coast. His employment indicates the rapid growth of the railroad lines and other transportation infrastructure required for economic developments in the area. In tandem with investments from other countries, US interests in Indonesia grew exponentially throughout the 20th century. In the field of oil, for instance, US investments ballooned from US$500,000 in 1914 to US$357,000,000 in 1959. Rubber was another valued export. In the 1920s, the United States imported roughly 45 percent of Sumatra's east coast rubber exports. In fact, US investments in rubber grew from US$400,000 in 1909 to US$44,000,000 in 1959, a reflection of the demand for rubber with the growth of the US automobile industry.[36]

Frances Gouda with Thijs Brocades Zaalberg, *American Visions of the Netherlands East Indies/Indonesia: U.S. Foreign Policy and Indonesian Nationalism, 1920–1949* (Amsterdam: Amsterdam University Press, 2002), pdf ebook, https://www.jstor .org/stable/j.ctt45kf5g, 67. Traces of these early interactions still exist today. For example, Albert S. Bickmore, a US naturalist who was instrumental in the founding of New York's American Museum of Natural History, gave a Batak prayer staff to the museum as part of its initial collection. See Gould, *Americans in Sumatra*, 138, 140.

35   See 163, this volume.
36   Gould, *Americans in Sumatra*, 79; Gouda with Zaalberg, *American Visions*, 76–77; Foster, *Projections of Power*, 55, 60; see, 153, this volume.

MAP 6   Medan and Pematang Siantar Region, featuring the locations of Pancur Batu, Medan, Tanjung
          Morawa, Tebing Tinggi, Pematang Siantar, and Kisaran

As a result of its foundational nature in the region, the interimperial plantation economy in which the US took part also would manifest itself in the next
generation of the family, in the life of my grandfather Gerhard L. Tobing. After
the Japanese left at the end of World War II, Tobing was employed in Siak Sri
Indrapura, but later fled to Tarutung due to political unrest. Then, Tobing looked
for a job to support the family, and found one at Katarina Hospital in Kisaran
on the east coast of Sumatra. Anne L. Foster notes how companies such as US
Rubber, Goodyear, and the Nederlands Koloniale Petroleum Maatschappij, a
subsidiary of Standard Oil, established housing, as well as medical and recre-
ation facilities for its employees, thus reshaping the geography of the region.
Rony remembered her father's place of employment at the former plantation hospital of Hollandsche Amerikaans Petroleum Maatschappij (HAPM),
situated among different Dutch and US properties. Indeed, US interests in
Indonesia would continue to have impact upon my family's trajectory a generation later. After Rony's brother Apoel Loembantobing earned a master's
degree in Southeast Asian Studies from Yale University in 1960, he trained in
nearby Naugatuck, Connecticut, for several months where US Rubber (later re-
named Uniroyal) was based. Finally, Loembantobing returned to Indonesia to

take up a job in Kisaran at Uniroyal.[37] The fact that different family members over time encountered this kind of economic infrastructure underscores how interimperialism was a normalized reality experienced by those in the region.

3   Multilingualism and Interimperial Temporality

How did interimperialism manifest itself in people's lives on an everyday basis? In this section, I chart how multilingualism emerged as one modality through these processes, as a strategy undertaken by my family to negotiate this environment. While definitely a course of action that came through privileged educational access, multilingualism is also a lens through which we can consider how people navigated the reality and simultaneity of multiple empires.

For Rony's and my grandparents' generational cohorts, multilingualism was a regular part of the interimperial climate during this time, especially because of war. For example, Rony went through multiple different linguistic environments as a student from the 1930s onward, even before her eventual employment and study at Yale University in the late 1950s, when English became her fifth linguistic environment. While Batak was the language she learned at home, Tobing also began teaching her Dutch as a young child. In fact, before World War II, Rony went to a Dutch-language elementary school in Siantar for a few years. After the Japanese arrived and Rony's family migrated for reasons of safety, Rony then attended a two-year Malay-language school in Bengkalis, the *Sekolah Sambungan*, for fourth and fifth grade.[38] Rony recalled the transformation in the curriculum after the Japanese arrived, as school was then taught in Malay and Japanese: "I had to learn the Japanese language including the writing, *katakana*, *hiragana*, and *kanji* [kinds of Japanese script], everything Japanese."[39] Later in 1945, when Rony was sent back to her father's home village as World War II continued, she learned Batak as a language in junior high school. By 1949, she went to study at the OSVO (Opleiding School voor Vak Onderwijzeressen), the teachers' training school for home economics for three years. When Rony entered the OSVO, she began with a Dutch-language curriculum which changed to Indonesian during her last year of study because of the Indonesian Revolution. As she recalled, "For me, it was not difficult because I had studied Malay in Bengkalis, which later became Indonesian. But those

---

37   See 216, 234 this volume; Foster, *Projections of Power*, 88.

38   Prior to the declaration of independence in 1945, what became Bahasa Indonesia (the Indonesian language) was known as Malay. See 181, 187, 198, 203, 207–209, 233–235, this volume.

39   *Katakana* and *hiragana* are kinds of Japanese scripts. See 209, this volume.

students who were in a Dutch school before had a really hard time switching languages."[40] During their final six months, when the students learned how to teach, they were expected to instruct in Indonesian as it had been chosen as the common national language in 1945. Schools such as the ones attended by Rony had to transition to the new political times.[41]

Rony was not the first in my family to have this multilingual facility, as these processes had already been established in previous generations. On the most fundamental level, learning different languages expanded one's educational and economic potential. For instance, in order to have increased prospects at the beginning of the 20th century, Tobing's father, my great-grandfather, migrated with his uncle, and taught himself Dutch so that he could get a better job by passing the *Klein Ambtenaars Examen*, which was like having a diploma from a Dutch elementary school. This was how Tobing's father was able to find a job on the rail system.[42] Several years later, due to imperial standards of race and language, Tobing's husband, Gerhard L. Tobing, pursued Dutch-language learning in the course of his educational career in Indonesia, and also went to the Netherlands for advanced study. Commenting on the hierarchies of colonial education, Tobing recalled about his education,

> After my husband got his degree in Leiden, he felt much more able to stand up against the Dutch. According to him, he didn't learn much more there than he learned at the STOVIA, because the knowledge they learned was taught by the Dutch doctors too. But [at that time,] he had to go to Holland to have the same diploma as the Dutch doctors, as the Dutch diploma was required for him to move up in his career.[43]

Rony also related that her father's education in Indonesia was not held in the same accord as an education in the Netherlands, and those doctors earned far less than someone who had graduated from a medical school in the Netherlands.[44]

Language also was essential for physical survival. As Tobing remembered about the violence of the Japanese Occupation:

---

40   See 224, this volume.
41   See 224–225, this volume; Joseph Errington, *Linguistics in a Colonial World: A Story of Language, Meaning, and Power* (Malden, MA: Blackwell Publishing, 2008), 133; Kees Groeneboer, *Gateway to the West: The Dutch Language in Colonial Indonesia, 1600–1950: A History of Language Policy* (Amsterdam: Amsterdam University Press, 1998), 263, 283.
42   See 153, this volume.
43   See 178, this volume.
44   See 202, this volume.

There was resentment, but you can't show that. Otherwise you could just be beaten or hung up until you tell them whatever is happening. Or you would be put in prison or even killed.

As she recalled, at one point her husband brought a towel bar to his office. Tobing asked him about his intent, and related the following:

He said, "Well, I'll put this on my desk. If a Japanese tries to touch me, I'll kill him with this." I said, "Before you do it, you will be killed first." He said, "Well, anyhow I feel safer if I have this. This is my security."[45]

Both Tobing and Rony remembered Gerhard L. Tobing studying Japanese to communicate with the military regime. Tobing reported that he spent three months learning the language well into the night. She discussed his concentrated study of the language, "He said, 'If I don't understand them, they could get angry.' Because they didn't speak any other language than Japanese."[46] Rony also noted the necessity of her father learning Japanese, "There was not always a translator around, so my father was learning medical terminology in Japanese so he could explain things to the Japanese."[47] Despite his language facility, my grandfather was called in for questioning by the Japanese authorities for an entire day, and came back to the family with impaired health. As Rony recounted, "He was tortured by the Japanese, and he became very ill. My mom had to nurse him for about three weeks until he was back to normal. He never told me what happened to him then."[48] My grandfather's silence about these issues likely was a rejection of this memory, as well as a way to protect his daughter from the knowledge of what he had endured.

My family's emphasis on multilingualism not only became part of their apparatus for addressing interimperialism, but it also became a position of linguistic authority from which critique could be made regarding arriving foreigners. For example, Samuel Munson and Henry Lyman were two American Baptist ministers from New England who ventured to northern Sumatra to proselytize among the Toba Batak in 1833, and were allegedly cannibalized.[49] In 1985, Tobing related their history and their inability to speak Batak: "They didn't know the language, they only had an interpreter. They were not prepared.

---

45   See 185, this volume.
46   Ibid.
47   See 210, this volume.
48   Ibid.
49   Munson, Thompson, and Lyman, *Memoirs*, v, 62, 64–65; van Bemmelen, *Christianity, Colonization*, 192.

They couldn't tell the people what they wanted."[50] Tobing's comments in 1985 were intended to explain the obvious to her American granddaughter: the importance of having proper language skills if you were trying to convert people. As linguist Joseph Errington argues about the essential nature of language in the colonial encounter:

> Talk was one of the lowest common denominators for colonial dealings where some humans made others targets of their efforts to persuade or awe, threaten or coerce, and who in turn resisted or cooperated, retreated or collaborated.[51]

The crucial nature of language was something profoundly important to Tobing. Indeed, a significant part of her professional career was devoted to facilitating the language acquisition of others.[52] However, this deployment of multilingualism as a strategy was due not just to individual proclivity, but also a reflection of the unequal hierarchies wrought by interimperialism. While on the one hand, having many languages was a reflection of Tobing's elite class status, on the other, it was an indicator of the requirement of colonials to learn the languages of multiple colonial authorities.

Through analyzing Tobing's and Rony's narratives, I began to see the emergence of what might be called an interimperial temporality regarding multilingualism, the sense that one had to prepare the language skills needed to negotiate future regimes. During the Japanese Occupation, for example, Gerhard L. Tobing continued to teach his children foreign languages in anticipation of the end of the occupation, a skill that would become immensely important later in their lives. As Rony wrote, her parents were concerned about the extent of the children's education during war. She remembered,

> Since we were taught a limited curriculum, mostly Japanese in school, my dad arranged to teach math and English to my brother and me. My dad also taught German to my brother Apoel. My dad knew the Dutch, German, and English languages—he knew everything.[53]

Rony's father tutored her brother and her secretly at great risk. He would educate them for two hours in the afternoon in a storage room, while their dog

---

50   See 151, this volume.
51   Errington, *Linguistics in a Colonial World*, 2.
52   See 190–191, 193, 195, this volume.
53   See 210, this volume.

Hector kept watch in case a Japanese soldier came by.[54] I see my grandfather's teaching of these languages to the children, even despite the possibility of extreme reprisal from the Japanese, as an indication of the essential nature of language for education and professional mobility at the time. In addition, I also see it as a hopeful strategy, an awareness that there would be a time when the occupiers would leave and the war would end.

This sense of interimperial temporality shaped the increased importance of my family continuing to study English at the beginning of the Cold War, a strategy that would dramatically affect their future ability to migrate to the United States. Significantly, Rony commented on how their previous multilingualism had an impact on my family members' ability to learn English: "I think because we had learned Dutch already, that helped us in learning English as a second Western language."[55] In Tobing's case, after her husband was killed by the Dutch in 1947 and she became a widow with four children to support, she sought English-language study as a mode of economic survival. As a reflection of the growing importance of the United States and the English language as a medium of instruction during this period, Tobing took evening lessons in English while a teacher in Medan. Although Tobing already had a double shift of teaching in the morning and the afternoon, she enrolled in further instruction for advanced training in the English language. In addition, Tobing decided to undertake an intensive program in Jogjakarta on the island of Java in order to learn English.[56]

These lessons were learned by the next generation as well. Rony wrote that when Tobing needed to enroll Rony's young sister Demak in kindergarten in the late 1940s, Tobing originally had a Dutch school in mind for Demak. However, Demak asked en route to the school, "Please, may I not go to a Dutch school because they killed Papa?"[57] As Rony related, Tobing then took Demak to the Methodist English School. English became Demak's first language of instruction from kindergarten onward, and she was taught by American teachers. This path would change Demak's life, not only because she had superb English-language skills and American-accented English, but she would end up going as a teenager to finish high school and then earn her college degree in the United States.[58] On one level, this memory is a poignant story of a little girl who mourns her father. And on another level, it also illustrates the role of in-

---

54   Ibid.
55   See 229, this volume.
56   See 189–190, 191, 226, this volume.
57   See 230, this volume.
58   See 192, 235–236, this volume.

terimperial temporality, the fact that Tobing's daughter, even as a young child, was aware that there were other options for education and language than a Dutch-language school.

This knowledge of interimperial temporality, that one empire follows another, is indicated further in a comment Tobing made about later generations of the family studying in the United States. Tobing reported that when her husband left for Leiden University in 1937, he told Tobing that she needed to take the children to the Netherlands for a Dutch education after they completed high school. She remembered:

> Well, his ideal came true. Even if it was not Holland, it was the United States. All the four children had the chance to study in the United States. And I am very grateful, I never expected them to go there.[59]

The fact that H.L. Tobing related this demonstrates an awareness of imperial succession. It also shows that these strategies and issues were transferable across empire, a knowledge honed by lives lived in an interimperial context.

4   The United States Cold War

The decision of my various family members to study English reflects the growing prominence of the United States in Southeast Asia. While the United States had interests in Indonesia throughout the 20th century, World War II and the US Cold War became important turning points for the United States in Southeast Asia. In fact, the region of "Southeast Asia" was a World War II construct: the US State Department formulated the first "division of Southeast Asian affairs" during this period, reflecting the geopolitical stakes of the region. After World War II, the North American continent, unlike other major powers in Europe and Asia who ended the conflict with countless dead and their cities in ruins, was relatively unscathed, with its industrial infrastructure still intact and its military troops stationed across Europe and Asia. National security in the global realm was a critical part of these issues, especially in the context of the United States' desire to curtail the power of the Soviet Union and to address the rising power of newly independent nations.[60]

---

59   See 171, this volume.
60   James A. Tyner, *America's Strategy in Southeast Asia: From the Cold War to the Terror War* (Lanham, MD: Rowman & Littlefield, 2007), 1, 6, 8, 48; John Bowen, "The Development of Southeast Asian Studies in the United States," in *The Politics of Knowledge: Area Studies*

Although the history of Indonesian migration to the United States during the Cold War still remains to be written, we can begin to trace out some different elements of these issues, all of which reflect the militarized conditions of the times. For instance, there were the maritime laborers. Rony remembered two Batak relatives in New York City who had left Dutch ships, part of the waves of Indonesian maritime workers who moved through many parts of the world. Their histories reflect a segment of Indonesian American history being studied by historian Greg Robinson, yet another way we can begin to see how the United States figured in the larger interimperial history of Indonesian migration. These processes were especially pronounced from 1945 to 1946, when hundreds of sailors began protesting in US ports about having to work on ships carrying arms and equipment for Dutch military forces seeking to retake Indonesia, in tandem with the political resistance of Indonesian maritime workers in other areas of the world. Disembarking from both British and Dutch vessels, about 400 Indonesians arrived in ports such as New York and San Francisco, prompting centers to open up to help this transient population. A number joined the US military, as registered aliens could volunteer for service.[61]

An even greater wave of Cold War migration happened in the following decades, with the arrival of Dutch Indonesians in Southern California, as well as other sites. In 1949 with Indonesian independence, many Indos (Indonesians of Dutch and Indonesian ancestry) decided to retain their Dutch citizenship and leave Indonesia.[62] Because of their migration to the Netherlands, several were able to complete a secondary stage of their migration from Holland to the United States, while others went to Australia, New Zealand, Brazil, and Canada. Whereas some arrived immediately after the war, refugee legislation

---

and the Disciplines, ed. David L. Szanton (Berkeley: University of California Press, 2004), 391; Alfred W. McCoy, *In the Shadows of the American Century: The Rise and Decline of US Global Power*, Kindle ebook (Chicago: Haymarket Books, 2017), under "Introduction: US Global Power and Me"; and under Chapter 1 "The World Island and the Rise of America," "America's Axial Geopolitics" section.

61   See 233–234, this volume. While most of the maritime laborers were detained by the US government at Ellis Island in New York, some were held at Terminal Island in Los Angeles. Eventually, the sailors were sent by the government to Crystal City, and in March 1947, about three hundred were deported. Greg Robinson, "The Great Unknown and the Unknown Great: The Incarceration of Indonesians in the United States: An Untold Story," *Nichi Bei Weekly*, January 8, 2015. Available at: https://www.nichibei.org/2015/01/the-great-unknown-and-the-unknown-great-the-incarceration-of-indonesians-in-the-united-states-an-untold-story/ (accessed January 4, 2018), 1–2.

62   Greta Kwik, *The Indos in Southern California* (New York: AMS Press, 1989), 40–43; Azlan Tajuddin and Jamie Stern, "From Brown Dutchmen to Indo-Americans: Changing Identity of the Dutch-Indonesian (Indo) Diaspora in America," *International Journal of Politics, Culture, and Society*, 28/4 (2015): 357.

in the 1950s and early 1960s enabled the movement of thousands to the United States. These migrants were named as refugees because their originating country of Indonesia had relations with the Soviet Union, and at the same time, they held Dutch passports which enabled them to travel to the United States as Europeans, thus avoiding the race-based quotas in the pre-1965 immigration laws. By 1962, roughly 30,000 had migrated, who in turn sponsored the migration of some 30,000 relatives and friends.[63]

Another strand of migration were those Indonesians sent to the United States through exchange programs, or other programs started during the Cold War era. Indonesia was especially important as a focus for the US government because it was the site of direct rivalry between the United States and the Soviet Union. In 1948, the United States began connecting with Indonesian military forces, and offered training and assistance to its police in 1950. The United States sought to train army officers, in both Indonesia and the United States, a significant way to expand its influence, initiating another trans-Pacific migration flow. Through exposure to American curriculum and modern technology, these officers not only would gain more affiliation and orientation to the United States, but they also would receive education and instruction to counter Communist influence, in keeping with US Cold War objectives. In her autobiographical narrative, Rony further remembered other community members in Washington, DC, whose occupations reflected this international relationship between the United States and Indonesia, such as those who worked at the Indonesian embassy, or for programs such as the Voice of America.[64]

Most familiar to me are the Cold War-era migration of Indonesian students and teachers to the United States, as this was my parents' and grandmother's cohort, as well as the next generation, the children of their cohort from 'back home' who were studying in the United States. Envisioned as the 'softer' way to influence countries in contrast to overt military action, US educational channels were seen as instrumental in exerting influence in other countries. In the late 1950s, for example, the Ford Foundation gave grants to

---

63   Kwik, *The Indos*, 69–70; Tajuddin and Stern, "From Brown Dutchmen," 350, 359. DOI: 10.1007./s10767-015.9197-z.

64   Bradley R. Simpson, *Economists with Guns: Authoritarian Development and U.S.-Indonesian Relations, 1960–1968* (Stanford, CA: Stanford University Press, 2008), 4–5, 9; Simpson, *Economists with Guns*, 32; Odd Arne Westad, *The Global Cold War: Third World Interventions and the Making of Our Times*, Kindle ebook (Cambridge: Cambridge University Press, 2007), under chapter 1, "The Empire of Liberty: American Ideology and Foreign Interventions," "Modernization, Technology, and American Globalism" section; see 237, this volume.

Indonesian educational institutions, sent American professors and students to Indonesia and Indonesian professors and students to the United States, trained Indonesian English teachers, and also provided American advisors and equipment. The Asia Foundation offered funds for cooperative training centers, educational materials, scholarships, and other support until the Indonesian government stopped the foundation's work. Government funding also was invested in US universities such as Yale and Cornell to produce scholarship and language instruction which would contribute to the United States' mission overseas. In addition, institutions such as the Rockefeller Foundation, the Carnegie Endowment, and especially the Ford Foundation, supported language and academic programs. With all of these developments, both university and government agencies were invested in training elite students from the Third World, especially with the expectation that these students would return home and wield considerable influence in aligning their home countries to US politics, its economy, and its way of life.[65]

The backdrop to these issues was that Indonesia was emerging as an important area of foreign policy attention. Increasingly, as the Cold War took shape, the United States became further invested in Indonesia and concerned about its susceptibility to Communist control. The US also weighed the potential impact to its interests if there were shifts in the regional power balance, especially due to possible alliances with China or the Soviet Union. In fact, Indonesia was a location of direct competition between the United States and the Soviet Union. Due to its population numbers, geographic size, and strategic location, Indonesia was of vital concern, especially when positioned against its neighbor to the north, the Philippines, which was an American ally and former colony, and part of a mutual defense treaty. As a result, up to the mid-1960s, government officials were more focused on Indonesia as opposed to Vietnam. In tandem with these efforts, the United States also tried to wield

---

65   Mary Yu Danico, ed., "Indonesian Americans," in *Asian American Society: An Encyclopedia* (Thousand Oaks, CA: SAGE, 2014), 518–520; Jonathan H.X. Lee, Fumitaka Matsuoka, Edmond Yee, and Ronald Y. Nakasone, eds., *Asian American Religious Cultures* (2 vols) (Santa Barbara, CA: ABC-CLIO, 2015), 517–518; Gould, *Americans in Sumatra*, 133–134, 158–160; David L. Szanton, "Introduction: The Origin, Nature, and Challenges of Area Studies in the United States", in *The Politics of Knowledge: Area Studies and the Disciplines*, ed. David Szanton (Berkeley: University of California Press, 2004), 8–9; Westad, *The Global Cold War*, under chapter 1, "The Empire of Liberty: American Ideology and Foreign Interventions," "Modernization, Technology, and American Globalism" section; Madeline Hsu, *The Good Immigrants: How the Yellow Peril Became the Model Minority* (Princeton, NJ: Princeton University Press, 2015), 11; McCoy, *In the Shadows of the American Century*, under "Introduction: US Global Power and Me."

its power through other means. The United States Information Agency (USIA) began in 1949 with Voice of America radio broadcasts in both Indonesian and Vietnamese. Working alongside the CIA, USIA ran the Voice of America radio program, organized libraries and published literature in the form of pamphlets and books, produced films, and conducted 'exchange-of-persons' programs.[66]

Developments continued to escalate by the late 1950s. In 1957, the Eisenhower administration poured millions of dollars into regional rebellions that challenged President Sukarno's power and the political balance. As the United States indicated its support of a government with an anti-communist administration, rebels organized what would become the dissident Pemerintah Revolusioner Republik Indonesia (PRRI, Revolutionary Government of the Republic of Indonesia). By 1958, the Eisenhower administration gave direct support through air cover to the rebels, stationing the US Navy at the ready in case reinforcements were needed in Sumatra. Despite the US supply of weaponry and other personnel support, the rebellion did not succeed, and Sukarno imposed martial law and consolidated power in what he named 'Guided Democracy,' thus discontinuing Indonesia's parliamentary democracy. As it happened, Rony still was in Indonesia at the time of the PRRI rebellion, working as a language teacher and cultural informant, and she remembers fleeing the area due to the military unrest with two American scholars whom she was then assisting.[67]

US intervention would undergird the repression that would unfold in 1965 and 1966, when a group of lower-ranking Indonesian army officers who belonged to the September 30th Movement kidnapped and killed six army generals and one lieutenant. The officers stated continued loyalty to Sukarno, and that their actions were to prevent a takeover by a "Council of Generals" that was supported by the CIA. In response, General Suharto and the Indonesian military, with the backing of the US government, moved against both Sukarno and the Indonesian Communist Party (Partai Komunis Indonesia, PKI), resulting in unprecedented levels of violence and the rise of authoritarian military rule.

---

66   Tyner, *America's Strategy*, 6, 8, 48, 134; Audrey R. Kahin and George McT. Kahin, *Subversion as Foreign Policy: The Secret Eisenhower and Dulles Debacle in Indonesia* (New York: The New Press, 1995), 9, 16–17, 33, 125–126; Simpson, *Economists with Guns*, 4–5, 9–11; John Roosa, *Pretext for Mass Murder: The September 30th Movement and Suharto's Coup d'État in Indonesia* (Madison: The University of Wisconsin Press, 2006), Introduction, "The Movement and the United States" section; Tony Day, "Honored Guests: Indonesian-American Cultural Traffic, 1953–1957," in *Heirs to World Culture: Being Indonesian, 1950–1965*, ed. Jennifer Lindsay and Maya H.T. Liem (Leiden: Brill, 2012), 121–122.

67   Kahin and Kahin, *Subversion as Foreign Policy*, 121–122, 140, 175; Tyner, *America's Strategy*, 136–137; Simpson, *Economists with Guns*, 33–34; see 232, this volume.

In 1965 to 1966, enormous violence, killings, and confinement took place over several months, with the deaths of some 500,000 alleged members of the Indonesian Communist Party and related groups. Around a million were imprisoned. When this violence occurred, most held affiliations to entities that were within the law, and did not bear weapons.[68] Tobing and Rony did not directly experience the events of 1965 and 1966, as by then they already were in the United States. In 1985, Tobing did tell me a few stories about what she heard had taken place, in a hushed tone. Scholars like Geoffrey B. Robinson have made critical interventions in our understanding of the devastating events which ensued, transforming our knowledge of what happened.[69] My immediate family members, however, were not swept up in this history, especially because of their time of migration to the United States.

However, I can speak to how the labor represented by my family's migration to the United States is an indicator of the interimperial environment already prevalent in Indonesia. It also illuminates the rapidly growing interests of the United States in the region during the Cold War. Hence, as opposed to seeing my uncle and Rony only as foreign students or language teachers who migrated due to educational opportunity, I want to shift the analysis to also note their simultaneous labor as knowledge workers within a landscape of US militarized interests. I find these issues quite graphically suggested by Rony's route to the United States in 1958 when she migrated to Yale University to work as a language teacher. At the time, Rony was traveling to take on a one-year position as an Indonesian language teacher at Yale University, a program which itself had emerged during World War II and the Cold War era to address growing US interest in the region. Indeed, the airplane route that Rony took to travel to the United States reflects the militarized transportation infrastructure developed through the US empire and its interests in the Pacific. Leaving Indonesia, Rony flew to nearby Singapore, then on to Saigon, Manila, and Guam, then Wake Island, and finally to San Francisco. What I find interesting is how most of the stops on her flight illuminate a map of US interests in the Pacific, not only the US expanding role in Vietnam, but also its former colony of Manila in the Philippines, the organized and unincorporated territory of Guam, the unorganized and

---

68   Geoffrey B. Robinson's *The Killing Season: A History of the Indonesian Massacres, 1965–66* (Princeton, NJ: Princeton University Press, 2018), 3–5; Tyner, *America's Strategy*, 137; Kahin and Kahin, *Subversion as Foreign Policy*, 224–226, 229; Simpson, *Economists with Guns*, 32.

69   See Geoffrey B. Robinson's *The Killing Season* for his recent analysis of this period and its aftermath.

unincorporated territory of Wake Island (also part of the Marshall Islands), and then finally the major military port of San Francisco in the United States.[70]

As my family history indicates, if the United States sought to build ties with countries in Southeast Asia as part of its larger campaign against Communism, it also needed knowledge workers through which to facilitate its aims. By knowledge workers, I am referring to the language teachers and cultural informants who familiarize US personnel with a foreign culture. As 'native informants,' my family members had specific skills that were useful for US involvement overseas as well as government organizations in the United States. Even though the labor of language teachers and cultural interpreters goes regularly unacknowledged, their history helps to illuminate the United States' sustained interest in Southeast Asia, and enables a broader and more nuanced understanding of the relationship between the United States and this region. With American dominance and intervention in the Pacific, the United States needed workers to translate and interpret, to make it possible to achieve its political, economic, and military aims. Furthermore, whether or not scholars from the US in the Cold War had direct ties to US militarism, their labor was produced within a larger framework of government funding for area studies programs, and the unfolding of US involvement in war in Vietnam and elsewhere in Southeast Asia. This context is valuable in terms of reading the ways that my family became incorporated into the US project of area studies during the Cold War.

In my family's case, migration to the United States was an extension of the already established interimperial environment in which they operated. For one thing, the US scholars who sought to employ them benefited from their multilingualism and knowledge of different cultures. In the mid-1950s, geographer Karl Pelzer from Yale University went to Nommensen University in Medan to find Batak speakers who could interpret in English. As Tobing remembered,

> Mrs. Pelzer, Karl Pelzer's wife, came to my house, and she chose Apoel for their research, to go with her to Bakara, to Tarutung, to Lintong Nihuta, all those places, to interview people about matters like the *adat*. And when they came back, Mr. Pelzer asked Yale University for support to have a young man to go with him to America as an assistant to finish his book.[71]

---

70 See 233, this volume. For more information on the program at Yale University, see https://cseas.yale.edu/history-southeast-asia-studies-yale (accessed October 19, 2019). Malay was taught earlier in the program's history, and later became known as Indonesian.

71 See 191, this volume.

Her son's English-language skills were pivotal to his opportunity to travel to the United States, as Tobing recalled:

> So Pelzer interviewed people for the position. When he did, some boys would answer Pelzer's question, "What did he say?" with the response, "Oh, that is not so important." But with Apoel, Apoel could interpret because he liked to talk. Apoel knew English, Batak, Dutch, and a little German. And so they asked to have Apoel go to America.[72]

As this excerpt suggests, it was important that Apoel not only had facility across multiple languages, but also was effective in engaging with different parties as well. Apoel was given a scholarship to go to Yale and migrated there in 1956 to finish his bachelor's degree.[73] Tobing's comments indicate the importance of Apoel knowing multiple languages, including Indonesian, and his ability to navigate among various cultural sensibilities. Her comments further suggest how family members understood the pivotal role of those who could interpret language and culture, an awareness that also is demonstrated in Rony's memories of that period.

As suggested by the clarity and detail of Rony's autobiographical narrative, Rony was also a skilled cultural informant with well-honed observation skills that began when she was a small child. Even as a youngster, Rony not only observed what was going on around her, but she began to analyze it too. For example, when she was a young girl, one of Rony's earliest memories is of listening to the stories told by elders in her father's ancestral home in the village.[74] Later on when she returned to Pearaja as a young teenager during World War II, Rony continued to develop her understanding of the Batak community. Rony explained how she gained her cultural knowledge by paying close attention to what was going on around her:

> I started to learn things about Batak culture by observing. No one really told me what was going on. They were all busy. But as a little girl and then as a young teenager when I lived there, I often was present at the ceremonies. If there was a family wedding, naturally I was there with my mother or another family member. Over there, people would just say "Let's go,

---

72   Ibid.
73   See 191, 232, this volume.
74   See 199, this volume.

let's go," and you go there in a group and after everything, you go home as a group too.[75]

Hence, it was assumed that Rony would participate in community ceremonies and gatherings.

Years later, Rony's multilingualism as well as her knowledge of the Batak language and culture would reshape her future academic and employment prospects. During the 1950s when Rony was in college, she was a cultural informant, research assistant, and language teacher for two US scholars, who were conducting research on a Batak village. Rony then was an Economics student at Nommensen University, and she took some time off from her studies to "help" the Americans, as she explained it. As is clear from Rony's discussion of her labor, Rony understood how her contributions were indispensable for the couple's work. Rony gave Batak language lessons to the female researcher, and then would accompany her so she would have the opportunity to converse with the women in the village.[76] As the linguistic intermediary between the scholars and the Batak community, Rony was cognizant of how race and postcolonialism shaped the reception of the Americans when they would attend ceremonies, especially as she acted as translator and cultural informant. As Rony recalled:

> Because the couple were the white people, the Westerners, the Batak looked up to them, and they treated them with deference. They would give the couple good seats, and they would talk to them.[77]

Rony was well aware of her centrality in the couple's research process, as well as her possible effect on its outcome. For example, she maintained her professional autonomy by not fully disclosing her political status, as she thought it would have an impact on the research produced. Rony explained:

> The elder who rented the couple their house knew my mom and the whole family, and knew that I was a descendant of Raja Pontas. At one gathering, he came to me and said, "Everybody know who this girl is?" And then he said, "She is the daughter of Dr. Gerhard Tobing, and the great-granddaughter of Raja Pontas from Pearaja, Tarutung." All the

---

75   See 221, this volume.
76   See 230–232, this volume.
77   See 231, this volume.

people were surprised because they hadn't known my full background. I was kind of embarrassed. I guess he knew that I would not reveal who I was.[78]

Previously, Rony had opted not to disclose her identity because she did not want it to affect the scholars' research. As Rony noted,

Because I thought that if I did, the people in the village would change their attitude to me and I wouldn't get the information that the researchers needed [...] I didn't want them to know that I was from an educated and middle-class family. The couple knew something about my background, but they didn't know exactly where I was from as I had never really told them. I wanted them to accept me as I was. After that the villagers treated me differently.[79]

As Rony's actions show, Rony knew that the realm of language was suffused with relations of power, especially because of its immense necessity.

These connections to scholars would lead to my family's eventual migration overseas to Connecticut. When Yale needed an Indonesian language teacher for its program in Southeast Asian Studies while Apoel was a student there, Apoel suggested Rony for the one-year position. Two years later, Rony and Apoel taught Indonesian during the summer at Cornell, another burgeoning center for Southeast Asian Studies, and earned enough money to bring their sister Demak so that she could go to school in the United States. Upon the advice of Rony's mentor, Isidore Dyen, Rony decided to continue to teach Indonesian at Yale and earn a master's degree in Southeast Asian Studies, which is how she met her future husband, A. Kohar Rony, in 1960.[80]

A. Kohar Rony had taken another route to travel to the United States, but his journey was structured by US imperialism and Cold War interests as well. He attended Methodist English School in Palembang, South Sumatra, the southern campus of the school which Demak Tobing also had attended (Demak Tobing was a student at the Medan campus in North Sumatra). Kohar Rony was especially influenced by two young American teachers, Albert and Dorothy Hamel. When his cousin Saleh Zen won a scholarship to attend college in Florida through a UNESCO fellowship, Kohar Rony too applied for

---

78   See 231, this volume.
79   Ibid.
80   See 232–236, this volume.

funding and was able to travel to the United States on scholarship to Monterey Peninsula College in 1954. Later, to stay in the United States, he gave up his student status to work in the Monterey Defense Language Institute, and subsequently was recruited by the US Army where he further served as a language teacher, a reflection of the permeable border between education and the US military during that time period. After his discharge, Kohar Rony was able to obtain a bachelor's degree in Communications at the University of California at Berkeley through GI benefits. He then won a Ford Foundation scholarship to enter a master's degree program in Southeast Asian Studies at Yale University, which is where he met my mother. As Southeast Asian Studies graduate students, one of the classes that they took together was a Vietnamese language class, where they were students with Huỳnh Sanh Thông three times a week for a whole year. Professor Thông, who originally had come to the United States in 1951 and began teaching at Yale in 1957, would become known for translating *The Tale of Kieu*, and would earn a MacArthur fellowship in 1987 for his brilliance and dedication to Vietnamese culture.[81]

In the meantime, after Apoel graduated from Yale with a master's degree, Apoel found employment with Uniroyal. While Apoel returned to Indonesia, my parents remained as knowledge workers in the United States. Rony continued to teach Indonesian in New Haven. Kohar Rony also was in demand because of his academic background and Indonesian language skills. In the summer of 1962, for example, my father acted as an interpreter and a guide for an Indonesian through the State Department. Then his advisor, Harry Benda, recommended Kohar Rony for a job at the Southern Asia section at the Library of Congress, where my father became a reference librarian in October 1962. In 1967, my mother joined him at the Library of Congress and also began working as an Indonesian cataloguer. Both of them would remain there as knowledge workers for several years until their retirement in the early 2000s.[82]

But it was not just my parents who taught Indonesian at Yale. Rony had brought H.L. Tobing, my grandmother, to the United States to give her an opportunity to travel and work in another environment. Rather than remain in Washington, DC, at home with Rony's family, Rony contacted Professor Dyen and found out that there was an Indonesian-language teaching opportunity at Yale. Rony remembered helping her mother move to New Haven, and the new life that Tobing enjoyed due to her full-time job as a language teacher

---

81 See 235, this volume; unpublished manuscript of A. Kohar Rony's autobiography in author's possession; "Huynh Sanh Tong, 1926–2008," https://cseas.yale.edu/huynh-sanh-thong https://cseas.yale.edu/huynh-sanh-thong, accesed 19 March 2020.

82 See 235, 237, 239–241, this volume.

as well as her involvement with the Lutheran church. Tobing even taught Indonesian in the Netherlands for one summer.[83] That Tobing taught the English language in Indonesia and then later the Indonesian language in the United States reveals the vital importance of knowledge workers at the interface of different empires.

As I have shown in this section, the migration of different members of my family must be read within historical developments of the US Cold War. My family members moved to the United States at a time when the US was intensifying its involvement in Southeast Asia, and Indonesia was an important target of US activity. As scholars such as Catherine Choy, Madeline Hsu, and Odd Arne Westad have discussed, students and other representatives from the Third World like Rony were instrumental in the US's Cold War efforts, especially because of their potential to advocate for a United States-style modernity and political economy upon return to their home country. In the interim, they also could make contributions to the US economy through their labor and professional expertise.[84] My intervention here is to underscore that the ability of my family members to migrate to the United States during this period was a product of US involvement in an interimperial environment in Indonesia. In assessing my family history over the course of several decades, it is easier to see how the migration of family members as knowledge workers during the Cold War did not emerge out of a vacuum. Their ability to move across different cultural and linguistic arenas was already well developed when the possibility arose for them to go to the United States.

5   Conclusion

As this chapter has demonstrated, Indonesian American history offers us another way of conceptualizing Asian American migration, precisely because of its insistence on an interimperial framework in which migration to the United States was not historically central. A close analysis of my family history underscores my supposition that my family's experience with US empire was not a break from the past, but a continuation of an interimperial present. Hence, addressing our eventual migration to the United States cannot be understood

---

83   See 192–193, 195, 238–239, this volume.

84   Westad, *The Global Cold War*, under chapter 1 "The Empire of Liberty: American Ideology and Foreign Interventions," "Modernization, Technology, and American Globalism" section; Catherine Ceniza Choy, *Empire of Care: Nursing and Migration in Filipino American History* (Durham, NC: Duke University Press, 2006), 64–65; Hsu, *The Good Immigrants*, 11.

without taking into account the multiple imperial environments of the Dutch, German, and Japanese empires. My discussion indicates the importance of shifting our geographical framing in order to locate the United States within an interimperial context, and to follow the overlap of empires.[85] In underscoring this interimperial positioning for the United States, my project thus occupies a different space from many other Asian American Studies projects for which the United States was a dominant migration destination. For example, while discussions of Chinese American community formation rightfully place it in the context of a diasporic movement to multiple sites around the world, including countries in Asia, Europe, and Latin America, many Chinese American Studies projects privilege the US context, and center around sites such as San Francisco and New York City. Filipinx American migration to the United States represents another model, where the United States was *the* primary destination because of the incorporation of the Philippines into the US empire. As a result, the narrative trajectory of Filipinx American Studies is shaped by its historical gaze from the postcolonial United States. Vietnamese American Studies too is fundamentally implicated by these issues, especially because of the United States' massive presence during the Vietnam War. These kinds of framing hold great sway in a US national context, especially as Chinese Americans and Filipinx Americans form the two largest Asian American groups in the United States, with Vietnamese Americans representing the fourth biggest community.[86] My point here is not to minimize the interimperial context in which these other communities developed, but rather to provide an analysis as to why Indonesian American history might not register in the same way as the histories of these other groups. Indonesian American migration thus demonstrates another way to consider US/Asia relations, as well as patterns of Asian American community formation in the United States.

Addressing the role of Indonesian American migration during the US Cold War reminds us of the significance of departing from standard ways to measure the "importance" of a community through population statistics, permanent settlement, and visibility. Rather than insisting on these kinds of numbers and legibilities, tracing the different strands of Indonesian migration to the United States leads us to other ways of seeing. For example, focusing on interimperialism in the case of my family's history illuminates the significance

---

85   See Denise Cruz, *Transpacific Femininities: The Making of the Modern Filipina* (Durham, NC: Duke University Press, 2012), for a crucial work on the simultaneity of empires in shaping ideologies in Philippine culture.

86   See https://www.pewresearch.org/fact-tank/2017/09/08/key-facts-about-asian -americans/ (accessed January 8, 2020).

of multilingualism. Language was one major way that people on the ground could navigate empire, and was a profoundly sought-after commodity that also enabled one to pursue education and employment. This knowledge of the crucial nature of language as a strategy for negotiating imperial and interimperial environments is seen again and again in my family's history. This strategy is quite dissonant from my own experience of being born and raised in the United States during the Cold War era, where monolingualism in English was regularly taken for granted. It was precisely their multilingual capabilities that made my family members so valuable in an interimperial context, as language was so critical to the operation of all of these empires, including the United States.

Furthermore, although the migration of language teachers and other knowledge workers like my family members might seem relatively small, it is important to discuss their pivotal significance. Language teachers in a sense are nodal workers, who provide indispensable knowledge at the intersection of different networks. Their labor not only provides an essential tool in order to access another culture, but they also can have an impact on multiple sectors at the same time. As language teachers in the US during the Cold War, my family would help train a generation of scholars in language acquisition. In addition, in their work at the Library of Congress as an area specialist in the case of my father and as a cataloguer in the case of Rony, my parents also were part of the apparatus to make knowledge of Southeast Asian Studies available not just at the federal government level, but to scholars and the general public as well.

From that standpoint, I argue that my family's experience underscores how the movement of knowledge workers can be seen as migration undertaken in the militarized context of the Cold War, and should be placed adjacent to the experiences of other postcolonials, immigrants, and refugees who arrived in the United States through US military intervention overseas during this era. In their trans-Pacific journeys forged by US empire, my family members joined streams of other kinds of migration, such as displaced survivors of US militarism in Korea like Korean adoptees, or the Asian and Asian American military workers who labored on both sides of the Pacific.[87] Like these migration

---

87   Grace M. Cho, *Haunting the Korean Diaspora: Shame, Secrecy, and the Forgotten War* (Minneapolis: University of Minnesota Press, 2008), 11; Catherine Ceniza Choy, *Global Families: A History of Asian International Adoption in America* (New York: New York University Press, 2013); Susie Woo, "Transpacific Adoption: The Korean War, US Missionaries, and Cold War Liberalism," in *Pacific America: Histories of Transoceanic Crossings*, ed. Lon Kurashige (Honolulu: University of Hawai'i Press, 2017), 161–177; Simeon Man, *Soldiering through Empire: Race and the Making of the Decolonizing Pacific*, Kindle ebook (Berkeley: University of California Press, 2018), under "Introduction," "The Work of Soldiering" Section; Choy, *Empire of Care*, 64. See also Yến Lê Espiritu, *Home Bound:*

streams, my parents' paths to the United States reflect patterns of US military involvement in the Pacific and overseas. By making groups such as Indonesian Americans more central to the larger history of Asian Americans, we not only can envision alternate models of migration and community formation, we also can better discern the wide range of strategies that Asians took as they went to and from the United States. In the process, we also can illuminate other ways of seeing the US and its history as an interimperial power.

Filipino American Lives across Cultures, Communities, and Countries (Berkeley: University of California Press, 2003); Yến Lê Espiritu, *Body Counts: The Vietnam War and Militarized Refuge(es)* (Berkeley: University of California Press, 2014).

CHAPTER 2

Gendered Knowledges
Patriarchies and the Politics of Belonging

1 Introduction

In her autobiographical narrative, Rony relates an early memory of being at her grandmother's home with her mother and brother in Pearaja, her father's village, when she was about five years old and her father was away studying advanced medicine at Leiden University in the Netherlands. She remembered that while her brother and other cousins were happily playing outside in the yard, her grandmother insisted that she sit quietly in a chair in the house, even though she wanted to join the other children. As she waited, confined to the space of the chair, her grandmother explained that she had to sit there because she was a *boru ni raja*, meaning that she was a daughter of a *raja*, descended from the males of the family, and hence subject to special restrictions. Rony recalled watching the other children running around outside and enjoying themselves, including her brother who did not have the same rules as a son in terms of physical movement. Even her female cousins played outside because they were descended from the daughters in the family, while she was descended from a son.[1] Patrilineal descent, as evidenced by Rony's experience, was central to the Toba Batak culture in which Rony was raised, whose precepts her grandmother was enforcing in this political moment.

I open the chapter with this story to show how gender and patrilineality structured everyday life for Rony and Tobing, even at the most foundational level. In contrast to Chapter 1, which mapped the broad ways that interimperialism shaped family strategies, this chapter on gendered knowledge closely examines Tobing's and Rony's narratives to determine how personal knowledge on an intimate scale can be used to examine women's history. Focusing on their two narratives is a deliberate strategy precisely because of the complexity of their experiences as women, which spans over a hundred years, great distances, and multiple political regimes. In many ways, their experiences are singular, not only because of their class status, education, and religion, but also because of their identities as Toba Batak women. Hence, despite my conviction of the worth of their histories, my goal in this chapter is not to argue that

---

1 See 203, this volume.

their experiences are necessarily representative of Indonesian or Indonesian American women.

Instead, I am interested in analyzing how their experiences resulted in the formation of gendered knowledges—a constant in my grandmother's and mother's lives—about what it meant to regularly negotiate one's secondary status as a woman through male-focused hierarchies. As young women, both Tobing and Rony navigated competing but converging gender hierarchies, both in their home Toba Batak culture and through the cultures of domesticity being promulgated by the Dutch and German empires. Although very different in nature, central to both were hierarchies that privileged men's choice and movement while promoting the notion that a woman's place was in the home. These dynamics were illuminated in sharp relief when their lives drastically changed following my grandfather's death during the First Police Action, when the Dutch tried to regain their former colony of Indonesia in 1947.[2] However, Tobing's and Rony's narratives also demonstrate that there were ways to traverse, if not contest, these hierarchies, even despite the most formidable of barriers. In these processes, Tobing and Rony developed alternate forms of political autonomy, which, while predicated on these gendered knowledges, offered new possibilities for them to chart their lives, and to imagine these possibilities for future generations.

2   The Toba Batak Culture as Political Location

Let me start then by providing background on the Toba Batak and Dutch colonial cultures that Tobing and Rony experienced. To begin, it is important to situate the experiences of my grandmother and mother in the context of Toba Batak culture and its patrilineality, and the expectations placed on women and girls.[3] Back in 1985, when Tobing was discussing these issues of gender, she remembered an old saying in the Toba Batak culture, which helps to illuminate some of the challenges that she faced. She recalled how people would react to the gender of new babies:

---

2   See 187–189, 217–218, this volume.
3   Sita T. van Bemmelen, *Christianity, Colonization, and Gender Relations in North Sumatra: A Patrilineal Society in Flux* (Leiden: Koninklijke Brill NV, 2017), 63–71; Jan S. Aritonang, *Mission Schools in Batakland (Indonesia), 1861–1940*, trans. Robert R. Boehlke (Leiden: E.J. Brill, 1994), 49.

In the old days, they say if it is a boy, "*Taho ma i.*" "*Taho ma i*" means "very fortunate, very lucky." And if it is a girl, they would say "*Ngoluna i ma.*" "*Ngoluna i ma*" means "As long as it lives." "A son is worth more than a girl."[4]

As Tobing's comments show, there was an intense weight placed on gender, even from the outset of one's life.

This awareness of the gendered differences between men and women was a constant in Tobing's and Rony's lives, and reinforced by Toba Batak culture, as well as the other cultures with which they came into contact. As discussed in Chapter 1, Tobing spent her initial years on the east coast of Sumatra away from the Toba Batak region due to her father's job on the railroad system. Thus, as a ten-year-old, Tobing had the opportunity to observe other cultural practices, such as when she saw a young Muslim woman who had been divorced multiple times. The situation of this woman made such an impression on her that she recalled it six decades later. As Tobing observed, without the status and protection of marriage, women had a far more precarious existence. Tobing commented,

> But when the husband got another wife, she had to leave and she had to take care of the children, usually because the stepmother wouldn't take care of the children and she didn't have the *marga* [clan system] like the Batak had.[5]

Tobing's reflection both underscores the difficulties that women faced if their husbands wanted to remarry, as well as the significance of having a communal support system available.

Similarly, Rony recalled a childhood story of her father delivering twin girls for a Chinese Indonesian family during the Japanese Occupation, and the family requesting that her father take them into his household. The fact that the family felt compelled to give up the girls for the survival of the family during wartime is heartbreaking, and illuminates the lesser worth placed on female children. Rony's father did not have the milk that the babies needed, so he was not able to help with this situation, even though Rony offered to care for one of the girls. Sadly, the babies died, likely because the family lacked the necessary

---

4   See 156, this volume.
5   See 163, this volume.

FIGURE 11   "Het dorp Pea Radja bij Silindoeng in de Bataklanden," [Pearaja Village in
Silindung in the Batak Region]
SPECIAL COLLECTIONS, LEIDEN UNIVERSITY LIBRARIES, PART OF KITLV A38,
KITLV, 12140, CA. 1890

nutrition to give them.[6] As Tobing and Rony came to know, male-focused hierarchies were a seemingly naturalized part of their environment within their
home cultures, and also across the other cultures that they experienced.

Within the Toba Batak culture itself, Tobing and Rony faced an intense
patrilineality. These issues are embodied in the very way that Tobing began
telling the family history as a story of male ancestors, without accompanying
discussion of our female ancestors. For example, Tobing started with a story
of an ancestor, Ompu [an honorific title used for the rank of grandparent]
Sotaronggal, who had four sons, one of whom was Raja Pontas, from whom
we are directly descended. Raja Pontas was the leader of the area, and also allowed the German missionary Nommensen to start his mission on family land
in Pearaja, the ancestral village. This focus on male ancestors was a reflection
of the absolute priority placed on having sons. The birth of sons to continue
the family line was considered paramount; it connected a man to his forebears
and linked him to the generations to follow. According to the *adat*, sons made
it possible for parents to gain rest and honor in the afterlife. Therefore, sons
inherited the land and other property. Sons also were needed to increase the

---

6   See 205, this volume.

family wealth and build resources for the family. Producing male heirs thus was seen as a vital accomplishment for women, especially as families gained political status and security through male offspring.[7]

In contrast to the treasured status of sons, daughters were considered more expendable, as they were expected to leave the family household as young adults in order to marry. In this male-focused social system, a woman's status was determined by her relationship to the men in the family, particularly to male ancestors and fathers, and later husbands and sons. From the outset then, Tobing had a secondary position as a daughter. For example, when her younger brother Johan was a year old, the family went home to the village of Simorangkir so that he could be named Namora Sojoangon and recognized within the family. Tobing remembered the necessity of return migration to the home village to hold the ritual: "It is a big name because it is one of the great-great-great-grandparents. You have to have a ceremony with the killing of a buffalo."[8] The water buffalo sacrifice indicates that this was a ceremony with the highest honor. No such naming ceremony was held for Tobing, despite the fact that she was the first-born child in the family.

Given the focus on men to inherit and become heads of the family, most families prioritized sons instead of daughters for educational opportunities. In this regard, it was an unusual decision for Tobing's parents to educate her not on the east coast of Sumatra where the family resided, but back in the Toba Batak region in northern Sumatra. A woman's education was typically considered to be secondary to a man's. Even if daughters were allowed to go to pursue education, it was not expected that they would continue past elementary school. Tobing remembered being one of a handful of girls attending school at the Hollandsche-Bataksche [Dutch-Batak] school, and that most young women married before they were twenty, an age considered "already too old" for becoming a wife.[9]

As Tobing's comment shows, marriage and family were essential goals for young women, especially as females gained status as adults through becoming married women. However, this recognition also was conditional upon remaining within the Toba Batak community: women were supposed to marry a man from another Toba Batak clan, and thus consolidate political connections. Rony noted that although young, unmarried women were required to follow the traditions of *adat*, they were "not really counted in the *marga*, in the clan"

---

7   See 151, this volume; van Bemmelen, *Christianity, Colonization*, 16, 127, 133–134.
8   See 154, this volume.
9   See 165, this volume.

until they were married.[10] These issues were pivotal because alliances built through these marriages were central to the construction of the Batak social system.[11] According to Tobing, the wife-givers were called the *hula hula* while the wife-receivers became the *boru*, which means daughter. Political connections were further consolidated as extended family members also were obligated by this relationship. As Tobing explained,

> So then the whole clan or family is your *boru*. They have to help you in case there is something that is necessary to be helped, while you are helping the *hula hula*. And the *hula hula* of course has *hula hula again* ...[12]

These connections with their attendant obligations forged strong bonds among different families.

The importance of these political connections was imbedded in Toba Batak culture, as can be seen in the way that Tobing, the oldest of eleven children, named all of her siblings in the course of relating her family's history in 1985. Tellingly, while all of her siblings were discussed in relation to key life events or their careers, her sisters were identified specifically by the families into which they married, and thus now belonged according to Batak culture. These familial connections by marriage became a foundational part of her sisters' identities, as well as a mapping of the family's political connections. In characterizing her siblings, Tobing did not feel it necessary to mention the families into which her brothers married however, as men retain their own political position and identity with marriage.[13]

Upon marriage, while a new daughter-in-law had some status because of her marriage to a son, she still was expected to be in a subservient position within the household, especially to her mother-in-law. However, a daughter-in-law could gain greater political authority through the birth of sons, and eventually, by becoming a mother-in-law herself. Conversely, if daughters stayed unmarried within the family household, their status diminished as they got older, not only because they were perceived as taking resources beyond their expected term of dependence, but also because they did not have their own households or children. Widows had a precarious political existence, because the *adat* law enforced strict rules regarding wives who had lost their husbands.

---

10   See 221, this volume.

11   Clark E. Cunningham, *The Postwar Migration of the Toba-Bataks to East Sumatra*. Cultural Report Series, No. 5 (New Haven, CT: Yale University, Southeast Asia Studies, 1958), 17–33.

12   See 155, this volume.

13   See 153–155, this volume.

Rony remembered that when her grandmother was widowed, she was required to remarry a family member in order to stay in the household. As she said, "Women had to stay in the family or go home. That's what the *adat* said." The social code thus naturalized male dominance as a central precept within Toba Batak culture.[14]

In keeping with these cultural priorities, most women's labor focused on the household, especially by addressing the family's needs. For example, Tobing's mother married at sixteen, and gave birth to eleven children. Rony remembered her grandmother's extensive work in watching over the family and running the household:

> My grandmother had to do a lot, especially because they did not have running water and it was kind of hilly ... I never saw her working in the rice fields, but she had rice fields too and helped there as well. Even after they harvested the rice, they made the field into a pond and raised fish for sale. And all other times, she was weaving too. She wove the *ulos* [woven ceremonial Toba Batak cloth] and once a week on Saturday mornings, she walked to and from the market and would sell the *ulos*. So that's how she had the money to buy meat, oil, salt, and other necessities.[15]

Thus, Rony explains how her grandmother had considerable physical labor in her daily routine of caring for everyone, in addition to weaving and working in the rice fields. In her narrative, Rony also discusses how her grandmother took care of the family through her emotional labor, and was an especially loving and nurturing person. Hence, a central part of her grandmother's work was attending to the physical needs of running a household, as well as facilitating the bonds among people in the household.[16]

3   Colonial Domesticity

The Toba Batak culture was not the only cultural context which Tobing and Rony experienced. As Toba Batak women in the unfolding decades of the 20th century, they both came of age during a critical era of massive political

---

14   See 200, this volume; van Bemmelen, *Christianity, Colonization*, 171–174.
15   See 219, this volume.
16   See 219–220, this volume. For more on women's labor as well as women's access to land, see Janet Rodenberg, *In the Shadow of Migration: Rural Women and Their Households in North Tapanuli, Indonesia* (Leiden: KITLV Press, 1997), 43–46, 101–113.

and economic change in Indonesia which included multiple wars—one of the reasons why their stories are so important to tell. Members of this generation lived in a compacted time of different empires and military actions, as well as rapidly changing social norms.[17] In the Philippines context, Denise Cruz names these kinds of processes "transpacific femininities," as Filipinas were shaped in their modernity by the interactions of the Philippines with Spain and the United States, as well as with Japan. Similar to the patterns that would unfold in Tobing's and Rony's lives, Denise Cruz discusses modernities that would include Filipinas being able to use multiple languages, engage in travel to different sites, and obtain specialized degrees whether in the United States or the Philippines.[18] These changes became manifest in Tobing's life as well. In contrast to her own mother and her future mother-in-law, Tobing's education and labor prospects were different due to her specific circumstances, including her early upbringing away from the Toba Batak region and her advanced colonial education. Tobing's challenge then became how to reconcile the new gendered practices she learned through Dutch colonial education with the Toba Batak practices she encountered at home and through moving back to the Toba Batak region during other periods in her life.[19]

The cultures of domesticity that Tobing and Rony learned as elite young women traveled across different generations and political regimes, and regularly was a factor in their lives.[20] In the critical period between 1870 and 1945 in which both came of age, domesticity was an ideology of "bourgeois respectability" promulgated across multiple empires.[21] Ballantyne and Burton argue that these issues were "a constitutive feature of imperial and colonial encounters in the context of global modernity," as empires spread ideas and domestic practices around the world.[22] Thus, both Tobing and Rony gained firsthand

---

17   Susan Rodgers, ed. and trans., *Telling Lives, Telling History: Autobiography and Historical Imagination in Modern Indonesia* (Berkeley: University of California Press, 2005), 3–4, 7.

18   Denise Cruz, *Transpacific Femininities: The Making of the Modern Filipina* (Durham, NC: Duke University Press, 2012), 6.

19   See 159–161, 166–169, 178–180, 202–203, this volume. For the influence of modernity on changing 20th-century gender roles prior to World War II, see Elsbeth Locher-Scholten, *Women and the Colonial State: Essays on Gender and Modernity in the Netherlands Indies, 1900–1942* (Amsterdam: Amsterdam University Press, 2000), 32–38.

20   Frances Gouda, *Dutch Culture Overseas: Colonial Practice in the Netherlands Indies, 1900–1942* (Amsterdam: Amsterdam University Press, 1995), 112–117; Rita Smith Kipp, "Emancipating Each Other: Dutch Colonial Missionaries' Encounter with Karo Women in Sumatra, 1900–1942," in *Domesticating the Empire: Race, Gender, and Family Life in French and Dutch Colonialism,* ed. Julia Clancy-Smith and Frances Gouda (Charlottesville: University Press of Virginia, 1988), 211–212.

21   Tony Ballantyne and Antoinette Burton, *Empires and the Reach of the Global: 1870–1845* (Cambridge, MA: Belknap Press, An Imprint of Harvard University Press, 2014), 333–334.

22   Ballantyne and Burton, *Empires and the Reach of the Global,* 334.

FIGURE 12 "Pastoren und Lehrerfrauen der Gemeinde Pearadja, Sumatra" [Pastors and Teachers' Wives in the Pearaja Local Community, Sumatra]. Figures 12 and 13 demonstrate the introduction of cultures of domesticity and women's education to the Pearaja area by arriving missionaries.
AMS DER VEM. ARCHIVE NUMBER: 203–436

FIGURE 13 "Krankenpflegerinnen Pearaja" [Pearaja Caregivers]
AMS DER VEM. ARCHIVE NUMBER: 203–98

knowledge of ideologies that emphasized that a woman's place was in the home, and underscored the centrality of women's identities primarily as wives and mothers. Furthermore, as young adults, they each graduated from specialized training programs in Java which prepared them to be teachers regarding domesticity for other young women.[23]

These issues were realized in Tobing's daily educational experience following her migration to the Toba Batak region as a young girl. After initially attending school in Tarutung, Tobing furthered her education in Sigompulon in sixth grade as the Dutch educational system had started a girls' dormitory with a German missionary, Zuster [Sister] Frieda Lau, as the dormitory mother.[24] The availability of the dormitory reshaped the intimate spaces of home and households for these young women, sending them to a more public educational environment under the surveillance of colonial educators and missionaries. It thus exposed them on a daily basis to European education and culture regarding issues of domesticity. In these new educational spaces, girls were introduced to colonial educational curriculum in the classroom, and also were trained for their future lives as female heads of households. The young women received lessons in the 'modern' way to clean the house and take care of the household, as well as to do needlework or use a sewing machine. In the process, women like Tobing developed skills that they would continue to perform throughout their lives. For example, Tobing felt a natural affinity to sewing and needlework, a talent that she traced to her mother's enjoyment of this kind of labor, and one that was later passed down to younger generations of the family too.[25] Thus, colonial activities were transmitted from one generation to the next, even as enjoyable labor.

The training of these young women was even more far-reaching than simply reshaping their household activities because there was a focus on moral education as well. Inculcating young women in these kinds of moral teachings presumably would have an impact on their role within the family, and how they raised the next generation. These lessons influenced the impressionable young women under Sister Frieda Lau's tutelage. As Tobing recalled:

> When we were in seventh grade every Saturday night, four of us girls would go to Zuster [Sister] Frieda Lau's room for half an hour or an hour to talk. I remember what she taught us about boys: "Girls are like butterflies. A butterfly, if someone holds the wings, then the glittering thing will

---

23   See 165–169, 222–225, this volume.
24   See 166, this volume; van Bemmelen, *Christianity, Colonization*, 464–465.
25   See 166, 219, 224, this volume.

stay on the fingers." Well, I took it literally. So when I was in Java [where Tobing later was a student], if a boy held my hands too long when he shook my hand, I would snatch my hands away! I was so naïve. I was then fourteen years old.[26]

As this passage shows, Zuster Frieda Lau was teaching the young women about expected social behavior and the fragility of the reputations of young women, as well as the proper kind of interaction they should have with young men.

Unlike many in her generational cohort, Tobing was supported by her family to continue her education beyond elementary school and to consider a profession. This is why Tobing had such an unusual and pioneering educational trajectory.[27] In pursuing her education, Tobing had ambitions of becoming a teacher or a midwife, the highest occupations to which young women at that time could aspire, following prescribed options for women's education. As she recalled, Tobing thought being a midwife was a good option as one still could practice this profession as a married woman, in keeping with the cultural norm that young women needed to marry and become wives and mothers.[28] In 1926, however, Tobing passed the exam to enter the Meisjeskweekschool voor Inlandsche Onderwijzeressen (MKS) in Salatiga, Java, which was a school for educating native teachers for four years with the Dutch language as the medium of instruction. Only twenty-four young women were accepted every year from all over Indonesia, highlighting the national reach of the school and the prestige of being admitted as a student.[29]

FIGURE 14
Inscription from H.L. Tobing's [Hermina Simorangkir] 1928–1930 schoolbook, when she was a student in Salatiga
TOBING FAMILY COLLECTION

26　See 166, this volume.

27　See 161, 167–168, this volume; For more background on advanced education for Toba Batak women, see van Bemmelen, *Christianity, Colonization*, 474–476.

28　See 167, this volume. Aritonang addresses the range of schools established for Bataks in the late 19th and early 20th century in Aritonang, *Mission Schools in Batakland*, 169–175.

29　See 167–168, this volume.

In keeping with the emphasis on domesticity, the curriculum focused primarily on the domestic arts, as students learned cooking and sewing, and other subjects such as batiking as well. Tobing even recalled an exam in ironing, in which students also demonstrated that they knew how to fold garments.[30] The level of detail in the tutelage that the young women received demonstrates how the colonial curriculum sought to restructure even the most mundane of household tasks. The school itself was a reterritorialization of space, with thorough control over the young women's daily experiences, as Tobing noted:

> We lived in a square dorm with a courtyard in the middle, and a place for a teacher to guard us in each corner. The rooms in the front part were classrooms. On the sides were the dorms.[31]

This layout suggests the kinds of surveillance enacted upon the young women by school authorities, as well as the contrast in the young women's relationship to their immediate environment compared to what they would have found in their home villages. Social relations were scrutinized and regulated too, especially the students' interactions with young men. Tobing recalled how she and her classmates would meet young male students through opportunities such as a conference in the city of Solo, also on Java. In accordance with the school's protected environment and its regular surveillance, Tobing reported that the principal would censor the letters the young women might write in order to discourage budding relationships.[32] Despite the multiple forms of social regulation, however, the young women forged new ideas for their futures, including marriage. Tobing recalled,

> When I was young, when I was at school in the 1930s, we didn't want to have the bride price. Because we thought we were "sold out," something like that. We thought we were bought by the husband's family. We, the first girls who went to school in Java, wrote something about that. But when we married, we did the same. It was the same with all the ceremony and so on. No one dared to go outside that.[33]

This story underscores the kinds of societal pressures brought to bear upon these highly educated young women to adhere to customary ideas about marriage and family, even as they might have considered other alternatives. It also

---

30   See 168, this volume.
31   Ibid.
32   See 169, this volume.
33   Ibid.

shows how they negotiated gendered cultures across their experiences in both educational and home environments.

In a parallel experience to Tobing's education a generation before, Rony attended the Opleiding School voor Vak Onderwijzeressen (OSVO) in Jakarta—the teachers' training school for home economics—from 1949 to 1952 when she was a young woman. She remembered her three-year OSVO education in detail, with the initial six months serving as an introduction to necessary subjects like cooking and washing, as well as their theory and practice. In addition, the curriculum included other subjects like childcare and psychology, as well as the study of the Indonesian language. Since Rony had to choose between a cooking and sewing curriculum and she knew how to sew already, she chose the cooking track, learning European and Asian cuisine.[34]

Rony's schooling at the OSVO was the first time that she lived independently away from a family unit. Despite the fact that the female students lived in an outside school setting in a dormitory, it was a very protected environment. Rony was aware of not only the surveillance within the school, but also from the surrounding community, and that shaped her actions to some extent. For example, she had male acquaintances who would visit or with whom she would correspond, but she avoided dating. In part, this was because Rony was shy as a young woman, but it also was due to Tobing's strict training regarding morality. Rony explained that her mother cautioned her about developing relationships with men, especially because of the scrutiny of young women within the Batak community.[35] Furthermore, Rony was extremely aware of her vulnerability due to her youth and gender: "I had to take care and watch out, to be guarded and vigilant, because I was a young woman alone in the city."[36] Rony recalled an earlier time during World War II where she was chased by an inebriated Japanese soldier, which left an impression upon her about the danger that young women faced.[37]

After graduation from the OSVO, as a condition of her government scholarship, Rony taught in Siantar for three years, from 1952 to 1955, as a home economics teacher at the SKP Kristen (Christian Home Economics School).[38] As she explained: "In the home economics schools, the expectation was that the girls would be introduced to modern ways, up-to-date living."[39] As a teacher, Rony was required to offer junior high-level courses similar to those she had

---

34   See 223–224, this volume.
35   See 226, this volume, and 203, for another example of this scrutiny.
36   See 226, this volume.
37   Ibid.
38   See 226–228, this volume.
39   See 227, this volume.

taken at the OSVO. Since she had learned the cooking track, she taught different aspects of cooking and household maintenance: "nutrition, setting the table, figuring out a menu, food preparation, housecleaning, everything that has to do with the house, the tools you use."[40] In 1954, she also started teaching in another home economics teachers' training school called SGKP—Sekolah Guru Kepandaian Puteri—with an Indonesian-language curriculum.[41] The fact that both Tobing and Rony received such intensive lessons regarding domesticity during their educational training was a testament to the pervasiveness of gender hierarchies that emphasized that a woman's place was in the home. Furthermore, their experience underscores how domesticity and colonial ideologies continued from one generation to the next, even as they were updated by modern practices and concepts. These issues also highlight how gendered knowledges regarding one's place in the family, home, and workforce were transmitted to younger generations.

4   Converging Gender Hierarchies

In this historical context, what I find striking is not the conventional dichotomy between the traditional culture of the Toba Batak in contrast to the modern culture introduced by Dutch colonialism, but rather the convergence of gender hierarchies across both Tobing's and Rony's experiences. Central to these hierarchies were three main precepts: the secondary status of women compared to men, the emphasis on women's roles in the household and the family, and the regular surveillance and containment of women's movements. Rather than a break in experiences, these were key ways in which the Toba Batak culture and colonial and postcolonial cultures of domesticity reinforced each other in both Tobing's and Rony's experiences. Both had the same effect: the placing of women in a seemingly naturalized, constrained position within the home.[42]

To begin to map out these convergences, I turn now to Tobing's experience as a young wife in the 1930s, during which these issues are illuminated in sharp relief due to the change in Tobing's experiences from when she ran her own household during the early stages of her marriage, to when she lived in her

---

40   See 228, this volume.

41   Ibid.

42   Dawn Mabalon offers an important parallel perspective regarding the expectations and surveillance of Filipinas in the United States. Dawn Bohulano Mabalon, *Little Manila Is in the Heart: The Making of the Filipina/o American Community in Stockton, California* (Durham, NC: Duke University Press, 2013), 151–169, 173–181.

husband's village from 1937 to 1939 in her mother-in-law's household. As discussed, in the early 1930s, Tobing moved to Amuntai, Borneo (now Kalimantan), to join her husband, Gerhard L. Tobing in his government post as a medical doctor. In many ways, Tobing's role as a new wife was the very portrait of colonial modernity, as both Tobing and her husband represented the Indonesian elite.[43] Tobing reported about her spouse's expectations for her work: "My husband thought that it was most important for me just to take care of the social life [in addition to the house and family], as that was needed for men with power and influence."[44] Although Tobing yearned to fulfill the professional aspirations for which she had worked so hard, Gerhard L. Tobing discouraged her from taking on paid employment outside of the home, and offered to pay her the same amount that she would have earned as a teacher. Thus, despite Tobing's professional ambitions, Tobing's husband emphasized that her primary place was within the family and the home. In keeping with this, one of Tobing's important memories of this time period is her performance as a hostess to the

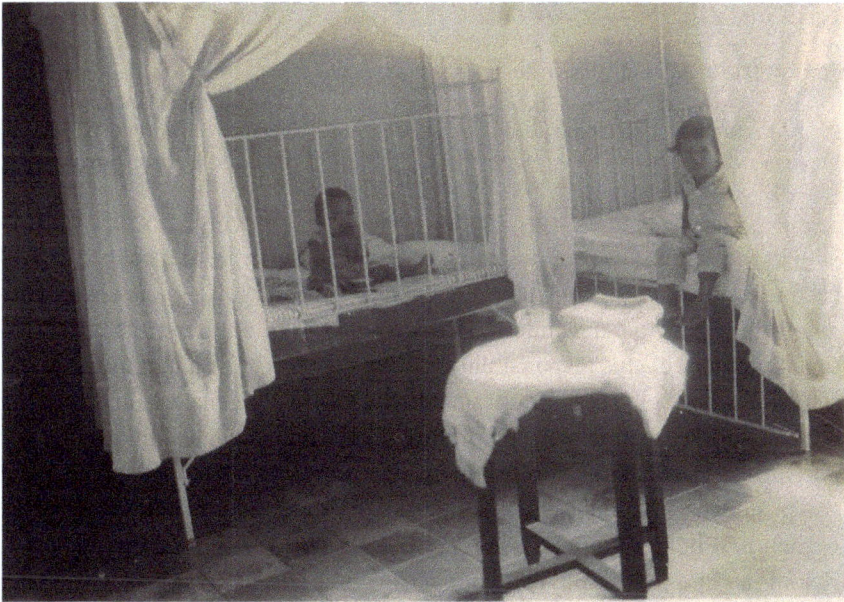

FIGURE 15   Minar T. Rony and Apoel Loembantobing in their cribs, c.1933. Their beds show
the introduction of new kinds of spatialities in domestic arrangements
TOBING FAMILY COLLECTION

---

43   See 171–173, this volume.
44   See 171, this volume.

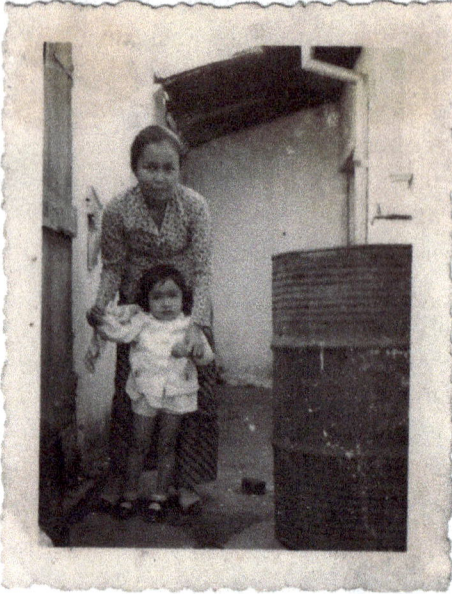

FIGURE 16   H.L. Tobing and Minar T. Rony,
              c.1934
              MINAR T. RONY COLLECTION

FIGURE 17   The back of the previous photo, with
              the inscription in Minar T. Rony's
              adult handwriting, "With Mama"
              MINAR T. RONY COLLECTION

elite in the Amuntai community due to her husband's role as a colonial medical professional. As a young wife at eighteen years old, Tobing was expected to
entertain the Dutch and Indonesian personnel.[45] Tobing reported about the
social pressure of this responsibility, "I didn't want to give a bad image of my
school or of myself as an Indonesian doctor's wife."[46] In accordance with her
social position as a doctor's wife, Tobing sought innovative techniques for her
parenting as well. For example, shortly after Rony was born, Tobing's husband
was posted in Semarang, Java, and they took the modern transportation of a car
to their new home. Tobing reported in detail about how she constructed a car-
rier for her one-month-old daughter because she had to find a way to keep her
daughter safe in the automobile. As young children, Apoel and Rony also had
cribs, as seen in Figure 15, which represented the introduction of new kinds of
spatial arrangements for child care. For these and other matters, Tobing's regular consultation with books and magazines illustrates the spread of domestic

---

45   See 170–173, this volume.
46   See 173, this volume.

ideologies through print culture, and the far-reaching and continued effect of her Dutch-language education, which emphasized these issues.[47]

After similar posts in Java at Semarang and Magetan, Gerhard L. Tobing decided to take advanced medical study at Leiden University in the Netherlands from 1937 to 1939. This decision illuminates how migration processes themselves were gendered, with men having far more mobility than women, as in the case of the contrast in experiences for Tobing and her husband.[48] While Gerhard L. Tobing went to study at Leiden for twenty months to pass a Dutch certification exam and then to prepare for an ear, nose, and throat specialty, Tobing traveled with her children to her husband's family village of Pearaja to stay with her mother-in-law. Unlike her husband, who as a male doctor was able to maintain his cosmopolitanism and independent career and study in a Dutch colonial metropole, Tobing was expected to return to his family household while he was away and remain part of a family unit. Her migration to Pearaja underscores how women were expected to maintain traditional ways, no matter how modern they had become, and uphold normative behaviors.[49] As seen by this situation, women such as Tobing faced intense gendered scrutiny about their proper role within the family household.

During this period, Tobing had an especially challenging time. Due to her birth family's migration to eastern Sumatra, she was not familiar with the Batak way of life. Since she was not raised or educated to work as a woman in the village, it was hard for her to perform the most basic of tasks, such as preparing ground for planting. Tobing explained,

> My mother-in-law would say to people, "Well, my first daughter-in-law's hoe is only her fountain pen. She can't even hoe the ground once. But my second daughter-in-law can have a plot of ground hoed as big as a winnow, about three yards square, with one hoe."[50]

The physical labor of being a woman in the village was very unfamiliar to Tobing in all ways, especially because it was a rural, agricultural economy. In 1938, Tobing was twenty-seven years old with many accomplishments, but still

---

47   See 174, this volume.

48   See 177–178, this volume; Rodenburg, *In the Shadow of Migration*, 10.

49   See 178–180, 202–203, this volume; Mabalon, *Little Manila*, 154–165, 173–174; Cruz, *Transpacific Femininities*, 7; Lan P. Duong, *Treacherous Subjects: Gender, Culture, and Trans-Vietnamese Feminism*, under "Introduction," "Treacherous Subjects: The Films and Literature of the Vietnamese and the Vietnamese Diaspora" Section, Kindle ebook (Philadelphia, PA: Temple University Press, 2012).

50   See 178, this volume.

expected to do the necessary but rudimentary tasks of village life. One task that was especially onerous was the feeding of pigs:

> I cried sometimes while squeezing the mash: "Is this now a doctor's wife's job? Is this now a teacher's job?" I had my teaching diploma, and yet I had to take care of these pigs![51]

Rony also remembered in her autobiography how her mother found delivering food to the workers in the fields difficult, even though it was an expected part of the daily routine. Rony commented, "My mom, the city girl, had a hard time doing all that and adjusting to that way of life."[52] As this story shows, Tobing faced many challenges not just because she grew up away from Batak culture, but also because she was accustomed to a privileged life in which her education and professional achievements were acknowledged. This was not the case in the rural village of her husband's family.

In the village, Tobing encountered more pressure to adhere to the Batak way of life in terms of her daily labor, as well as to attend to her family responsibilities. At one point, her mother-in-law called for a 'magician woman' to administer to her, as she just had two children at the time. Within the Toba Batak culture, childbearing and having many sons was seen as a central responsibility for married women. But as a Christian, Tobing did not want the consultation at all. She related in detail:

> I was told that I was possessed because I didn't have many children like the villagers did. I had only two, and my youngest child Minar was already five years old. My mother-in-law thought I should be examined by a magician woman. And then the magician woman came, and all these other women let her see their palms, like a soothsayer. But I said, "No, I don't want it. I believe in God and I don't want anything to do with these kind of people."[53]

These stories show how education and cosmopolitanism had different meanings and costs for men and women. Even so, Tobing continued on in the village, not saying anything back to her mother-in-law out of respect. She related:

> I wrote to [my husband in] Holland, "I want to leave the house, I want to go to Java." But then, what could my husband do? Choose between his

---

51   See 179, this volume.
52   See 203, this volume.
53   See 179, this volume.

mother and his wife? He wrote me a letter and said: "Whoever shall fight to the end, he or she will pluck the sweet fruit." For me it meant "You stay there, put." Then I stayed on, but it was really with heartbreak.[54]

Tobing was doing her best to observe the male-focused hierarchies of the Toba Batak culture, especially as upheld by her mother-in-law, even though it came at great personal cost.

Like Tobing, Rony also experienced similar issues during her life regarding the privileging of men in terms of opportunities and resources, the emphasis on keeping daughters within the household, and the constant social surveillance that women faced. Rony's gendered knowledge as a daughter was well honed from the outset, especially as her closest sibling in age was her brother Apoel, who was older than her by only two years. Hence, the difference in gendered expectations was quite apparent. Unlike Apoel, who enjoyed exploring and outside sports, Rony's movements were far more monitored and she was expected to stay close to home and not emulate her brother. Rony recalled: "I would follow him, and then he would say, 'You go home because you're a girl. You're not supposed to follow me with the boys.'"[55] Rony explained that Apoel had more opportunity to engage in these kinds of activities because of gendered roles and assumptions, including the allotment of different kinds of tasks. When the family lived in Bukit Batu during the Japanese Occupation, for example, Apoel would go with his male friends to sell produce in Singapore, traveling by boat over the Straits of Malacca. In contrast, while Rony also was expected to help in the family enterprise, her activities were confined to the local space of home. Hence, one of her primary responsibilities was to take care of her younger sister Demak, as well as to practice domestic skills such as sewing, including embroidery.[56] These required responsibilities shaped both her social identity and her ability to move within the community, as she did not have the same freedom enjoyed by her brother Apoel.

These expectations were in place both within one's home, and in the homes of other members of the extended family. For example, during World War II, Rony and her brother were sent to her father's village to live with their grandmother for safety as well as for education. In her grandmother's home, Rony was supposed to help in the household and to do the tasks obligated of a young woman, including washing clothing and sometimes cooking. It was a challenging time, as her grandmother had suffered a stroke and did not always

---

54   Ibid.
55   See 203, this volume.
56   See 213–214, this volume.

recognize Rony as her granddaughter. While Rony adapted to the village way of life, her brother Apoel found it more difficult to adjust, and asked to live in Siantar where he would be able to live in a more familiar urban environment.[57]

These patterns of household labor continued as she became older. As a daughter, Rony tried her best not to make demands on the family's resources, and to do her part with what was needed to maintain the home. She was used to having regular household chores, and putting others first, including visitors to the house. It was assumed, for instance, that Rony would care for relatives who stayed in the house by cooking or offering them a place to sleep. As an example of the expectation for young women that their needs came second, Rony remembered one time when another relative used her bedroom, and afterwards her best sweater went missing. She commented on the incident, "I mentioned it to my mother. Her answer was, 'She came from the mountains. It must be very cold there. She must have a better use for it than you.'"[58] In this way, Tobing was teaching Rony about the belief that young women should put other people in the family before themselves, especially older relatives.

For both Tobing and Rony, the pervasiveness of gendered hierarchies became especially pronounced with the death of Gerhard L. Tobing in July 1947. After the Japanese left Indonesia in 1945, Tobing's husband had a job in a hospital in Kisaran, and went regularly to Tanjung Morawa and other nearby clinics in the region in 1946 and 1947. The Dutch tried to return to Indonesia despite the declaration of Indonesian independence. As the Dutch approached the region in July 1947, Gerhard L. Tobing was on duty, and Dutch troops shot at his car. When they realized that he was a doctor, Gerhard L. Tobing and his driver were taken to Tanjung Morawa, but it was too late to save them.[59] Tobing was in Siantar when she received a visit from the Red Cross notifying her of her spouse's death. Rony, who was staying with her paternal grandmother in Pearaja at the time, recalled what it meant to learn the news: "My mother wrote me a letter about what had happened. I could see that tear drops had been flowing on the letter, and I could see the places where her tears had dried."[60] Gerhard L. Tobing's death would transform the lives of Tobing and their children.

When her husband was killed, Tobing's economic situation became far more challenging. As a thirty-six-year-old widow who needed to support four

---

57   See 215, this volume.
58   See 230, this volume.
59   See 187–188, 217, this volume.
60   See 217, this volume.

children during those tumultuous times, she struggled to build a new life for the family. She shared vivid memories of the precarious nature of that era:

> Independence came in 1945, my husband was killed in 1947. It was like a dream. Everything was so fast, and you had no support from anybody. The Red Cross, yes. But since, there were so many people, they could only give salted fish, some bad rice.[61]

Tobing would sell one of her sarongs [length of cloth wrapped around lower part of body and fastened at waist] or other belongings so that she could "survive with the children." Given Tobing's difficulties in living in the village during an earlier era, it is not surprising that she chose not to return to Pearaja, especially because she was concerned about how she could provide for her family. Tobing noted that returning to Tarutung only would give her limited income from a rice field, in addition to a small pension as a widow with children. Due to these reasons, Tobing decided to support herself and remain in the city.[62]

As a widow, Tobing continued to be defined by her husband's identity: "My husband died in 1947, but I still went on with his name, the wife of Doctor Tobing. You are behind the husband, being the doctor's wife, even after his death." At first, through the help of a relative, Tobing sewed nurse uniforms for a Medan hospital. After six months, she sought to become a teacher, but encountered resistance as a working single mother from the school administration. Tobing had to promise that if she was unable to come to work, that they could bring in another teacher and pay that person Tobing's salary for the day. As Tobing commented, "At that time, I was fighting for my job." Tobing observed that the initial years were the most difficult because she was a teacher for two elementary school classes at Josua Institut. In addition, she took classes in the afternoon for a more advanced teacher's diploma so she could better support the family. During that time in 1947, Tobing was reluctant to secure a job at a government school as the Netherlands was still an occupying force.[63]

Meanwhile, Rony remained in Pearaja for about six months. Tobing assumed that family would help her daughter, however, as Rony noted, "But this didn't really happen."[64] After she lost her father, her status changed considerably. Rony remembered,

---

61   See 189, this volume.
62   Ibid.
63   See 189, 218, this volume.
64   See 218, this volume.

When my dad was alive, there were many who would talk to me, but once
he was dead, it was as if I didn't exist anymore. Some people did not acknowledge me, even when I met them on the street. They would not talk
to me. They would turn their heads so they wouldn't have to look at me.[65]

Rony was experiencing political erasure because her father was no longer
there, a fact which underscored how female identities were so tied to the status of their male relatives. Consequently, she especially cherished the relatives
who did try to look after her and saw her as a person. She recalled in detail how
two distantly related uncles would visit, even though they had to walk a long
way from their village in Sumur to see her. Rony related that although they did
not have many material resources to share with her, their "kind, loving words"
had great meaning for her. Another crucial support during this period was her
maternal grandmother, whom Rony would find on Saturdays following school,
selling *ulos* [woven spiritual cloth] in the marketplace. Her grandmother saw
to her welfare, giving her some money so that Rony could purchase her weekly
groceries in the absence of funds arriving from her mother.[66]

After her father's death, Rony's prospects as a daughter became much more
limited. In order to search for further options for her family, Tobing went to the
provincial office of education to find a scholarship for her son Apoel. Instead,
she was offered a scholarship for her daughter to become a teacher in a home
economics program, an indication of how prevalent domesticity continued to
be as both an ideology and a curriculum, and how it was sanctioned by the government as a form of training for young women. Rony recalled how her mother
expressed to her that the scholarship "was a good opportunity" and that her
mother could then better support Apoel in his study at a high school. Rony was
devastated because she had hoped to go to medical school. At that point, she
already had applied to enter senior high school, and was planning to pursue
medical training in Medan at the Universitas Sumatra Utara [North Sumatra
University].[67] Thus, the gendered knowledge that the males always came first
was a regular reality in Rony's life across the different contexts in which she
lived. This became especially apparent after the death of her father when the
family had far fewer resources to support her education.

As my discussion shows, both Tobing and Rony faced parallel gender hierarchies across their household and educational experiences. Their different environments upheld ideas of male patriarchy, in which women were defined in

---

65   Ibid.
66   See 218–220, this volume.
67   See 221–222, this volume.

relation to the men in their lives, and a woman's central roles were to be wife, mother, and household caretaker. These politics of home were constructed and normalized in both Toba Batak and Dutch colonial culture. Despite their gendered knowledges of a woman's place, however, Tobing and Rony made regular decisions about how to maximize their choices, as the next section explores in greater detail.

5   Negotiation and Challenge

Although gendered hierarchies were a persistent component of life, Tobing and Rony strove in important ways to find alternate forms of political autonomy. Whether through the support of key family members or through finding other spaces or resources for themselves, both sought methods to surmount these inequalities. The barriers they faced as women though were often quite considerable, and challenging them might exact an accompanying high price. At the same time, a close analysis of their histories suggests that they sometimes found the means to alter or even evade gender hierarchies, albeit temporarily.

For instance, a focus on their recollections reveals that despite the favoring of sons, family members sometimes would circumvent these hierarchies to offer privileges to daughters. As previously discussed, Tobing's father wanted to send Tobing back to Tarutung when she was a young girl to give her expanded educational choices. Although there were other schools available in eastern Sumatra, Tobing's father insisted that she should learn Batak culture as well as Christianity. Tobing recalled that her father treated her in a similar way to her brothers. As she remarked, "I didn't feel the insecurity of being a girl. So I think that my father was very far ahead of his peers."[68] The backing of her father was instrumental for Tobing's ability to pursue her education, and an important factor in her being able to go to school in Salatiga as a young woman. His support of Tobing further can be seen through the fact that he accompanied her on the long journey to her school in Salatiga, and later made the trip again to Surabaya to attend her wedding.[69]

Not surprisingly, given the male-focused cultures through which they moved, political help from men was especially important in sanctioning new kinds of work and leadership, such as when Tobing attained greater prominence in the fields of education and politics in Medan in later years. After World War II, Tobing was a teacher in Medan from 1948 to 1964, as well as the principal of

---

68   See 161, this volume.
69   See 167–168, 170–171, this volume.

a training school for kindergarten teachers, the SGTKPWKI (Sekolah Guru Taman Kanak-Kanak Persatuan Wanita Kristen Indonesia), which she had helped to found in 1954.[70] Tobing acknowledged the aid she received to take on these responsibilities:

> That teaching was the nicest thing that could happen to me because I had support from everyone. The first was my own sister's husband, R.M. Simanjuntak, and then there was Marcus Tobing, he always called me Ompung, and Martin Siagian, he was at one time the inspector of the Department of Education in Medan. Mangara Manik, Melanthon Siregar, there were many who supported me.[71]

Part of the reason for this support, contends Tobing, was because of the expectation that a woman should be the head of the kindergarten teachers' training school, as it was considered labor more appropriate for a woman. Regarding her leadership, Tobing commented, "They trusted me wholly."[72] As in other stages in her life, the political support of men proved instrumental in enabling her to aspire to these kinds of positions.

By the same token, Tobing's narrative suggests how women's leadership positions might be conceptualized in relation to home and family, as was the case for Tobing. When she spoke of the changes after the Indonesian Revolution, tellingly, she says of Sukarno, the first president of the Republic of Indonesia, "He urged women to be strong, to assist their husbands."[73] Tobing became involved with the PWKI, the Persatuan Wanita Kristen Indonesia, the Indonesian Christian Women's Association. Ironically from today's standpoint which more fully recognizes the additional labor undertaken by single parents, Tobing's colleagues thought she would be a good leader because she was an educated widow who did not need to contribute time to her marriage and her husband. In fact, Tobing was reluctant at first to take on this leadership, but her colleagues told her that they would support her.[74] Rony recalled that Tobing won an election to become the chairman of the PWKI Sumatra Utara, [Indonesian Christian Women's Association, North Sumatra], and discussed the labor required of her position:

---

70   See 189–191, this volume.

71   See 191, this volume.

72   Ibid.

73   See 190, this volume.

74   Ibid. For a discussion of Sukarno's analysis of women's involvement in the new nation, see Mary Margaret Steedly, *Rifle Reports: A Story of Indonesian Independence* (Berkeley: University of California Press, 2013), 52–54.

On Sundays, she would have all these things going on because they were so busy.... After I left for the United States in August 1958, she also became a state representative to the provincial assembly for a while as a member of the PWKI, belonging to the Indonesian Christian Party, Partai Kristen Indonesia. The acronym is Parkindo. My mother was unusual in getting involved in politics. She was one of the first to get active and be involved. She was a good leader.[75]

Significantly, as shown in Tobing's case, the wake of the Indonesian Revolution brought the promise of new possibilities for women in political office.

Like Tobing, Rony also had a special relationship with her father, who had nurtured her independence and ambitions since she was a young girl. At a time when women's education was a secondary priority, her father supported her desire to enter the professional medical field.[76] Rony explained, "I always wanted to be a doctor like my dad. He encouraged me in this dream."[77] In the midst of the Japanese Occupation, Rony regularly visited her father at his hospital as it was near her school. In fact, her father allowed Rony to observe his work in the hospital, as long it was appropriate for a young girl to see.[78] This demonstrates her father's acknowledgment of Rony's medical ambitions, as well as displays his conscious decision to encourage her in a field that was very much male-dominated. Although Rony's interest in the hospital was unusual for the time period, Rony's mother Tobing accepted it because Rony was being looked after by her husband and Tobing knew her daughter would be safe.[79]

This kind of paternal guidance became one of the most enduring legacies that Rony received from her beloved father. She remembered her final conversation with her father years later when she was fourteen years old, a few months before his death. In this interaction, Gerhard L. Tobing encouraged his daughter to always strive for education and gave her words of advice regarding her eventual marriage. She recalled,

---

75 See 229–230, this volume.
76 See 204–205, 211–212, this volume. Analysis of women involved in the early 20th-century medical profession, including women receiving medical training as doctors, can be found in Liesbeth Hesselink, *Healers on the Colonial Market: Native Doctors and Midwives in the Dutch East Indies* (Leiden: KITLV Press, 2011), 218–220, PDF ebook, DOI: 10.26530/OAPEN_400271.
77 See 211, this volume.
78 See 211–212, this volume.
79 See 205, this volume.

My father said to me that I should always pursue my education as that
was the one thing that no one could take from me. That was my *senjata
hidup*, the most important thing in life [your livelihood]. He also said that
I should be twenty-five before I got married, because that was when I
would be mature, physically as well as mentally. The man that I chose
should not smoke, drink, or gamble.[80]

Looking back, Rony thinks her father was prescient about the importance of
having this final conversation, especially as they had not had previous in-depth
conversations before about how her life might unfold. This conversation would
stay with Rony for the rest of her life.[81]

Tobing and Rony learned that there was yet another way to achieve political autonomy: migration. Migration conferred possibilities for education and
work, and it relieved women of some of the responsibilities that were required
of females in terms of their daily duties within the Toba Batak culture. For example, when Tobing and Rony went to school in Java—Tobing in Salatiga and
Rony in Jakarta—both of them had much more freedom to make their own
decisions about what they wanted to do with their time.[82] Furthermore, it was
an opportunity to escape at least some of the surveillance and judgment faced
by women within family and community settings.

These processes are seen most clearly in the migrations that Tobing and
Rony undertook to go to the United States. Rony left for the United States first
in 1958, in part because she was not yet ready to get married. With her son
Apoel already in the United States for his studies, Tobing placed pressure on
Rony to become a wife within another Batak clan. As Rony wrote, her mother
began suggesting that it would be helpful to be accompanied to ceremonies
by a married daughter. As Tobing and Rony both knew, a married daughter
would provide more political and economic support within the Batak community through expanding and strengthening a family's inter-clan alliances.
However, while Rony had a Batak suitor at the time, she was reluctant to
marry. So, when she wrote to her brother Apoel about her situation, Apoel replied with information about a teaching job opportunity at Yale. Rony asked
for his help to take the one-year position: "And that is when I told him about
my situation, that I had a suitor who kept visiting. I wrote him, 'Please get
me out of here because Mama wants me to get married.'"[83] Apoel supported

---

80   See 216, this volume.
81   See 216–217, 228, this volume.
82   See 167–169, 222–226, this volume.
83   See 232, this volume.

his sister and was able to help her secure a one-year teaching position in the Indonesian language at Yale. Throughout these developments, the sanctioning of her departure by male relatives still was key. Rony commented that although she had a suitor who was hoping for an engagement prior to her departure, a male relative advised her mother to allow Rony to go abroad for the year.[84]

Without the surveillance of the Batak community in New Haven, Rony had more freedom to make choices about the course of her life, including her decision to develop a relationship with her future husband, A. Kohar Rony, a fellow Indonesian. As she remembered, her future husband Kohar was a persistent suitor.

> And I thought, "Well, since Kohar is around, maybe I should consider him." He wasn't a smoker, a gambler, or an alcoholic, which was what my dad had told me to think about if I was considering getting married. And Kohar seemed to be nice, as he was taking me to church every Sunday.[85]

Significantly, as Rony was half a world away from the extended family, she did not have to face the social scrutiny and censure for being involved with someone who was not Batak, especially as her brother Apoel by then had already returned to Indonesia. As she recalled, "This was my chance at marriage, as I happened to be here, and he happened to be there."[86] Even so, Tobing still had to explain Rony's decision for not marrying within the Batak community to others back in Indonesia. When Rony and her fiancé decided to get married, Rony's uncle (Tobing's brother-in-law) was a graduate student at SUNY [State University of New York] Oswego, and Rony asked whether he would be part of the ceremony to give her away. Afterwards, Tobing wrote a letter to Rony saying that she could not approve of the marriage because Rony's prospective husband was not Batak. So Rony told her uncle that she would understand if he did not want to be at the wedding. She reported, "His answer was, 'Oh no, your mother wrote me a different letter, and said to make the best of the situation.' I was surprised."[87] Rony realized afterwards that her mother felt pressure not to give her approval in public because of the social code of the Batak clan.[88]

As it turned out, Rony would go on to extend the possibility of migration and a different way of life to Tobing as well. In 1964, through Rony's intervention,

---

84   See 232–233, this volume.
85   See 235–236, this volume.
86   See 236, this volume.
87   Ibid.
88   See 155–157, 236, this volume.

FIGURE 18
Minar T. Rony at 35 Cave Street
in New Haven, 1959
MINAR T. RONY COLLECTION

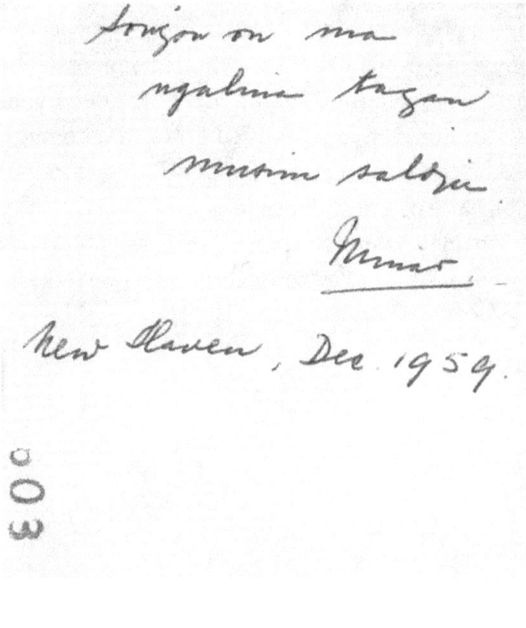

FIGURE 19
Writing on back of previous
image. The note in Batak reads,
"This is how cold it is during
the winter. [Signed] Minar. New
Haven, Dec. 1959"

Tobing was able to come to the United States to teach the Indonesian language at Yale too. Tobing would reside in the United States for fifteen years before finally returning home to live in Pearaja. Tobing valued her years in teaching students at Yale and stayed until 1979. Along with participating in the campus community, Tobing was an active member of her Lutheran church, joining the Women's Club and taking part in Friday potlucks and craft activities. Importantly, due to Tobing's extended work history in the United States, Tobing also was able to achieve more economic autonomy. As a result, Tobing could travel back forth between Indonesia and the United States regularly during her retirement years.[89] Rony commented about Tobing's independence during her senior years, "I was glad that I could help my mother in this way."[90]

The possibilities afforded by migration reshaped Tobing's life because of her extended absences from Indonesia, and also because it transformed her manner of living in Indonesia when she returned to Southeast Asia. In her retirement, Tobing divided her time between the United States and Indonesia, staying in Pearaja on her own terms. Tobing felt strongly about the need to remain in the village during the last part of her life. As Tobing explained: "Even though I could stay in Medan or Jakarta, I wanted to come back to the village because this is the inheritance of my husband's family."[91] Tobing credited her mother-in-law for instilling in her a sense of place in Pearaja. As she continued,

> From 1937 to 1939, when my husband was in Holland to study, I was in Tarutung and my mother-in-law was in this house. And I had to respect her for all her teachings and wise remarks in the past. That was actually maybe the main reason that I came back. She planted in me the love, or the awe, the respect for our grandparents' effort to have this village established. So when I became older, I thought I should come here. I have to take care of my husband's property, to keep and preserve it for my own children. Because that is the custom according to my mother-in-law then.[92]

It is important to note that Tobing chose not to return to the village at an earlier era in her life because she wanted to better support her children as a single mother after the death of her husband. That she did so at the end of her life speaks to the connection and responsibility she felt to the land and to her offspring, especially to the male descendants who would inherit the land.

---

89   See 192–195, 238–239, this volume.
90   See 239, this volume.
91   See 197, this volume.
92   Ibid.

Despite all the challenges she has faced and her departure to make a new life in the United States, Rony also remains tied to the ancestral village and the land through a sense of familial connection. She has returned regularly to the village and provided intergenerational support so that other members of the family can build that connection too, myself included. Most recently, in the last few years, she has returned to the village every year providing an opportunity for me to accompany my mother. Over the decades, my ability to write this book has been structured by these returns, whether I was a new college graduate in 1985 living with Tobing in the village, or by accompanying Rony in 2017, 2018, and 2019 back to Pearaja. Despite her secondary status as a daughter, Rony's pride in being a Toba Batak woman is a central part of her identity.

6   Conclusion

In the end, one of the main lessons I have learned from addressing Tobing's and Rony's narratives together is that culture is not immutable, and gender hierarchies are not inevitable. While this may seem an obvious lesson to many—at least to those of us who write women's history—it is important to underscore that in the case of Tobing and Rony, both faced a very strict social code within the Toba Batak culture. In addition, due to the historical context in which they came of age and the colonial cultures of domesticity with which they came into contact, Tobing and Rony faced extremely gendered environments from all sides which consolidated a decidedly subordinate position for women. Through focusing closely on Tobing's and Rony's narratives, however, it is possible to see how they negotiated change in the face of many challenges, even as they attended to their labor both within and outside the home.

By doing so, it is easier to see how memorykeeping, which is the focus of the remainder of the book, emerged as so essential for Tobing and Rony precisely because of their lesser political status as women in male-dominated societies. As women's memorykeeping is not perceived as a material legacy that coheres to male descendants, as in the case of the family land or home, it is possible to develop it as an independent political space. Thus, for Tobing and Rony, memorykeeping arose as a political strategy, binding together gendered knowledges through intergenerational storytelling and artifact collection that became portable across time and space. Their memorykeeping was not only produced through gendered knowledge, but it also became gendered knowledge in itself, as the subsequent chapters reveal.

PART 2

Curating Time

∴

CHAPTER 3

Stories and Silences
Telling the Past

1 Introduction

As discussed in Chapter 2, Tobing and Rony grew up in a Toba Batak culture
that privileged sons more than daughters because sons carried on the family
line. While daughters were important to the family project, they were seen as
ultimately expendable because they were expected to marry out to another
family. It was the heirs of the men, especially the male heirs of men, who were
considered central in Batak culture, and they were the ones who were supposed to inherit the land. Thus, patrilineality was a governing precept of the
Toba Batak culture in which both were raised. For example, according to the
old rules that Rony learned about as a child, if a woman was widowed, she
was supposed to marry again within her husband's clan, or return back to her
original clan and village.[1] Daughters, as Rony well knew, were secondary in the
political framework of the family.

Such gender hierarchies have a foundational impact on women's memorykeeping. Not all women, of course, are family memorykeepers. But for those
women who are, such as Tobing and Rony, to be a family memorykeeper is a
specific political positioning. It is a site of alterity in a male-focused authority
structure which renders women both integral and subordinate in the scheme
of things. As Rony demonstrates throughout her narrative, she is a 'provisional
insider' because she is a daughter, and thus occupies a more tenuous positioning.
However, as bearers of knowledge, women memorykeepers understand their
importance and essential nature to the family project. The phrase 'provisional
insider' references both Rony's status as well as her political vision and obser-
vations, as someone who is both *of* and *not of,* a positionality that enables her
to have a particular kind of critique. On the one hand, this positionality allows
her to witness how people might deploy privilege derived from male lineage to
claim authority and power, invoking the *adat* to maintain their position, while
the daughters are relegated to secondary status. But on the other hand, this perspective also suggests a possibility that there might be another way, in which
daughters do not have to be marginalized in Toba Batak culture behind sons.
These processes became particularly apparent in Tobing's and Rony's lives due to
the major political, economic, and social changes happening in the 20th century.

---

1 See 199–200, this volume.

© KONINKLIJKE BRILL NV, LEIDEN, 2021 | DOI:10.1163/9789004436237_005

FIGURE 20   Minar T. Rony as a toddler, ca. 1933–1934
             TOBING FAMILY COLLECTION

FIGURE 21
H.L. Tobing, Apoel
Loembantobing, and
Minar T. Rony, ca. 1935
TOBING FAMILY COLLECTION

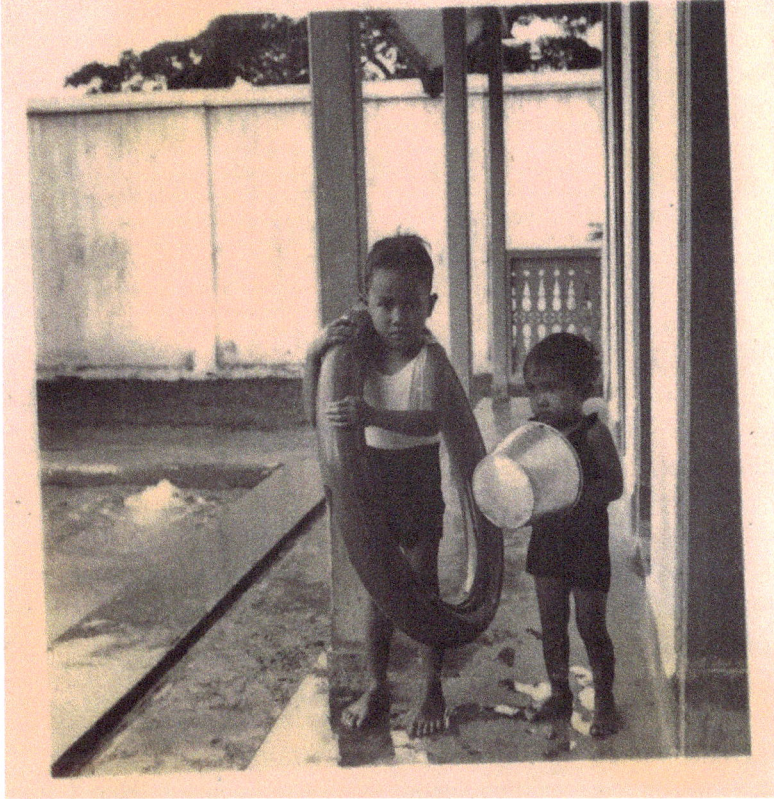

FIGURE 22   Apoel Loembantobing and Minar T. Rony, ca. 1935
TOBING FAMILY COLLECTION

In this chapter, I explore how women's memorykeeping creates an autonomous space for the critique of patriarchal structures and expectations, not only because of the perspective afforded by women's differential position, but also because women's memorykeeping allows their historical and cultural knowledges to be preserved over time, usually away from direct, public gaze, to resurface at another time and space in which it is safer to deploy this critique. As Ann Laura Stoler argues,

> Treating governance through the microphysics of daily lives has redirected historians to new readings of familiar archives and to new genres of documentation. It also has changed how we read—for discrepant tone, tacit knowledge, stray emotions, extravagant details, "minor" events.[2]

2   Ann Laura Stoler, *Haunted by Empire: Geographies of Intimacy in North American History* (Durham, NC: Duke University Press, 2006), 6.

Following Stoler's lead, my call in this chapter is to take women's memorykeeping seriously as a form of knowledge production and truth-telling, and to do so by a close analysis of my grandmother's and mother's life narratives, produced over thirty years apart.

2   Searching for Archives

This journey of women's memorykeeping involves an inversion of focus, a pivot from more recognized archives like those in government agencies or university libraries, to see how different methodologies might yield insights not revealed through more accustomed modes of inquiry. The conventional route for scholarship based on archival work is to find a rich, untapped collection in an institutional setting like a university or library archives, and then to develop research that emanates from those sources. Historical training underscores that we should treat the document as primary, to see it as a kind of truth, to take seriously the provenance in which it appears in a collection. In past decades however, scholars have emphasized that documents are cultural productions developed in specific historical contexts, and hence should be understood and treated as manifestations of their own historical period.[3] Furthermore, archives themselves narrativize history, requiring scholars to undertake counterstrategies in how they read the archives.[4]

Those of us who document populations that have undergone colonization know that histories told through empire generally depend upon the records of male colonial administrators and government officials. These histories tend to emphasize the destruction of indigenous culture in favor of Christian conversion, as well as uphold European models of masculinity and femininity. In addition, they often emphasize the perspectives of male leaders of higher social standing and with more institutional resources than others. Investigating women's histories through these kinds of archives thus requires deliberate strategy, especially given gendered hierarchies where women's experiences are devalued in institutional memory. To address women's experiences, for instance, we often have to investigate alternate sites of memory, as well as read across the grain in the archives. Aisha Finch, for instance, argues for the need

---

3   Michel-Rolph Trouillot, *Silencing the Past: Power and the Production of History*, Kindle ebook (Boston, MA: Beacon Press, 1995), 54.

4   Lisa Lowe, *The Intimacies of Four Continents* (Durham, NC: Duke University Press, 2015), 2; Ann Laura Stoler, *Along the Archival Grain: Epistemic Anxieties and Colonial Common Sense* (Princeton, NJ: Princeton University Press, 2009), 1–5.

to navigate the multiple violences represented by colonial archives, to lay bare "imperial fictions" and utilize "conceptual dexterity" to catch the most discreet of nuances.[5] Here, I want to be sure to highlight that women's counternarratives are still narratives and not necessarily 'authentic truth.'[6] Nevertheless, these issues call us to take seriously the production of knowledge through women's storytelling. They also push us to consider how personal collections produce different kinds of insights than institutional archives, which are privileged in the writing of history.

My challenge in addressing this project is further compounded through the difficulties in naming and articulating Indonesian American history, as our group's community formation largely is not found or recognized in the United States as a subject in formal archival settings. While the United States has had a regular interest in the region that became Indonesia, much of the material in US archives was produced through US investment 'over there' in Indonesia. For example, one can investigate the archives in Salem, Massachusetts, to locate records on the spice trade, or anthropological studies of Indonesia deposited at the Smithsonian Institution, or the growth of area studies in the Cold War era at places like Yale University and Cornell University. Other sites to search would include the archives of companies with business interests in Indonesia or universities in the United States where Indonesian students enrolled. All of these archival searches are important and immensely valuable. But these kinds of records tend to be from government and institutional perspectives, and one is hard-pressed to find the individual recollections of Indonesian women regarding their personal lives, much less those who have taken up long-term residence in the United States, in these archival collections.[7]

Women's memorykeeping, as demonstrated by Tobing and Rony, thus presents an immediate rebuff to these issues of selectivity and exclusion, requiring a pivot away from institutional memory and the knowledges produced through government categorization and institutionalized documentation. Whether featured in a formal institutional collection or not, women's memorykeeping is very much rooted in gendered relations of power. Typically, it manifests itself as gendered labor, an extension of the family project for which women bear the brunt of responsibility. Precisely because so much of women's

---

5 Aisha K. Finch, *Rethinking Slave Rebellion in Cuba: La Escalera and the Insurgencies of 1841–1844*, Kindle ebook (Chapel Hill: The University of North Carolina Press, 2015), 7, 10–12.

6 Yến Lê Espiritu, *Body Counts: The Vietnam War and Militarized Refuge(es)* (Berkeley: University of California Press, 2014), 3.

7 In her discussion of "the politics of our lack of knowledge," Lisa Lowe argues that "forgetting" illuminates "the more extensive erasure of colonial connections." Lisa Lowe, *The Intimacies of Four Continents* (Durham, NC: Duke University Press, 2015), 38.

FIGURE 23
H.L. Tobing with
Fatimah Tobing
Rony and Dorothy
Fujita-Rony,
ca. 1965. This
picture and the
next seem to be
taken on the same
outing
MINAR T. RONY
COLLECTION

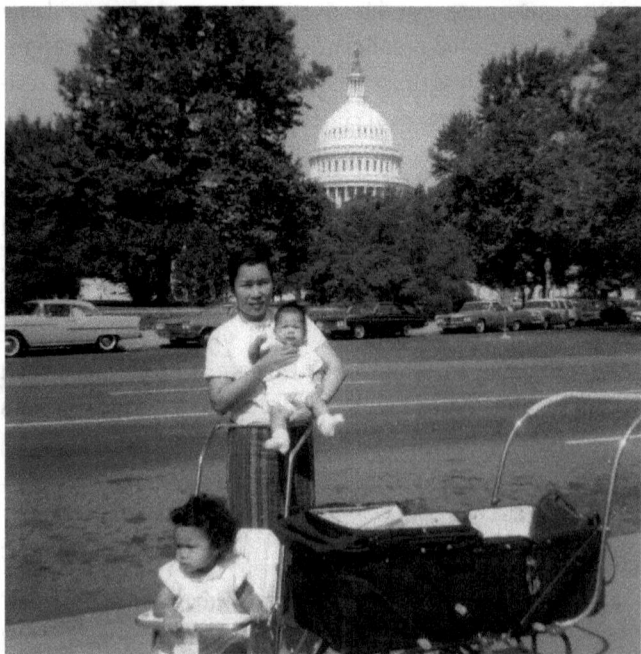

FIGURE 24
Minar T. Rony with
Fatimah Tobing
Rony and Dorothy
Fujita-Rony,
ca. 1965
MINAR T. RONY
COLLECTION

labor is considered of lesser worth, consumable, or disposable—childcare and preparing family meals are two clear examples of this—women's memorykeeping often is taken for granted, especially if it is treated as this kind of devalued labor.[8]

Reflecting its gendered nature, women's memorykeeping also might be underrated as affective labor, as a form of emotional labor involving the work of caring for another's feelings. In the US context, Micaela di Leonardo explains the role of this gendered activity in her discussion of kin work, the effort needed to build connections across households. di Leonardo delineates the affective and material work for these processes, labor that requires forethought and engagement to develop these kinds of social networks, and the use of resources to maintain something that others might not consider important, even though it brings personal satisfaction or other forms of power related to the familial context.[9]

As an extension of these issues, women's memorykeeping regularly manifests itself as intergenerational labor, in which women administer to both older and younger generations by preserving the past for the future.[10] In this form, women's memorykeeping becomes communal work that usually takes shape in private spaces in the home where it is not publicly observed. Thus, even if critiques of patriarchy or alternative knowledges emerge through memorykeeping, typically these discussions are not voiced in arenas beyond these private settings, which contributes to its lack of recognition. In some ways, memorykeeping might be considered similar to gossip, in that it is a communal activity that often is dismissed or not seen as important, yet also can emerge as a site of resistance and social critique.

Furthermore, there is a temporal dimension to Tobing's and Rony's memorykeeping, which I want to emphasize. Memorykeeping, as demonstrated by my grandmother and mother, is tied to the particular historical moments of empire, war, and revolution that they experienced as women, and their knowledge of the interimperial context due to the incursions of Dutch, German, Japanese, and US empires. Their memorykeeping should be viewed in the face of these political transformations, and also can be seen as a response to the ruptures and silences caused by imperial and gender hierarchies. As I have

---

8   This is also an argument that Micaela di Leonardo makes regarding kin work. Micaela di Leonardo, "The Female World of Cards and Holidays: Women, Families, and the Work of Kinship," *Signs*, 12/3 (Spring 1987): 440–453.

9   di Leonardo, "The Female World," 442–443, 451.

10   Long T. Bui, *Returns of War: South Vietnam and the Price of Refugee Memory*, Kindle ebook (New York: New York University Press, 2018), under Chapter 4, "Militarized Freedoms: Vietnamese American Soldiers Fighting 'Future Vietnams'," introductory section.

outlined in previous chapters, the first several decades of the 20th century in Indonesia was a particularly fraught time, especially because of multiple empires, militarism, and a changing global economy. Thus, women like Tobing and Rony transformed the ways they maintained different kinds of knowledges in the face of these evolving political developments. For example, empires shaped the kinds of technologies and print cultures being disseminated, as well as the languages in which they were produced. Tobing's and Rony's multilingual archival collections are reflections of the various imperial regimes which they experienced.

As a result of so much societal change, to be a memorykeeper in the sense of Tobing and Rony is not just personal inclination, it also is a fundamental and urgent responsibility. Khatharya Um tells us that family narratives emerge as a key space where history is not available elsewhere, as in the Cambodian and Cambodian American context.[11] While Um's analysis raises very specific issues to the Cambodian American community, especially given the genocide that so many community members have faced, her insightful commentary also sheds light on the experiences of other communities, including several Southeast Asian American groups. What compels us to take up these histories as an ongoing and critical part of our lives? And what makes it so difficult to do so? Um addresses these issues at length for the Cambodian American community, pointing out the difficulty of passing on memory when silence is the norm and a well-honed strategy of survival. In this kind of context, the terrain of memory connotes great peril, owing to the intensified urgency of preserving generational memory, as well as the difficulties of communicating these issues to younger generations, who might not want to believe what they hear.[12]

These strategies regarding memorykeeping urge us to take seriously our emotional and affective understandings of the past as they continue to affect us, and how we construct our knowledges about them.[13] In her research on the Vietnamese American community, Yến Lê Espiritu directs our attention to how people themselves contend with these issues of memories, and the choices people make to constitute these silences:

---

11   Khatharya Um, "Exiled Memory: History, Identity, and Remembering in Southeast Asia and Southeast Asian Diaspora," *Positions*, 20/3 (2012): 843, DOI: 10.1215/10679847-1593564.

12   Ibid, 842–844.

13   Raymond Williams, *Marxism and Literature* (Oxford: Oxford University Press, 1978), 132; Avery F. Gordon, *Ghostly Matters: Haunting and the Sociological Imagination*, Kindle ebook (Minneapolis: University of Minnesota Press, 2008), 188; Marianne Hirsch, *The Generation of Postmemory: Writing and Visual Culture after the Holocaust*, Kindle ebook (New York: Columbia University Press, 2012), 4, 34.

I also pay more attention to strategic and self-imposed silence than to the power-laden process of silencing, to the ways that subjugated histories are told "quietly" or told without words or sometimes safeguarded for future tellings, whether or not I grasp the reasons behind these decisions.[14]

In doing so, Espiritu encourages us to read silence as a way of narrating, and also to read *through* silences, and to recognize their temporal quality. By respecting the decisions of people to refrain from the telling of these stories, she is also addressing the possibility that there might be a future telling. Espiritu thus models for us a critically informed analysis of how to attend to the risks involved in releasing these stories, and to acknowledge the many truths that might be involved. As Grace M. Cho explains, "The act of laying bare the components of silence can allow for something new to come forth in its place, but that is not to say that it exposes a singular truth."[15]

3   What Is Said

I raise these theoretical discussions here not just to underscore my point about taking women's memorykeeping seriously as a form of knowledge, but also to emphasize the stakes involved in a close examination of Tobing's and Rony's stories. It is very clear through the telling of the stories, sometimes in the very way that the story is narrated on the page, that both Tobing and Rony confronted disparities produced by gender and empire in their own lives and those of the people around them. Even as they employed specific narrative scripts to explain their actions, they also produced alternative explanations or demonstrated ambivalence, as shown in the stories to follow. Their accounts also illuminate how silences could be strategic in duration, whether in the immediate moment when a story is withheld, or for a lengthy period of thirty years (or more) until a knowledge is ready to be released. It is from this vantage point of attending to their stories over some five decades that I want to argue that women's memorykeeping is a form of critique. I am interested in assessing how women's relationship to knowledge—whether to find meanings, tell stories, or maintain silences—are strategies to address their differential and often subordinate position in the context of their historical experiences regarding gender

---

14   Espiritu, *Body Counts*, 19–20.
15   Grace M. Cho, *Haunting the Korean Diaspora: Shame, Secrecy, and the Forgotten War* (Minneapolis: University of Minnesota Press, 2008), 17.

and empire. In this section then, I identify a few different stories, to explore some of the meanings in how they presented their narratives.

For example, both Tobing and Rony presented different originary moments to their narratives of family history. Tobing began by focusing on male lineage in the family, namely our family ancestor Raja Pontas, one of four brothers. She also related two moments of European male arrival, the first being the American Baptist missionaries Henry Munson and Samuel Lyman who appeared in the 1830s to promote Christianity and became martyrs for the cause, and the second being the German missionary Nommensen who spread the Lutheran religion in the area in the 1870s. Ironically, when Tobing told me about the origins of the family and she related the tale of the four sons including Raja Pontas, she accentuated the democratic nature of Toba Batak culture, that anyone could become royalty, although her explanation centered on men. In the telling of the story, my grandmother did not discuss the contradictory nature of a male-focused culture being 'democratic,' a reflection of her assumption of the intense patrilineality of Toba Batak culture.[16]

I think Tobing began with those stories because of her historical positioning in terms of the changes wrought by empire and modernity. The stories can be seen as a way for her to identify herself as a Toba Batak with a strong sense of self and belonging, yet one who also was educated and on the cusp of all of the tremendous changes transforming the world around her. As I read the narrative she presented, I am struck by Tobing's analysis of these events. She relates the tale of Munson and Lyman as part of the history of Christian conversions in the area, and also points out that the Americans did not know the language and could not communicate. By doing so, Tobing also implicitly questions American arrogance in arriving in a region to 'save' the natives when they did not know the language. In addition, she is responding to images of the Toba Batak as 'savages' and 'cannibals' in need of religious conversion, and to the negative portrayals of indigenous people. I remember being curious in 1985 about her knowledge of the practice of cannibalism. Eventually, she shared this story:

> I had an aunt, an old aunt from Lintong Nihuta. And she said, "When I was a child, maybe seven, eight years old, people would come with a *tabanan*, that means a person that they caught in the war [who became a prisoner or slave]. I have never seen that they ate the person. But I remembered that I played with the fingers cut from the person ..." She was about forty years older than I was, so around 1870 this happened then.[17]

---

16   See 151, this volume.
17   See 152, this volume.

While Tobing emphasized that these issues were in the past, even in the generation prior to her own, she nevertheless shared this story with me.

However, when she discussed the enslavement of prisoners during wars of the Batak people, Tobing also made a point of reframing the situation to emphasize the culpability of the United States in these processes as well. In telling this story, Tobing maintained the political high ground, pointing back to slavery in the United States, and saying that it was not as bad as what the Americans did, as she had seen the television miniseries *Roots*. As she commented, "And besides, they abolished that kind of situation with the coming of Christianity. Christianity came here in the 1860s. So it was recently here." She then went on to highlight the great changes that had taken place: "Like I told you, my mother-in-law couldn't read or write. Her son managed to get the highest education. He studied medicine in a university in Leiden, in Holland!"[18] In that moment, Tobing was emphasizing the enormous changes wrought by empire, and the ability of her husband's family to overcome barriers to higher education in the course of one generation.

Rony began her stories with a different framework, relating her earliest memories of being a young girl and listening to the oldest relatives in Pearaja in the yard in the early morning. As Rony remembered, "Every morning, the old people would come out of the house, sunning themselves in the yard, and they would tell stories."[19] The fact that Rony valued listening to the elders and hence was granted the knowledge of the story, also indicates key components of Rony's character in terms of her desire to build her relationship with the past. These strategies were instrumental in her role as a memorykeeper, as her girlhood practice as a listener insured that these stories would be brought forward to the next generation. Rony recalled the knowledge that she gained, as when relatives were keeping alive the stories of the resistance of Raja Si Singamangaraja and his forces in the face of alien colonial incursions into the homeland, as already discussed in Chapter 1.[20] These stories were a counternarrative not just to an imperial script about the need to 'save the natives,' but they also gestured to another narrative of time, the indigenous culture prior to the arrival of the missionaries. By doing so, the stories also situated Rony's generational identity within an alternate temporality.

In addition, both Tobing's and Rony's narratives provide evidence of their critique of the racialized hierarchies imposed by the Dutch empire in which the Toba Batak were seen as subordinate. For example, while others have argued that northern Sumatra came under Dutch rule relatively late because of

---

18   Ibid.
19   See 199, this volume.
20   See 27, 29, 199, this volume.

its location far away from the center of power of Dutch rule in Java, Tobing underscored that the Dutch found it difficult to contest the strength and integrity of the Batak *adat*. Tobing commented that while Dutch governance was already established when she was young, Batak rule nevertheless persisted in some realms:

> If you ask here, the Dutch didn't dare to do anything about the construction of the *adat* here because it was strong. We use their committee for criminals, but if it is for land dispute, we have our own government.[21]

With these comments, Tobing also was emphasizing the independence and continued integrity of Batak culture.

Rony was familiar with racialized categories too, especially as she attended a Dutch school at a young age. She was quite used to the ways that other students enforced the social boundaries, and relates in her autobiographical narrative:

> At this time as a little girl, I had my first experience of discrimination as an Indonesian in a Dutch elementary school and learned that we were second-class citizens in our own country. Eurasians and Chinese and also those Indonesians serving in the army were considered first-class citizens. I felt the discrimination clearly. Although the teacher didn't treat us differently because there were only two of us Indonesians in my third-grade class, the other students made it clear that there was a difference between the natives and first-class citizens. I remember the things that the other children said.[22]

Although these incidents had happened over seven decades before, Rony still had keen recall of how her fellow students treated her. She also remembered, however, how she and the one other Indonesian student excelled in math, especially as compared to their Dutch classmates:

> There were only two natives in the class, and we were the star students. The other Indonesian was the son of a Batak Karo, local royalty. The two of us always competed in math, which was a subject I liked. Whenever we had math, the teacher would ask questions and you would have to raise your hand if you knew the answer. There were the two natives who usually were raising their hands.[23]

---

21   See 163, this volume.
22   See 207, this volume.
23   Ibid.

With this story, Rony was making a comment about how racial superiority was an illusion, given the ability of the Indonesians to best their classmates in the subject of math.

In a similar manner, Tobing shared two stories that illuminated her opposition to the social rigidity of colonial society, as well as her sense of self as an elite, Dutch-educated Indonesian woman. When Rony and her brother Apoel were young, Tobing and her husband sought to place them in a Dutch-language school in Medan. However, Rony and Apoel were not allowed into the dormitory as *Inlanders* ["natives", can be in a perjorative sense] due to the social segregation of the times. Hence, Rony and Apoel went to school in Siantar from 1940 to 1942 so they could live with relatives.[24] Tobing was vehemently against this housing segregation, and complained to the highest-ranking civil servant, Assistant Resident Mynheer [Mr.] Dirks. Tobing recalled,

> I told him [Assistant Resident Mynheer Dirks], "I think it is unfair, see." I said, "How come my children can't swim there? They are not allowed to go to the dorm. I have to find a place for them to stay at the boarding house. Even swimming. Do you feel that they are dirtier than the other Dutch children?" I said, "Unfair. How could you accept that children of educated *Inlanders*, educated natives are not allowed to swim while a child born out of a Dutch and a *babu*, a maid, can swim there because it has the name of a Dutch?" I said. "My husband was Dutch-educated from Leiden. I had a Normal School, Dutch education too," I said. "And my children can't even go there!" "Well," he said, "what can I do? The one that donated the swimming pool, that was her restriction, the swimming pool was only meant for Dutch children."[25]

Here, Tobing demonstrates that she was upset that people were judged not by their educational or professional training, but by their ancestry. And she was especially incensed at the colonial rules that as long as a child had some Dutch ancestry and a Dutch name conferred by their father, they would be considered Dutch and accepted into the school. Tobing thus is making a critique in this passage of the social and racial practices of the Dutch colonial regime. She further commented about the alleged superiority of the Dutch women she encountered:

---

24   See 181–182, 207–208, this volume.
25   See 181–182, this volume.

Sometimes the Dutch women who came to Indonesia only finished elementary school, and they came to Indonesia. But they spoke Dutch and
they looked white, so they were the superior nation, right?[26]

She continued, however, with a telling comment that spoke to the falsity of
these distinction, "But I had my education too."[27] In posing this comment,
Tobing was both underscoring her sense of self and also indicating how her
education, which extended well beyond the level of elementary school, also
conferred class and professional resources.

In another story narrated by Tobing, which Rony also wrote about, Tobing
attended a Christmas service at Rony's school in Siantar. While both Tobing
and Rony were at the event, a Dutch girl classmate assumed that Tobing was a
maid because she was wearing Indonesian dress. Tobing remembered:

> Another time, I went to attend the Christmas service at their school. My
> daughter Minar played a role in the Nativity play. And then suddenly, a
> Dutch little girl nearby said, "Look, look Mama, a *babu*." Because I had
> my *kebaya* [blouse tunic] and sarong on. For the Dutch, you should have
> a gown, a dress like a European. Then you are a European. You are not
> supposed to wear native dress, for then they think you are only a *babu*, a
> maid. The mother said, "Pssssst ..."[28]

On one level, Tobing recognized the behavior of the Dutch woman and her
child as an insult, as she was assumed to be a maid despite her educational
attainments and her status as a fellow parent. In addition, the context of the
religious service also added to the indignity of the moment, especially as her
family was among the first Bataks to be converted to Lutheranism by the missionary Nommensen. But on another level, by not wearing Dutch-style clothing, my grandmother was making a statement about who she was. Later, even
when Tobing moved to the United States for fifteen years, her regular dress
continued to be a *kebaya* and sarong. In addition to feeling more comfortable
in her accustomed wear, her clothing also was a testament to her pride in being
Batak and Indonesian, even though she was in a foreign country.[29]

---

26 See 178, this volume.
27 Ibid.
28 See 182, this volume.
29 See Figures 50 and 51, this volume, for an example of Tobing's regular dress in the
    United States.

Rony wrote a slightly different version of this story:

> One time, my mother was wearing a *kebaya* and sarong and she went to a Dutch church with me in Siantar for the Christmas service. My Dutch schoolmates knew me from school but they were surprised to see my mother there. The Dutch girl from the elementary school I attended said to her mother, "What is the *babu* doing here?" I thought, this girl only knew one in *kebaya* as the help in the house, not as a person you socialized with. And the mom of my schoolmate said, "Shhh ..." And I think they were one bench behind. The mother understood that this was my mother, not my nanny.[30]

In her writing of the story, Rony was commenting on her classmate's provincial and colonial outlook that she only knew Indonesian women wearing a *kebaya* as servants. In doing so, Rony was addressing the fact that when her Dutch classmate saw her, she did not fully recognize her as Indonesian, with an Indonesian mother and father. She also pointed out her classmate's mother's complicity in acknowledging the situation and quieting the student, but not making a direct apology to Tobing.

To provide a further example of how stories might become a vehicle for social critique, I want to turn to another part of Rony's autobiographical narrative from when she was a young girl. Instead of confining his daughter to typical gendered behavior in which Rony would be expected to stay at home, Gerhard L. Tobing supported Rony in her desire to experience new activities out in the public sphere. As Rony recalled about that happy time in her life, "When we were in Bengkalis, I got to see my dad every day, and talk with him. My dad would give me advice regularly, and also let me try out different things that I wanted to do."[31] As Rony's father encouraged her independence, Rony was interested in becoming an entrepreneur and selling snacks in front of a local movie theater. Rony recalled,

> I decided to start my own business. I went on my bike to the countryside, and bought some sugarcane in long stalks. I had to clean the sugarcane and cut them about one foot in length, and I put them in a basket. As for the peanuts, our cook showed me how to roast them over the fire. Then

---

30   See 208, this volume.
31   See 210, this volume.

FIGURE 25   Gerhard L. Tobing in his medical office, ca. 1930. The cabinet is filled with medical
             supplies and equipment, and a Batak *ulos*, a woven Batak spiritual cloth, is hung
             on the wall by his desk
             TOBING FAMILY COLLECTION

> I had a basket of peanuts and a basket of sugarcane. The movies started at
> six, so at about five o'clock, I went to the front of the movie house, and sat
> at the edge of the street with my sugarcane and my peanuts.[32]

A passer-by recognized her as the doctor's daughter, and bought all of her
wares, thus freeing Rony to go to the movies. Later, Rony's father sent a member of the household staff to find her and bring her home. But tellingly, her
father did not get upset with her. Rony remembered, "He asked me, 'How did
you do?' So I told him the story. I don't think he expected that someone would
recognize me and buy me out."[33]

Due to the importance of this story in her autobiographical narrative and its
extended discussion, I began to realize that it was not just an anecdote about
her entrepreneurial initiative as a young girl, but it also was about her father
encouraging her to be independent and explore her interests. The poignancy

---

32   See 211, this volume.

33   Ibid.

FIGURE 26   In this photograph, Gerhard L. Tobing stands alongside his children
            on a carousel, c.1935
            TOBING FAMILY COLLECTION

of this story, of course, is that after her father's death, the family faced economic hardship and she was not able to achieve her dream of following her father into the medical field. The story then also is about Rony's continuing to hold on to a sense of possibility even though her original goals no longer seemed attainable.

4   And What Is Not Said

In my reading of Tobing's and Rony's narratives, silence does not constitute mere absence or negative space, but has real presence, and tells us something as well. Furthermore, not telling a story does not mean that it disappears, but might mean that it becomes dormant, kept below the surface of public recollection. In fact, there are many different reasons why silences might become the norm, and these silences can span over years. There are silences as delays because women feel they do not have the resources, at that moment, to confront the unequal relations that structure these silences. Sometimes, decades later, these issues reemerge because women have altered resources or political environments. On a basic affective level, sometimes silences exist simply because voicing a story might hurt another person's feelings. There were many stories that Rony did not share with others for decades, but now as a community elder with the principals long gone, she relates them in her autobiographical narrative. These issues remind us that silence does not equate consent and can be, in fact, a temporal strategy of resistance in which the telling is delayed.

In this section I assess how empire and gender shaped the narratives of my grandmother and mother in terms of strategic silences, both within the stories that they told, and in their decisions not to speak at times. For example, in her narrative, Tobing recounted several times when she chose silence in the moment as a way to negotiate gendered barriers. To illustrate this, recall that Tobing did not speak back to her mother-in-law, no matter how difficult things became for her as a young daughter-in-law unused to the village way of life. Here, silence was a strategy of staying in a situation in which she had minimal autonomy, and was under heavy surveillance in her mother-in-law's household. I suspect that the silence was also a matter of maintaining dignity for Tobing, in a situation in which her advanced education and experience did not prepare her for life in the village. After her father died, Rony too sometimes chose silence because she recognized that the family was going through difficult times and she did not want to burden her mother. As she remembered, rather than ask her mother for more money, she would seek help from other relatives, like her grandmother. On Saturday market days, she would go with a basket to find her maternal grandmother after the school day was over, as she knew that her grandmother would be occupied selling the *ulos* that she and her friends had woven:

> I would come to her place and say, "Hello Ompung, how are you today?" And she would say, "Hello, have you heard from your mom." And I would say, "No." And then she would say, "Watch my *ulos*, I will be back in a few minutes." She would leave, and when she came back she would have money for me to do my weekly shopping needs.[34]

Rony only revealed her hardship to her mother several months later, after she was reunited with Tobing in Medan, as she had not wanted to burden her mother unnecessarily.

---

34 See 220, this volume.

There also is silence not just in what goes unsaid, but also in what is not acknowledged by others. As discussed, Rony intended to become a doctor and wanted to attend the Universitas Sumatra Utara in Medan for medical school after high school. But when Tobing accepted a scholarship for Rony to go to the OSVO [Opleiding School voor Vak Onderwijzeressen, teachers' training school for home economics], she put those goals aside and kept silent. Rony remembered,

> Once my mother told me about the scholarship though, I didn't say a thing. I didn't tell her of my ambitions for medical school because I knew that she had to give my brother, as the oldest, the first choice. She wanted him to continue. I am sure that she thought that he would go into medicine. So my dad was gone, and so were my dreams. I had to adjust as the second child ... And I knew that my mother also was working very hard.[35]

Rony was keenly aware of how her mother was struggling to support the children as a single parent. Tellingly however, Rony did make an oblique comment about her deferred dreams in characterizing the curriculum at the OSVO. She remarked that she liked chemistry the most as it was a kind of science (unlike other subjects like washing), a reference to the fact that Rony had wanted to be a doctor and knew the kinds of premedical subjects that would have been required. Later, when she was a young teacher and had the chance to study economics, she seized upon that opportunity eagerly, even though it was not an area of expertise for her. As Rony noted, "I loved studying economics because it was not home economics. To me, it was a science that I could apply in my life where home economics was something that you used at home." Although she did not pass that exam, Rony went on to earn a degree in economics at Nommensen University.[36] What I find important about Rony's comment is that it is a rare instance where Rony actually revealed her yearning for a field of study that would fulfill her ambitions, unlike her customary silence about her deferred professional ambitions.

I also want to address another kind of silence that is demonstrated through their narratives, of selective telling, and sometimes, continued silence. As a young woman, I was well aware that there were some stories which my grandmother did not share with me, stories that might have been too private or maybe not appropriate for a young granddaughter of my age. Some I had heard about from other family members, and others I had pieced together through different fragments of family history. For example, in my childhood, I remember my

---

35   See 222, this volume.
36   See 223–224, 228, this volume.

Aunt Demak saying that my grandmother went on a hunger strike so she would be allowed to go to school as a little girl. I recall asking my grandmother about this in 1985, but she did not want to talk much about this story. I think she might not have wanted to discuss it because she did not want to portray herself as someone who broke the rules, and this kind of behavior certainly would not have been in accordance with a daughter's expected compliance to the family mandate. Age and generation matter, not just in terms of the stories you might be told, but also in how you understand those stories. Sometimes stories are not entrusted to you until you have lived long enough to comprehend them more fully.

There are also stories that are considered dangerous, such as what happened in the mass violence of 1965 to 1966, about which people might be silent. Although the historical events were twenty years in the past when I was staying in Indonesia, and Tobing had been in the United States during that time, my grandmother knew of people who had been imprisoned or lost, even though they were not immediate family members. In part, I am sure, she was trying to protect me from the knowledge of what had happened, or maybe she did not think it was important knowledge for me to carry forward. Like other violent events in which there is tremendous pain and suffering, the young often encounter silences about historical events which have occurred, that may only be broken decades later when others come forward to recover these knowledges.

But while some silences may continue, others may begin to be negotiated, or even stop. As my mother began to write her autobiographical narrative and share stories of her past, I began recognizing the purposeful way in which she was articulating her historical reality via this means. Although there were many stories that she decided to keep private, one of the main themes of her autobiography became her discussion of what it meant to be a *boru* [daughter], and to have secondary political status in a male-focused hierarchy. She also began to write more fully about the impact of growing up in a colonial and postcolonial society, as in her oblique critique of the US scholars to whom she gave cultural and linguistic assistance during the Cold War:

> I think it is hard for people from outside the village to fully understand Batak culture. Even I, sometimes, had to learn more about Batak culture by looking to others and following them, because I was born and brought up with a different background. I always tried to watch what was going on and try to understand it from the perspective of people in the village.[37]

---

37   See 232, this volume.

Even though Rony knew that these scholars had both racial and national privilege, she couched her analysis in more general terms regarding the difficulty of learning Batak culture as an outsider. These were issues that she had rarely voiced publicly, but now were being released by her into the space of this book project. Although understated, the fact that Rony even made this kind of critique in her autobiographical narrative is significant, given the great care that Rony took to use kindness and integrity in characterizing the events she witnessed and the people that she encountered. By sharing these stories, Rony not only relates her own historical experience, but also demonstrates how others also may challenge received 'truths' and posit other knowledges in their stead.

5   Two Pictures

Next, I turn to two photographs, as a different way on reflecting on these issues of stories and silences. From closely analyzing Tobing's and Rony's narratives and how they shared them, I want to move my focus to consider how these issues might be embodied within different archives, as well as by the artifacts that they contain. In particular, I want to consider how these issues might manifest themselves in an interimperial context.

Michel-Rolph Trouillot reminds us "... any historical narrative is a particular bundle of silences, the result of a unique process, and the operation required to deconstruct these silences will vary accordingly."[38] Trouillot helps us to understand that as much as stories are produced from historical evidence, they also emanate from compounded silences as well. Hence, the way we construct historical knowledge is both provisional and contingent. Trouillot's comments illuminate some of the complexities of undertaking interimperial archival research. On the one hand, there are the material realities of developing this kind of documentation over space and historical era. Investigating these issues for this project, for example, required following Tobing's and Rony's geographical knowledges, and traveling from the United States to see collections across the Pacific, as well as across the Atlantic. It also necessitated the use of multiple languages: English, Batak, Indonesian, Dutch, and some German too. In addition, and perhaps on an even more fundamental level, it requires a sustained understanding of the multiple hierarchies that produce and are produced by these different archival collections, not only the imperial context that positioned 'natives' through a particular racialized lens, but also how gender so fundamentally structured who was documented, and who was not.

---

38   Trouillot, *Silencing the Past*, 26.

FIGURE 27   "Vrouw en kinderen van Radja Pontas uit het dorp Pea Radja bij Silindoeng in de
Bataklanden," [Wife and children of Raja Pontas from Pearaja Village in Silindung,
Batak region]
SPECIAL COLLECTIONS, LEIDEN UNIVERSITY LIBRARIES, PART OF KITLV A38.,
KITLV NO.12145, CA. 1890

To explore these issues further, I want to offer the stories of two images of the
family, one from the Special Collections at Leiden University, and the other from
Rony's personal collection in Los Angeles. I first saw the initial family photo
of my great-great-grandmother Cornelia, who was married to my great-great-
grandfather Raja Pontas, and her children in Sita Van Bemmelen's book on gender and the Toba Batak.[39] With that clue, on our trip to Special Collections at
the Leiden University Library, we set aside time to look at that photograph, and
hopefully others. As it turned out, the photograph in question was the only photograph we saw in the Dutch administration records for the region that documents our family. In the photograph, my great-great-grandmother Cornelia is
seated, surrounded by three of her children, my great-grandfather Aris, and two
of my three great-grand aunts. My great-grandfather Raja Aris was the youngest of two sons of Raja Pontas, and he had three sisters. We know that one of
these sisters was named Hulda, but we do not know the names of the others, or

39   Sita T. Van Bemmelen, *Christianity, Colonization, and Gender Relations in North Sumatra:
A Patrilineal Society in Flux* (Leiden: Koninklijke Brill NV, 2017).

whether Hulda is in the picture. Our knowledge of this photograph then is structured by Trouillot's "bundle of silences."[40] To read the histories of the women, one must look for traces of their presence, and reinterpret their lives through the fragmentary glimpses we can find—glimpses that also are mediated through other frameworks. For example, in addition to the male-focused hierarchies previously discussed, the narrative of Christian conversation organizes our knowledge of this photograph, as one of the reasons why Raja Pontas and his family were documented likely was because of his relationship with the German missionary Nommensen. In yet another layer to this search, the names by which we know the women are Christian, imperial names, as names like Cornelia and Hulda are not Batak names. Thus, the women are recognized within the framework of Lutheran conversion, as opposed to their indigenous names as known within Toba Batak culture. These issues underscore the vital importance and complex challenges of recovering women's history in an interimperial context.

A month after we returned from Europe, we found another photograph in some family papers. In the image, my great-grandfather Raja Aris sits in a wooden chair, wearing a white buttoned-up shirt and a dark suit. There is a watch chain visible in front of his jacket, as well as a flat hat. He is barefoot. With one arm braced on the arm of the chair, he stares forward, off into the distance. We know that he died as a young man, one of the reasons why there was so much pressure on Gerhard L. Tobing to carry on the family name as the only surviving son (an older brother and an older sister had both died young). We are grateful that we now have two images of Raja Aris, as we are aware of how rare it is to have photographic images of the family from this period. I am not able to share the picture in this book because we were not able to locate its archival provenance. But we are glad, nevertheless, to have this second image. We also know that my grandmother must have been documenting the history of the family, for on the back of the photograph, Tobing had written the date when Raja Aris was born, and the *marga*s, or clans, into which the sisters married. Tobing's notes reflect the Batak cultural emphasis on the male line and the political alliances created when daughters married into other clans. Although Raja Aris's sisters are not present in the photographic image, Tobing did leave us a historical trace by noting this information, providing a trail for us to follow in the future.

These two images, taken together, demonstrate the nature of women's memorykeeping. The fact that my grandmother kept this last photograph and made some notes regarding its content, and our discovery of it decades later in family papers, illuminates the importance of women's memorykeeping over space and time. Both of the photographs analyzed here likely were taken in

40   Trouillot, *Silencing the Past*, 26.

the Toba Batak region during Dutch empire at the turn of the 20th century, when German missionaries were influential in converting some of the Toba Batak to Lutheranism. While one photograph traveled back to Leiden to become part of the Dutch imperial record, the other one of Raja Aris as an adult probably remained in Pearaja, and was passed down within the family. Luckily, both photographs were preserved despite the losses of World War II in the Netherlands due to German occupation, and in Indonesia under the Japanese regime. The second photograph became part of my grandmother's personal collection, which she carried to the United States because it was such an important artifact for her.

6   Conclusion

Silences in family history have dimension and depth, and transform over time. They create both temporal and historical space. Sometimes they remain full silences, sometimes they become partial silences shared with a few selected listeners, and sometimes the stories eventually emerge in a family gathering or even in a more public realm. Women's memorykeeping—the stories, photographs, and artifacts women collect—challenge all of these silences by creating an autonomous political space for memory which can be archived. By recognizing women's memorykeeping as an arena of knowledge production and labor, and by charting these silences as they remain hidden or become manifest, we have a better sense of the reasons why these memories are finally released into a different political space.

    The book came into being in the midst of all of these processes. When I first began compiling my grandmother's narrative, she was keenly aware that these stories were for posterity. I recognize now the importance of what it meant to have her granddaughter, born and raised on the other side of the world, listening to her stories of the past so intently. In that space of storytelling, she released stories to me about the personal details in her life, knowing that I would take them back with me when I returned to my home in the United States. As a skilled memorykeeper, my grandmother knew that I appreciated her stories, and that I would carry them forward, and find other people for whom they would have meaning. Although I do not think that I fully understood in 1985 what a precious gift my grandmother had given me, and by extension my mother who gave me the plane ticket to go to Indonesia, I have more comprehension of its significance now in my later years. In many ways, my grandmother was showing me the significance of memorykeeping; she

FIGURE 28
Minar T. Rony at Gerhard L. Tobing's grave
PHOTOGRAPH BY AUTHOR

was modeling it for me as well. In assisting my mother in writing her autobiographical narrative, similar processes also happened, as we prepared Rony's stories for eventual publication. As an older person now, I better understood the urgency of my mother's wish to write about her experiences, in terms of charting her own life, but also so that others that she knew and loved could be remembered. Through their stories—and sometimes silences—Tobing and Rony guide us in their journeys of what they have witnessed and undergone, and in the process have opened up a space for other people's stories to emerge.

CHAPTER 4

Artifacts and Memories:
Representing Meaning

1   Introduction

If the previous chapters of this book have focused on our connections to the
past, this fourth chapter looks more at how women's memorykeeping carries
knowledges forward through the collection of different artifacts. In particular,
I consider how migration shapes the various forms of meanings represented
by Tobing's and Rony's personal archival collections. Both Tobing's and Rony's
memorykeeping have been indelibly influenced by the processes of migration
in an interimperial context, producing multiple knowledges and representations. As a result, their collection and curation strategies for these artifacts create new ways of seeing and belonging. Rather than being merely an innocuous
group of photographs, documents, souvenirs, and other memorabilia, I contend that it is important to look deeper into what the artifacts represent in
order to understand their significance. These collections are a curation of time,
especially in the face of migration and loss, that can bring together memories from different eras in one's life and various places where one has traveled.
These issues are especially pertinent for women like Tobing and Rony because
of the sheer amount of social and political change they have experienced, particularly as a result of empire and militarism.

In this chapter, I address Tobing's and Rony's collections, asking what they
can tell us about women's memorykeeping in the face of the interimperial
environment they experienced, in which migration came to be an expected
and regular part of the course of their lives. I begin by considering how the
collection and maintenance of artifacts can be seen as a strategy for creating
autonomous political space, as a response to the massive political change they
experienced in the years leading up to World War II, and the devastating loss in
1947 of Gerhard L. Tobing—Tobing's husband and Rony's father. Subsequently,
I pay close attention to how their archival collections exemplify these issues,
identifying four categories of artifacts that emerge from their practices: biographical artifacts, recreated artifacts, cultural practices artifacts, and reintegrated artifacts. Finally, I conclude with a discussion of how Tobing's and
Rony's collections might be seen as a method of creating an archival legacy for
future generations by carrying the knowledges they have developed over the
course of their lives.

2   Knowledge as Legacy

When Tobing returned after her time away from Indonesia to live in the ancestral household, she was taking care of the family's past for future generations. While the lands were to be kept for the male heirs, Tobing maintained
an archives of knowledge for all the family, including the female descendants.
In that way, as Tobing's practices demonstrate, women's memorykeeping can
exist alongside if not outside of the patrilineal practice of the material inheritance of land or property. As discussed in Chapter 3, this kind of labor represents what Micaela di Leonardo has identified as "kin-work," an extension of
women's domestic roles for taking care of the family and household.[1] Tobing's
meticulously kept archival collection emerges as a strategic way to counter the
ruptures she faced due to war and migration, as well as because of patrilineality and the untimely death of her husband.

Tobing was unusual for her generation in her advanced educational trajectory, her extensive travels overseas, and her emphasis on the written word. These
themes shaped the nature of the books and documents that she maintained
and helps to explain why her collection is so rare and such an important intervention into the historical, archival knowledge of Indonesia and the United
States during the 20th century. Without a sensibility focused on the preservation of paper culture, it is more common for documents and other artifacts
to be left behind or thrown away. These issues are further compounded when
empire and patriarchy generate ruptures in family history, dispersing artifacts
to sites across the globe through militarism, empire, and family separation.

Tobing's memorykeeping highlights that remembering the past differs according to whether one remains in one location, or whether one has gone
abroad. The extraordinary level of Tobing's memorykeeping is not surprising,
because she underwent so many changes, and because keeping documents
was a way of holding onto a present reality in the midst of larger social and
political forces that might have seemed out of her control. For instance, I am
struck by the detail in her accounting when she was managing an agricultural
enterprise during World War II, and her meticulous record of all costs and pay-
ments, including what workers were owed. Also remarkable is the fact that
she saved this accounting book, so that decades later it could be found by her
descendants. I read her scrupulous care in documenting and then preserving

---

1   Micaela di Leonardo, "The Female World of Cards and Holidays: Women, Families, and the
      Work of Kinship," *Signs*, 12/3 (Spring 1987): 451.

this accounting book as a way for her to be able to control at least this part of her daily life, despite the upheaval of wartime.

The relative completeness of Tobing's collection is particularly notable in the face of regular family migration, and the political and economic turmoil caused by empire and war. While Tobing's and Rony's work as memorykeepers has been instrumental in the formation of our family archives, male privilege and patrilineality also structured our ability to find my grandmother's collection as it is tied to male inheritance of property; her husband, Gerhard L. Tobing, was the only remaining son, and the family house was considered his. Nevertheless, women's labor organized our ability to develop this family archive. Because other family members moved for better opportunities to urban areas in Indonesia or overseas, it was mostly Tobing and one of her distant nieces, my aunt, who remained at the house. Since Tobing's death, my aunt has been the caretaker of the house, and so Tobing's papers were left undisturbed for several years. And whereas other objects such as clothing or jewelry might have been moved or taken, the papers remained. While this was to some extent because of my aunt's care in maintaining the household, the fact that the papers were left intact in the cupboards also had to do with their being seen as having limited use value in the rural culture of the village. Other items, such as the weaving tools which I used in 1985, are no longer in the house as they were items that someone else found useful.

3   Memorykeeping as Response to Precarity

Although it is highly likely that Tobing's memorykeeping was shaped by her long stay in the United States and the processes that she witnessed there, in fact, her memorykeeping began decades before she migrated. I see Tobing's immense collection as a way for her to curate time because of the profound changes and sometimes losses she had sustained in an interimperial context. I suggest that memorykeeping was one of the ways that she was able to make sense of her own life, as well as carry on and take care of her family, even under conditions of extreme duress or loss. I also believe that the specific intensity of Tobing's memorykeeping was, in part, a response to the events of World War II; the Japanese Occupation played its part, but especially the violent loss of Gerhard L. Tobing in 1947 when the Dutch attempted to retake their colony.

To begin my discussion of the possible effects of war on memorykeeping, it is important to note how precarity and the threat of violence became the norm during the Japanese Occupation. Tobing remembered the devaluation of human life during the Japanese regime:

On a boat maybe with a capacity for eighty people, you would have 200. It was overcrowded and they didn't have enough plates. The Japanese just threw the rice, and these passengers would catch the food, the rice, in their hands or with a hat. I heard that is what they did. And I know in Bengkalis that these poor people then got dysentery, and they would just die on the edge of the road. And the prisoners would be the ones who would bury them because they had no relatives. In war, they didn't care. A chicken's life had much more worth than a human life. A chicken, if you kill it, you can eat it.[2]

With this stark statement, Tobing conveyed how life and humanity turned upside down during wartime.

During this time period, the lives of family members were in peril. Tobing remembered how many young men were forcibly conscripted by Japanese military forces, including her own brother. Due to fears that her son Apoel also would be conscripted, Tobing took the children to Bukit Batu for greater safety.[3] Both Tobing and her husband were in danger too due to their Dutch educations and high socioeconomic status. One of her husband's patients alerted them that the Japanese military forces sought to kill Indonesians of their class strata, and to prepare themselves and their families for their possible deaths. It was at this point that Gerhard L. Tobing hid many of the documents and photographs that would have incriminated them as Dutch-educated in the ground, in order to conceal their identities. As it turned out, the Japanese surrendered before Tobing and her husband were taken. By the time the materials were retrieved, however, it was too late as they had been irrevocably damaged because of the dampness of the soil.[4] The loss of the family's precious archival materials, however, would seem insignificant compared to what would come next.

Although the United States commonly marks the end of World War II with the surrender of the Japanese, in fact war continued on in Indonesia in the following years as the Dutch sought to return. This is when Gerhard L. Tobing lost his life. Tobing was one of three doctors who took turns going to the front to deal with casualties. On July 29, 1947, he was returning from attending to wounded soldiers from the Indonesian nationalist forces. After Japan's defeat in World War II, the Netherlands decided to retake its former colony, and

---

2 See 186, this volume.
3 See 183, this volume.
4 I also have discussed these issues in an article which includes a section on my own family archives. See Dorothy Fujita-Rony, "Illuminating Militarized Rupture: Four Asian American Community-Based Archives," *Journal of Asian American Studies*, 23/1 (February 2020): 1–27.

Sumatra was one of the prime spots for their return, with its plantations and oil fields. This military campaign to recapture Indonesia became known as the First Police Action. On that day, Gerhard L. Tobing was traveling with a driver and an aide after administering to the wounded, when his vehicle was shot. His two companions in the car, a driver and a nurse, were killed instantly. Gerhard L. Tobing was mortally wounded. They rushed him to the hospital at Tanjung Morawa to try to save his life, but it was too late.[5]

In their personal narratives, both Tobing and Rony gave extended, detailed stories about learning of his loss. Tobing remembers the soldier who came to her door to deliver the news:

> So he was killed on July 29, 1947. A week later, one of the Red Cross people came to the house in Siantar. And the man said, *"Mana Ibu Tobing, Nyonya Tobing?"* ["Where is Mrs. Tobing?"] *"Saya,"* I replied. ["Me."] They said, *"Ibu, ada kabar kurang baik. Jadi, ibu isteri Dokter Tobing?"* ["Ma'am, there is bad news. So are you the wife of Dr. Tobing?"] *"Saya."* ["Yes."][6] *"Dokter Tobing sudah meninggal."* ["Doctor Tobing has died."] Just like that. I was still standing there. He said it so bluntly. Not even "Sit down first."[7]

Rony, who at the time was in Pearaja staying with her paternal grandmother, remembers being reached by another family member to deliver the news to her grandmother a week later. Rony recalled what happened when her grandmother learned of Gerhard L. Tobing's passing:

> My *ompung* sat on a mat in the front room when she was told about it. My grandmother didn't say a word for maybe about five minutes. The news was repeated. And then my grandmother started grieving, she called out her son's name again and again and said things to him.[8]

In that moment, the course of Rony's life was irrevocably changed.

Although other widows might have been afraid to go visit the Dutch encampment because of the fear of continued violence, Tobing decided to find out more about what happened regarding her husband's death. As a result, Tobing wanted to go to the bivouac post where the Dutch army was stationed

---

5   See 187–188, 217, this volume.
6   Literally, "I" but in context it means, "Yes."
7   See 188, this volume.
8   See 218, this volume.

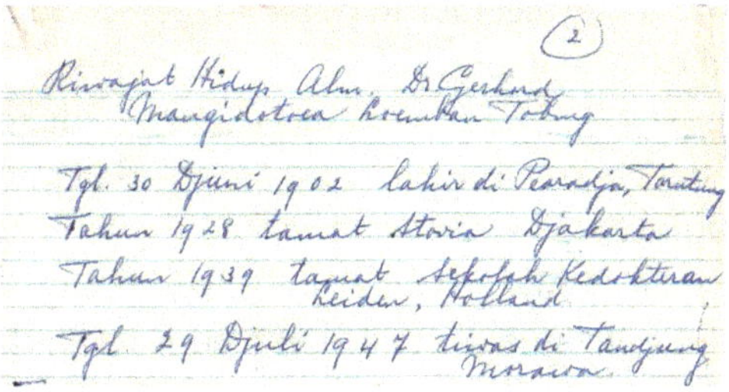
(2)
Riwajat Hidup Alm. Dr Gerhard
Mangidotoea Loemban Tobing

Tgl. 30 Djuni 1902 lahir di Pearadja, Taroetoeng
Tahun 1928 tamat Stovia Djakarta
Tahun 1939 tamat Sekolah Kedokteran
Leiden, Holland
Tgl 29 Djuli 1947 tiwas di Tandjung
Morawa

FIGURE 29
H.L. Tobing's notes on Gerhard L. Tobing's life
TOBING FAMILY COLLECTION

to find out more information. Accompanied by Apoel, Tobing spoke to the doctor who had treated her husband, who asked her for more information about Gerhard L. Tobing. As Tobing reported:

> Within the hour I got the statement that he was killed on the twenty-ninth by such and such. And he even gave the drawing of the place where he was buried, in the back of the hospital in Tanjung Morawa where he usually was working. And the Dutch doctor said, "We are sorry, but we didn't expect to find there a doctor. We thought it was one of the Army people." Because my husband had on Army dress too, not a doctor's, and he was on the road.[9]

In H.L. Tobing's papers in Pearaja, we were able to find the typewritten statement that she secured, which gave us important clues about what happened that day. Thus, on our most recent trip to the Netherlands, I also worked with my mother, aunt, and uncle on this information to begin our research about the circumstances of her husband's death. We did so as a way to honor our memory of Gerhard L. Tobing, and as a way to respect Tobing's efforts to do so as well.

Gerhard L. Tobing's death would have tremendous impact on the course of Tobing's and Rony's lives, not only because of his loss as a beloved husband and father, but also because his death would plunge the family into economic and political uncertainty, especially given the patriarchal nature of Batak culture and Indonesian culture as a whole. Prior to his death, Gerhard L. Tobing was an elite doctor, commanding power and respect by the nature of his position, as well as because of his personal authority and charisma. As Batak culture during this era was so male-focused, to be without this relationship drastically changed the status of Tobing and her children. Widowed with four children to

9 See 188, this volume.

support, Tobing struggled to keep the family together. Rony remembered about those days, "We were very poor and had just enough to eat."[10]

From Rony's narrative, I strongly suspect that it was the event of Gerhard L. Tobing's death that so changed the course of her life and propelled her toward eventual migration to the United States. If Rony had had her father's support, it is extremely likely that she would have been able to become a doctor and remain in Indonesia, even if she had studied abroad for a while for her medical education, as her father wanted her to do. In addition, if her father had remained the head of the household, Tobing would not have felt such pressure for Rony to marry in order to build political support within the Batak community through family networks. Tobing's and Rony's lives took another turn after Rony moved to the United States, as it also led to Tobing's lengthy sojourn there, when she became an Indonesian language instructor at Yale University.

Although this book has focused more on Tobing's and Rony's lives, it is important to note that documentation of my grandfather, in fact, drove this book project to come to its fruition. Rony's wish to honor her father was the impetus for us to embark upon a journey of memorykeeping that led us back to Indonesia and to the family village of Pearaja, and then on to Leiden and Wuppertal, to locate other archival fragments of the family's past. I underscore these issues of Gerhard L. Tobing's life and his untimely death by Dutch forces to demonstrate, once again, that if empire and gender structure women's memorykeeping in my family, it is not an innocent process. Indeed, the specter of military violence haunts the edges of this book, even as Tobing and Rony made decisions not to dwell on the past, but to carry on for the sake of the family and for themselves. It is a testament to Tobing's and Rony's strength that Gerhard L. Tobing's life and his gifts to his family and his community are emphasized in the stories and artifacts they kept. And it is to these processes that I will now turn, with a close examination of how different kinds of artifacts can represent and embody meaning.

4   The Labor of Artifacts

If space and location determine how a collection is developed, maintained, and understood in the context of the home village, the same is true for an artifact collection that is developed elsewhere. In both cases, the migration of household members can have major impact on how artifact collections are

---

10   See 218, this volume.

formed in these different sites. In this section, I explore how migratory knowledges might be symbolized and embodied by family artifacts, such as their ability to represent people who might be far away.

These issues highlight how archives are produced by social actors in specific historical contexts, and that their meanings are continually reshaped over time and space. Arjun Appadurai, for example, directs our attention to "the concrete historical circulation of things" so that we can better see "the things-in-motion that illuminate their human and social context."[11] Calling this process of making meaning an 'activation,' archivist Eric Ketelaar argues that these meanings shape how people understand the world around them, as well as their identities.[12] With each activation, the record changes and a new version is formed, which also affects future activations.[13]

These processes of making meaning through things also are very gendered. Adria Imada provides us with a memorable example of the complex meanings that can be held by objects in her discussion of a bracelet created by hula artist Kini Kapahukulaokamāmalu. Kini Kapahukulaokamāmalu engraved the names of German cities on coins in commemoration of her travel as a performer there in the late 19th century, transforming it into her own personal item.[14] This example highlights what is often the 'everyday' nature of women's memorykeeping. In addition, it can be a practice that does not require considerable expenditure, especially to preserve overall resources for the family. In fact, women's memorykeeping can be used to generate even more assets for family and community. In her history of second-generation Japanese American women, for example, Valerie Matsumoto documents the practice of 'compilation cookbooks,' in which groups of women submit cherished recipes, usually with the proceeds going to support an organization or an event.[15] Matsumoto's

---

11   Arjun Appadurai, "Introduction: Commodities and Their Political Value," in *The Social Life of Things: Commodities in Cultural Perspective*, ed. Arjun Appadurai, Kindle ebook (Cambridge: Cambridge University Press, 1986), 4, 5.

12   Eric Ketelaar, "Cultivating Archives: Meanings and Identities," *Archival Science*, 12 (2012): 19–33. DOI: 10.1007/s10502-011-9142-5.

13   Michelle Caswell, *Archiving the Unspeakable: Silence, Memory, and the Photographic Record in Cambodia* (Madison: University of Wisconsin Press, 2014), 16.

14   Adria L. Imada, *Aloha America: Hula Circuits through the U.S. Empire*, Kindle ebook (Durham, NC: Duke University Press, 2012), under Chapter 2, "Modern Desires and Counter-Colonial Tactics: Gender, Performance, and the Erotics of Empire," "The Grand Tour" section; Susan Stewart, *On Longing: Narratives of the Miniature, the Gigantic, the Souvenir, the Collection*, Kindle ebook (Durham, NC: Duke University Press, 1993), 136, 138.

15   Valerie J. Matsumoto, *City Girls: The Nisei Social World in Los Angeles, 1920–1950*, Kindle ebook (Oxford: Oxford University Press, 2014), 228.

discussion emphasizes the gendered nature of these processes in their preservation of memory, art, and labor in the service of others.

While Rony and Tobing also were known for their talent in preparing different dishes, in this chapter, I focus primarily on how their memorykeeping is enacted through their gathering of artifacts, particularly those that represent migratory knowledges. Although I will discuss their memorykeeping more generally, I also will pay close attention to Rony's artifact collection in the United States. Rony's preservation of family history is foundational to her identity, especially because of all the experiences her family has undergone. She writes,

> For me, it is crucial that people not be forgotten, and that my grandchildren know about the past and what it means to be Toba Batak. Whenever I am able to be with the oldest relatives now, I always ask them questions about the past and take notes about the family history. It is not so much for me as for the younger people, because I think it is important for them to know where they came from, and to learn about all the things that we have gone through as a family.[16]

As a result, Rony's personal collection has become a repository for these issues, not only in the stories that she has chosen to pass on through her autobiographical narrative, but also in her careful collection and maintenance of family artifacts, including photographs, documents, and other representations of the past. These issues are also very much shaped by her status as a daughter in the family. In previous chapters, I already have discussed that according to Toba Batak culture, the house and land go to the sons. However, the daughters are permitted to take what they can from the house. Rony explained in her narrative, "As a daughter, I am allowed to ask and be given things that are removable and can be carried away."[17] Thus, gendered issues of inheritance and property also have an impact on why memorykeeping through artifacts might become so important for women.

In assessing Tobing's and Rony's memorykeeping practices for this book, I have identified four different kinds of artifacts that underscore these knowledges: biographical artifacts, recreated artifacts, cultural practices artifacts, and reintegrated artifacts. These four categories represent the changing meaning of artifacts for people who undergo the processes of migration. *Biographical*

---

16   See 243, this volume.
17   See 204, this volume.

artifacts suggest memories of the people left behind whether in space or time. Photographs are among the most common of these biographical artifacts, although other artifacts too can serve as a reminder of a person, such as a person's favorite shirt or a cherished piece of jewelry. *Recreated artifacts* stand in for artifacts that were lost in a previous time, or that could not be taken during the migratory journey. They do not have to necessarily be valuable in themselves, as it is the meaning they hold which is precious. They could be, for example, dinner plates that remind one of one's childhood, or a lamp similar to one from a relative's home long ago. *Cultural practices artifacts* embody connection across generation and space through representation of meaningful cultural activity, such as cooking or music-making. These are important activities that can be carried to new sites, and again do not need to be activities requiring great expense. Finally, *reintegrated artifacts*, such as previously dispersed photographs that have been reconsolidated into one collection, represent the bringing together of different artifacts that have been spread out in multiple sites or that previously were not accessible because of the collections in which they were housed. While artifacts can move in diverse categories of meaning depending on the context, I name these categories to help illuminate the complex ways that artifacts might achieve different kinds of prominence through the processes of migration.

Let me begin with the category of biographical artifacts. Rony's stories of her father often have a common theme in which Gerhard L. Tobing encouraged her professional ambitions and nurtured her as an individual. For example, in a glass case in her living room, Rony has a collection of beer mugs that remind her of her father, a collection that has been in her possession for as long as I can remember since I was a young girl. None of them actually belonged or were used by her father, who passed away in 1947. But she collected them during her travels in Indonesia and Europe because she remembered how her father would enjoy a beer after a long day of work at the hospital, and once even allowed her a taste as a young girl because she was curious about what he was drinking. Hence, the beer mug collection reminds Rony of the companionable moments they shared during her father's rare times of leisure. Even beyond the direct memories they represent regarding one of her father's leisure activities, their significance also emphasizes the way that her father acknowledged her personhood. The fact that Rony's father was willing to allow her to taste beer indicates his recognition of her as a person who could be trusted, and his sense of possibility for her even though others considered her, as a girl, to be secondary.[18]

---

18   See 206, 242, this volume.

FIGURE 30   Beer mugs collected by Minar T. Rony that represent memories of her father,
Gerhard L. Tobing
PHOTOGRAPH BY AUTHOR

Another important biographical artifact for Rony is a golden cigarette case
given to her father by the Sultan of Siak for curing him of illness. When the
Sultan's customary medical healers could not help him, the Sultan turned
to Gerhard L. Tobing, who was able to bring him back to good health. When
Tobing passed away and Rony went to Pearaja for the funeral, Rony asked for
the cigarette case, because she was the only one left with memories of its significance and what it meant to her father.[19] This cigarette case became all the
more important to her because it was one of the things she was allowed to take
as a daughter. These issues remind us of how legacy can be shaped by male
privilege, and how further meaning might be invested in artifacts because of
these kinds of practices. It also demonstrates how women such as Rony have
a fundamentally different relationship to the past and family inheritance than
their male siblings and other relatives, one of the reasons why Rony and others
develop gendered knowledges about the meaning and collection of artifacts.

Gendered knowledge also imbues particular significance in a second category
of artifacts prevalent in Rony's collection that can be called *recreated artifacts*.
By this I mean newly acquired artifacts used to represent those that have been
lost in the past, and that are filled with the meaning of the original artifact, even

---

19   See 204, this volume.

FIGURE 31
Betel nut set kept by
Minar T. Rony
PHOTOGRAPH BY AUTHOR

though they are acquired in the present; the beer mugs I discussed earlier in this section fit into this category as well. Although Rony has faced many challenges and different kinds of losses in her lifetime, she does not live within this sense of loss and dwell on what was left behind or not to be, as can be seen by her narrative.[20] But this is where her memorykeeping is key, and perhaps restorative as well. This group of artifacts speaks directly to her continuing efforts to integrate these former parts of her life with her current, everyday existence.

For example, one year, Rony brought back a betel nut chewing set from a trip to Indonesia, consisting of a larger vessel and smaller equipment by which to engage in betel nut chewing. This set was particularly evocative because it drew her back in the past to when she was a young child visiting her father's village. As a little girl, she remembered seeing her grandmother chewing betel nuts in the morning, when the elders would sit in the yard and exchange stories about the past, including when the Dutch came in the late 19th century. Because her grandmother lived in Pearaja in the family home, the betel nut chewing set represents these memories, and are inextricably linked to Rony's recollections of her paternal grandmother and to the physical site of the home village in Pearaja.[21]

Another recreated artifact is a wind-up clock that marks the time in fifteen-minute intervals, pealing at the top of each hour with bell rings to mark the

20   See 225, 235, 236, 242–243, this volume.
21   See 242–243, this volume.

FIGURE 32 Porcelain and other souvenirs collected by Minar T. Rony that remind her of childhood
PHOTOGRAPH BY AUTHOR

hour of the day. I remember that Rony purchased the clock when I was young, and that she told me it reminded her of the clock her family had when she was small. It was a familiar sound in my childhood years in my family home in Maryland, and something that I associate with the family and the past as well because of its prominence in our home life. Its significance within our collective memory is one of the reasons Rony took the clock with her when she moved to Los Angeles after her retirement. As an adult now, I more fully recognize that the clock's marking of fifteen-minute intervals with its chimes was a fundamental organization of the passage of time. My mother's purchase of the clock and its centrality in our household insured that these rhythms from the past became part of how I marked the passage of the day and night as well. Furthermore, I also see how the clock can be taken to represent the colonial modernity introduced to the family in the early 20th century, which my grandfather embraced even as he sought to stay true to Toba Batak culture.

Yet another set of recreated artifacts is Rony's collection of Delft-style figurines and plates, the blue and white china figures of windmills, children, and other items inspired by the renowned manufacturers in the Netherlands. While she has a few of these figurines from her later travels to the Netherlands, most of these figures and plates date from the last decade of her residence in Los Angeles. The display shelf where she keeps this china has become more crowded over the past years because Delft china is a popular tourist souvenir for Americans and others visiting the Netherlands. As a result, examples show up regularly in the fundraising bazaar held in her retirement community, which she then purchases.[22]

In fact, when we visited the Netherlands and Germany for archival research, in the only free day we had in between our work at Leiden University and the Rhenish Mission in Wuppertal, we visited the town of Delft and took a tour of the facility. Rony has ambivalence to Dutch culture as a former colonial subject whose father had been killed by Dutch military forces. She also has written about the racism and segregation that she faced. For example, she remembers, as I discussed in an earlier chapter, attending Dutch-language school as a young girl and being called names by one of her classmates. She has not forgotten these events and they are central to her understanding of her life in Indonesia. However, as Rony recalls in her autobiography, Dutch culture also was part of her childhood memories of her home environment, an outcome of her parents' status as Dutch-educated elite during that time.[23] Her collection of this Delft-style porcelain thus demonstrates that she has made choices about the kinds of memories to assign to which objects, and how memories can be selectively reclaimed.

The third type of artifacts that I want to explore are *cultural practices artifacts*, or artifacts that tell the story of intergenerational cultural practices. These are artifacts that remind people of their relationships with other people and the connections between generations. In doing so, they bridge the ruptures that people might have encountered through, for example, war or migration. For a number of people, photographs of ancestors might serve that function, or perhaps cherished family recipes and foodways. Indeed, I have many memories of specific foods that my grandmother and mother made, and of watching their considerable labor in the kitchen be consumed rapidly by the family and visitors who so enjoyed their cooking. For this part of the discussion, though, I am particularly interested in the kinds of meaning represented by a category often labelled—and dismissed—as 'women's handicrafts.' Some of this labor might be for family use, such as the making of a garment or blanket for a child, which might be considered similar to other women's work like cooking or childcare. But other handicrafts, embroidery or tatting for example, also are part of this category too, and can be more decorative in nature, intended for display or to mark special occasions.

Both Rony and Tobing treasured all kinds of handiwork, such as sewing, crocheting, knitting, macramé, embroidery, needlepoint, and tatting. Spanning

---

22   See 242, this volume.
23   See for example, 200–202, 203, this volume.

FIGURE 33   Crocheting was a skill passed down by the women in my family, and I continue to
practice it today. This blanket was made by my grandmother, who taught me how
to crochet when I was a little girl
PHOTOGRAPH BY AUTHOR

the different time periods and empires of their lives, these arts were considered appropriate to teach girls and women because they were associated with the home and private space, as indicated in Chapter 2.[24] Thus, both Tobing and Rony learned these kinds of arts through colonial education curriculum during their girlhoods in Indonesia, due to the importance of women's domesticity in Dutch and German colonial culture of that time. Significantly, they continued to use these skills later in the United States because of the availability of similar domestic arts activities for women. For example, Tobing further developed her skills through arts and crafts classes offered at her church when she moved to New Haven in her later years.[25]

But the handicrafts were important beyond the way they had been incorporated into their learned school curriculum, for they also had meaning on an individual level. Women in my family took pride in these different arts, and Tobing and Rony actively taught and encouraged me to enjoy this kind of work as well. They often shared stories of how my great grandmother was very skilled in these activities, whether she was engaged in traditional Batak weaving, using a Singer sewing machine, or making macramé handbags. They also actively supported me to follow my interest in this kind of labor as it was through their efforts that I visited Pearaja in 1985 to study weaving.[26]

---

24   See 66, 68, 214, this volume.
25   See 166, 168, 195, 223–224, this volume.
26   See 166, 219, this volume.

I recognize now that the importance of these handicrafts is not just for the object itself, but also for the object as an embodiment of meaning. These meanings might include the affective emotions symbolized by the making of the handicraft, and the pleasure it gives the maker to create and present them to another. Or it might serve as a reminder of the joy of personal artistry, and the autonomous private space that making the handicraft confers, in the middle of a busy day of work and caring for others. And, as I already have pointed out, these handicrafts also could represent a form of continuity across the generations. In 1995 when we visited Tobing's home in Pearaja, I was touched to find one of my first crocheting efforts, a small bag made out of single-stitch crochet, hanging on the wall near her bed where she would see it every morning. It displayed a young girl's initial efforts in the craft. Made out of bulky thread with clashing colors from the leftover yarn of other projects, the bag was the work of a novice who was learning how to do simple stitches. I was glad to be remembered, especially as a daughter of a daughter. Now I recognize that the bag represented a grandchild who was across the Pacific Ocean, as well as a granddaughter who had learned and valued the art of crocheting and other needle arts, like generations of women before her.

Finally, the fourth type of artifact are what I call *reintegrated artifacts*, artifacts that are connected to the family in some way, but that were taken or stored elsewhere in another geographic site, and then brought back to be reintegrated into the family collection. On a familial level, these artifacts could be situated in different physical spaces because of the migrations that family members might have undergone, such as how my grandmother's and mother's archival collections are located on both sides of the Pacific. Part of our project has been to bring together photographs that were spread out in different personal collections. But there is another level by which we can consider migration knowledges within an interimperial context. Artifacts are formed by the migrations that colonial populations themselves might undertake in search of work and education; however, they also are produced by the processes of empire, which has an impact on how these artifacts are physically dispersed over space and time. For example, empires often generate voluminous documentation about a subject population, whether through written materials or images, and typically keep these materials wherever the imperial administrations are located. In this case then, migration knowledges might not be just about the knowledges communities produce themselves from moving to a different site. In fact, they can also be about people's awareness of the wider imperial context in which they made these movements, such as the decisions and policies of empires to send representatives to colonies, as well as to have colonials travel to imperial metropoles. This is especially true of the interimperial context which both Tobing and Rony experienced.

FIGURE 34   "Adatdansen door Toba-Batakkers, vermoedelijk in de Silindoengvallei bij
Taroetoeng," [Ritual dance of the Toba Batak in Silindung Valley, Tarutung]
SPECIAL COLLECTIONS, LEIDEN UNIVERSITY LIBRARIES, KITLV 101167,
CA. 1910. THIS PHOTOGRAPH LOCATED IN SPECIAL COLLECTIONS, LEIDEN
UNIVERSITY LIBRARIES, APPEARS TO BE IN THE SAME SEQUENCE AS THE
NEXT PHOTOGRAPH, WHICH IS LOCATED IN THE AMS DER VEM

This type of migration knowledge was the reason for our journey across
the Atlantic to Europe in the summer of 2018 to visit the Special Collections
at the Leiden University Libraries and the Archiv- und Museumsstiftung der
VEM [AMS der VEM] in Wuppertal, Germany. By undertaking this travel, our
archival efforts followed Rony's and Tobing's geographical knowledge which
spanned both the Pacific and Atlantic. In a counter migration to the flow of
these documents and photographs moving from Indonesia to Europe, we
sought to reunify materials that were related to family history and locate them
in one collection back in our homes in California. Our intent was not so much
to bring back the actual 'authentic' documents and photographs, but to return
with images and copies which could represent the past in an integrated collection. In a different context, Ricardo Punzalan has written about similar issues
in his discussion of the "archival diaspora" of Dean C. Worcester's ethnograph-
ic photographs, generated through his role in the US colonial administration
in the Philippines. Punzalan writes of the new archival strategy of "virtual re-
unification," in which separated constituents of a collection are recombined

FIGURE 35   "Heidnisches Fest, Sumatra" [Pagan Festival, Sumatra]
AMS DER VEM. ARCHIVES NUMBER: 203–156. RITUAL DANCE

through digitization technologies, an especially important strategy given that many archives might want to retain their original segment of these fragmented collections.[27] Our own archival process mirrors these issues in our attempt to negotiate the interimperial locations of family documents and photographs.

As migration knowledges embody specific geographical knowledges, it seemed logical to us—even familiar—to search for records across the Atlantic. In going to European archives, we retraced Gerhard L. Tobing's educational path back to Leiden and visited the sites from where imperialism emanated, retrieving artifacts that had been collected by these powers. Our ability to do so was further shaped by our intergenerational team of linguists, as Rony, alongside her brother Bistok Tobing and sister-in-law Arta Tobing, all spoke multiple languages.

In our case, it was a foregone conclusion that we should visit Leiden University because of its strong library holdings on Indonesia, especially its Special Collections. On one level, this is due to Leiden University's immense library and archives, and because of its stature as one of the oldest universities

---

27   Ricardo L. Punzalan, "Archival Diasporas: A Framework for Understanding the Complexities and Challenges of Dispersed Photographic Collections," *The American Archivist*, 77/2 (Fall/Winter 2014): 326–349.

FIGURE 36   Minar T. Rony and Bistok P.L. Tobing researching documents and
             newspapers at Special Collections, Leiden University Libraries
             PHOTOGRAPH BY AUTHOR

FIGURE 37   Artauli R.M. Pangabbean Tobing and Minar T. Rony reading
             documents at Special Collections, Leiden University Libraries
             PHOTOGRAPH BY AUTHOR

in the world, having been founded in 1575.[28] But on another level, the breadth of the university's Indonesia collection also demonstrates how documentation and knowledge production were considered integral to establishing control over areas of the far-flung empire. The colonial ethnographers and scholars who sought information about the Dutch East Indies and then brought back these knowledges to the Netherlands were part of a larger colonial adminis- tration who needed this kind of information to run its colony. They required myriad knowledges, whether in terms of assessing the need for military troops, the building of a transportation infrastructure to export raw materials, or the development of schools to train future administrative staff in Dutch language and curriculum.[29]

Hence, because of the careful ways that the colonies were scrutinized from the imperial center, copious amounts of information were sent to the

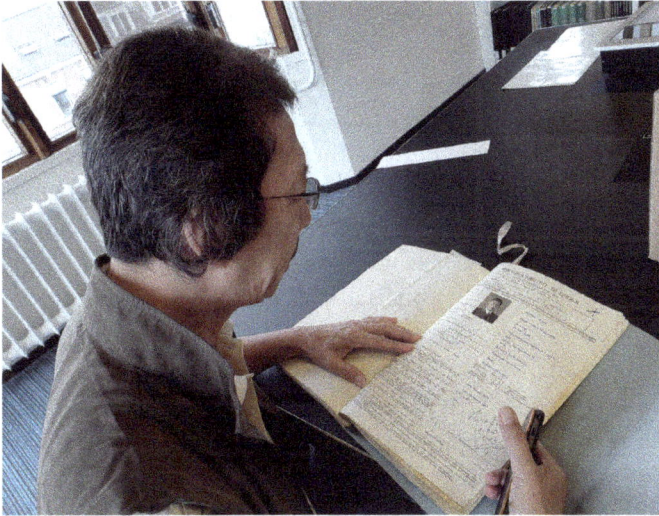

FIGURE 38   Bistok P.L. Tobing examining Gerhard L. Tobing's school
             records at Special Collections, Leiden University Libraries
             PHOTOGRAPH BY AUTHOR

---

28   "Indonesia and Leiden University have a shared history—and a shared future," June 19, 2019.
      Available at: https://www.universiteitleiden.nl/en/news/2019/06/indonesia-and-leiden
      -university-have-a-shared-history-and-shared-future (accessed January 13, 2020); Linawati
      Sidarto, "World's Largest Library on Indonesia Opens in Leiden," *The Jakarta Post*,
      October 23, 2017. Available at: https://www.thejakartapost.com/life/2017/10/23/worlds
      -largest-library-on-indonesia-opens-in-leiden.html (accessed January 13, 2020); "History,"
      https://www.universiteitleiden.nl/en/about-us (accessed January 13, 2020).
29   Ann Laura Stoler, *Along the Archival Grain: Epistemic Anxieties and Colonial Common
      Sense* (Princeton, NJ: Princeton University Press, 2009).

Netherlands from Indonesia, consisting of administrative records and periodicals. We were glad to discover articles that Gerhard L. Tobing had written for Batak newspapers during his schooling in Batavia (now Jakarta), as well as his school records for Leiden University, including his annual registration papers. Leiden University had added particular significance because in 1937, when Rony was five years old, Gerhard L. Tobing spent twenty months at Leiden University to study for the government medical examination, as well as to develop a specialty in ear, nose, and throat medicine. This research enabled us to have connection with the materials, especially since Gerhard L. Tobing had been lost several decades before. When he was killed in July 1947, his son Bistok was only three months old. Hence, the archival collection became a space for reconciliation on another level as well, where both Rony and Bistok Tobing could locate materials of their father firsthand.

It was Rony who suggested that we visit the AMS der VEM in Wuppertal. The connections through Wuppertal, like the linkages through Leiden, again highlight the global context in which our family history is situated. Globalizing processes in Wuppertal led to mission stations being developed in different parts of Africa and Asia. In our archival search, we concentrated our initial efforts on the administrative papers left by the Rhenish Mission, which involved such subjects as the establishment of the mission in its early years, the training of local leaders to be religious leaders, the spread of different congregations in the area, and the establishment of schools. As the mission regularly corresponded with the home mission in Wuppertal, it also generated a regular series of reports explaining developments within Pearaja.[30]

In the middle of our archival journey, we had the good fortune to be able to access Toba Batak photographs in their collection. While a few of the photographs show the 'old ways,' such as musical performance, most of the photographs document the transformed spatiality set up by the mission with the church at its center, and the new forms of education available to both young men and young women. Other images were important too, as they showed the mission and its surrounding buildings, the growth of the congregation, and the wider landscape in which the mission was situated. Although my family members, especially Rony, carefully went through the photographs, there were many that we could not identify. However, we did find some directly relevant to our family history, including two photographs of our ancestor Raja Pontas,

---

30   The AMS der VEM contains significant and rich files on the mission experience in Sumatra, including files of the mission stations, individual files for missionary leaders and staff, and reports of meetings and activities. See their comprehensive archival guide, "Indonesien, Sumatra."

FIGURE 39
Archivist Julia Besten
showing Minar T. Rony
the same image
of her ancestors
from Figure 29 at
the Archiv- und
Museumsstiftung der
VEM in Wuppertal,
Germany
PHOTOGRAPH BY
AUTHOR

one of which already was in Pearaja as part of the family collection. There also was another photograph of Si [The] Singamangaraja's family, the famous Batak king who had engaged in resistance against the Dutch.

While all of us on the research team pored over the old photos in both Leiden and Wuppertal, it was Rony, as the senior member of the research team, who actively sought to recognize relatives. She was too young to recognize most of the people in the photographs from the 1910s and 1920s, and all of us regretted that we had not traveled to Leiden and Wuppertal a few decades earlier with Tobing, who would have been able to identify many more. But in one of the group photographs, the rupture was closed, at least for a moment. Rony found a picture of her great aunt, Ompung boru Situmorang, as a young woman. This was the same *ompung* who had regaled Rony with stories about her experiences as a daughter-in-law to Si Singamangaraja when Rony was just a little girl listening to the elders spin tales in the early morning. In that moment, thousands of miles away from the ancestral village in North Sumatra, the photograph in Wuppertal created a space for Rony to lead us back into the past.

FIGURE 40   "Hinterblibenen—Sisingamangaraja" [Bereaved—Sisingamangaraja]
AMS DER VEM. ARCHIVES NUMBER: 203–423

FIGURE 41
Detail of photograph 40, "Hinterblibenen—Sisingamangaraja"
[Bereaved—Sisingamangaraja]
AMS DER VEM. ARCHIVES NUMBER: 203–423

Taken in Sumatra and preserved in Germany, we were able to get copies of the photographs for Rony so they now can 'return' to the family archives. In a technological update to Rony's memorykeeping practices, one of my ongoing projects has been to bring many of the images together for her into one slideshow: the family photographs that she kept from the United States and Tobing's collection from Pearaja, which I also scanned. Some of these photographs are from the early days of Tobing's marriage, and some of them are photographs of ancestors. Now there are also photograph groups that we have discovered in the Special Collections at Leiden University Libraries, and the AMS der VEM in Wuppertal. So far, it has been a generative space, bridging past gaps; going through the photographs creates a new kind of collective space and restores social knowledge. Seeing the images curated in this way often evokes long-forgotten memories and provides possibilities for the emergence of new stories. In assisting her in reconciling these images and artifacts, I recognize that I am engaging in a gendered process of memorykeeping myself, of bringing together various photographs and reminiscences that have been separated over time, space, and distance.

The different kinds of artifacts that I have discussed in this section— biographical artifacts, recreated artifacts, cultural practices artifacts, and reintegrated artifacts—all point to strategies for memory forged through loss and migration in some way, and in doing so, also show the power of continued reclamation for future generations. As these processes indicate, objects of profound memory do not have to be of considerable monetary worth—or even the original artifact itself. It is the memory that has been invested in the object, and what it represents to the storyteller and the listener, that ultimately makes the artifact important. Furthermore, the fact that many of these artifacts are not original and inherently replaceable speaks of their value in terms of their meaning within the context of gendered knowledge.

They further underscore the importance of women memorykeepers, and the critical nature of maintaining gendered knowledge through artifacts. Part of the reason, for example, that we know precisely the places and dates of Gerhard L. Tobing's life is because my grandmother prepared a one-page summary of his biographical record, which she left in her archival collection. While it likely was used for legal or administrative matters during her widowhood so that she could negotiate the Indonesian government bureaucracy, Tobing saved this precious record for younger generations who would discover it decades later. The occasion upon which we found it also was inspired by a memorykeeper from the following generation, my mother, who insisted that Gerhard L. Tobing not be forgotten, even though she is the only immediate family left who has direct memory of him. And that role has been passed on to the next generation, as represented by myself. When one of my relatives recently wanted to confirm some dates in my grandfather's life, because I had scanned the record and could call it up immediately, I was able to provide him with that history. Intergenerational memorykeeping thus has far-reaching impact, and can help to unify family memory and knowledge, even when the memorykeeper herself no longer is with us or we live in different parts of the world.

Our project has demonstrated that in addition to the knowledge that is communicated to younger cohorts, the modes of memorykeeping labor also can be passed on. Looking back now, I can see that both my inclination and instinct for memorykeeping came easily to me; I was drawn early on as a young person to the processes of public history, including personal narratives and artifact collection. It also explains why I began working in a history museum soon after college and then returned to graduate school to study US immigration and labor history. My professional choices make sense in light of my intergenerational legacy of women's memorykeeping, despite the fact that I grew up in the United States and am a child of the diaspora, living far away from the family's original home in northern Sumatra.

5   Conclusion

I have focused on artifacts in this chapter as a way to discuss how knowledges are carried and change through space and time through migration. In the nature of 'diaspora,' the reference point becomes the homeland, around which various migration streams have emanated. Typically in this kind of framing, the culture and language of the homeland are privileged, and the new communities that have formed elsewhere are seen as lesser, as derivative.[31] But for Southeast Asian Americans in the 20th and early 21st centuries, these processes are especially fraught because of the processes of empire. I am one of the lucky ones, in that I can visit my parents' homeland, and through my mother, have an intergenerational connection to the past. Many others cannot do so, whether because of political circumstances or economic resources, despite other privileges that we might enjoy due to living in the United States.

---

31   Mariam Lam, "Foreword," in *Southeast Asian Diaspora in the United States: Memories and Visions, Yesterday, Today, and Tomorrow*, ed. Jonathan H.X. Lee (Newcastle upon Tyne: Cambridge Scholars Publishing, 2015), xxvi.

My mother is now the only one left in our immediate family with direct knowledge of what happened before World War II. As a result, there are yet other questions that emerge in these processes of reclamation concerning the role of geography. In my final questions for this chapter, I want to ask what it means when the deepest knowledge of the 'homeland' is carried by our community elders who now live somewhere other than Southeast Asia, and have spent the greater part of their adult lives away from their birth country. Does that knowledge become invalidated or lessened because the elders no longer live in their country of origin? And what happens when they tell stories of the past to younger generations in the new languages of the destination to which they have migrated?[32] These processes will continue in the next decades, as those who make home in new lands as adults become the elders of our communities, particularly for those under conditions where they feel they will not return to their countries of origin in Asia. Reframing these knowledges not just as products of a diasporic culture, but in an alternate framing as 'migration knowledges' enables us to think more fully about how knowledges travel, take on their own autonomy, and become histories and archives in their own right. While some might believe that migration knowledges are lesser, perhaps not as authentic as those generated from the homeland, others of us understand that they are one of the most vital ways through which we can access a past that already has irrevocably changed, and which otherwise might not be remembered. This is the reality of our interimperial histories and the everyday archives that are made through women's memorykeeping. Maintaining gendered knowledges across geography and time, women memorykeepers such as Tobing and Rony enable us to see that artifacts not only can represent the past, but they also can convey knowledges that can accompany our migrations into the future.

---

32   Khatharya Um, "Exiled Memory: History, Identity, and Remembering in Southeast Asia and Southeast Asian Diaspora," *Positions*, 20/3 (2012): 831–850. DOI: 10.1215/10679847-1593564.

PART 3

Memorykeeping

∵

Prologue to Part 3
A Journey and a Path

My intent for this prologue is to introduce H.L. Tobing's and Minar T. Rony's narratives, in the third part of this book. The original impetus for this project began in 1985, as a way to learn about women's weaving in my maternal family's home village of Pearaja. Growing up, my mother, grandmother, and aunt had nurtured my love of crafts—crocheting, embroidery, tatting, needlepoint, and macramé—skills which I had learned from the women in my family since I was a little girl. As a teenager in high school, I had taken a weaving class, and my mother asked me to show my work to my grandmother when she was visiting in 1984. Recognizing my interest in these kinds of skills, my grandmother asked me if I would like to go to Indonesia to learn more about weaving in the home village. So after I graduated from college in 1985, my mother gave me a ticket, money for expenses, and a new suitcase, and off I went to Indonesia. After traveling for a month and a half with family, I went to stay with my grandmother in Pearaja.

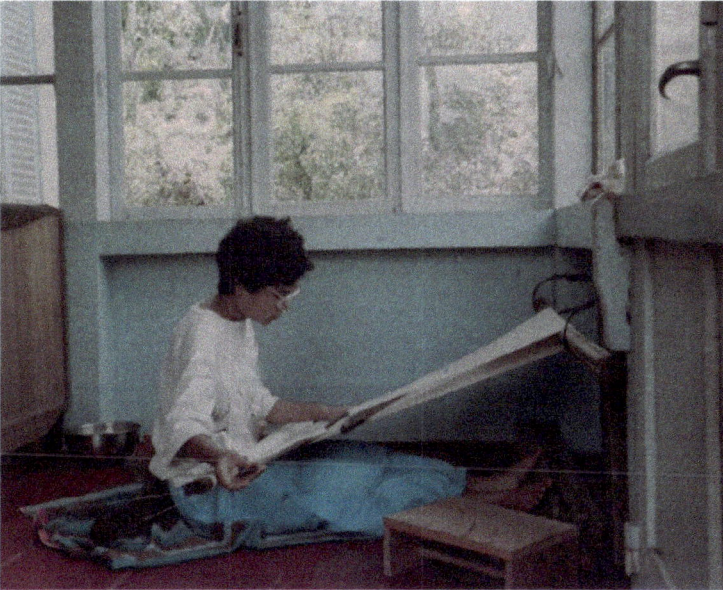

FIGURE 42   The author learning weaving in Pearaja in 1985
DOROTHY FUJITA-RONY COLLECTION

© KONINKLIJKE BRILL NV, LEIDEN, 2021 | DOI:10.1163/9789004436237_007

At the time that I first traveled to my grandmother's village to learn about the culture, I was newly graduated from Yale College without set plans for the following year. Looking back now some decades later, I am better able to understand how my migration to Pearaja was a manifestation of an earlier pattern of return to the home village. In 1985 though, I was like a fish out of water—with rudimentary Indonesian and not knowing the Batak language or culture. And, even though the village was in the town of Tarutung and hence not as rural as other sites in Indonesia, it still felt very rural to me, as my immediate experience had been growing up in the Washington, D.C., suburbs and then attending school in New Haven. But this positionality was to shape my experience in a crucial way which I had not anticipated prior to leaving the United States: it propelled me to document my grandmother's memories and discussions of family history. As an English language speaker, my main companion in Pearaja was my grandmother. Having just learned about US social history and oral history in college, it only was a small leap to decide to compile her stories into a narrative. I had a typewriter and plenty of time. Although I was studying weaving, this still left a good part of the day when I had my own schedule.

And so the project began. In some ways, my lack of knowledge of the Batak culture made it easier for my grandmother to explain the history as there was so much that was new and different than what I was used to in the United States. In other ways, the intricacies of Batak culture would be confusing. Moreover, I rapidly had to learn a geography of Indonesia based not only on the current names of sites, but also the former names under colonial rule. However, my grandmother was a storyteller and a teacher, and the memories of the past flowed. Furthermore, she was a grandmother who very much wanted her American granddaughter to understand why being Batak was so important. Through her words, we moved back and forth across time, from the earliest stories she was told by relatives, to stories she told of her present life in the village.

After my stay with her in 1985, I did not return to Pearaja again for ten years. In the intervening period, I was busy with a new job at the New York Chinatown History Project, now the Museum of the Chinese in the Americas, and then I went back to Yale to begin graduate school. I saw my grandmother a few times when she visited the United States, and she attended my wedding in 1994. It was a tremendous blow when she passed away at the end of that year. In 1995, I returned for a visit with my mother and my Aunt Demak, and we stayed for some days in the family home in Pearaja. We lost Aunt Demak just a few years later, and because my Uncle Apoel also had passed in 1990, my mother became the last of the immediate extended family to remember the years before World War II.

In 2014, several months after my father passed away, my mother had a heart attack. Although she made a good recovery, I decided it was time to prioritize working with her on the family history. Hence, I began traveling each weekend to visit my mother and scan her photograph collection. At first, I naively thought that it would only take a few weekends to scan and organize her photographs. Once I began doing this, however, the days quickly became months. My mother's photograph collection consisted of nearly a thousand images collected over her lifetime.

In the meantime, my mother also wanted to write down what she remembered about her father, as she was the last one left with clear memories of his life; her only other remaining sibling, my Uncle Bistok, had just been a few months old when my grandfather was killed. As she began the process of documenting her memories, the other recollections came back as well, and soon it became a full-fledged autobiographical narrative. In terms of her lifespan, it also was the right time for my mother to begin addressing her personal history. Now that she no longer had the responsibility to care for others on a daily basis, my mother had more choices about her regular schedule, and she had more resources to devote to her own projects. After a lifetime of putting other people first, she felt ready to write her own history.

And so, my mother began compiling her memories of the past. She originally started jotting down notes in longhand. But it soon became apparent that typing out her recollections on the computer would be much more practical in terms of compiling her narrative. As a result, I became her transcriber and administrative assistant. Although my mother had used a computer in her former career at the Library of Congress, she now had been in retirement for several years, and it was much easier for her to have me take on this labor. It also made it more convenient for her to edit and correct the typed pages.

Taking on another role, at that point I became my mother's companion in her overseas travel. In 2017, after being away from Indonesia for more than two decades, I accompanied my mother back to Pearaja to the ancestral home, along with my Uncle Bistok and my Aunt Arta. One of my mother's hopes was to find my grandmother's papers. Before the trip, we were not sure what remained, and we steeled ourselves ahead of time for the prospect that nothing might be left. But, in fact, stored away for decades in the upper cabinets, we found a treasure trove of my grandmother's papers and photographs. Because of the overwhelming amount of materials, in that initial trip, we only brought back the photographs we had discovered and the oldest documents. Thankfully, my cousins in Jakarta purchased supplies to house the documents and artifacts, and allowed me to set up shop at their house so we could organize and categorize materials.

Because we had left roughly half the collection in Pearaja, our research team—comprised of my mother, myself, my Uncle Bistok, and my Aunt Arta—returned the following summer in 2018, along with another aunt and uncle, to visit Pearaja and finish taking care of the collection. This time, my son Theodore accompanied us as well. As result of that trip, we brought home the remaining documents and photographs to my cousins' home in Jakarta for safekeeping. My family helped me purchase a scanner in Jakarta so I could preserve photographs and documents. This time, I focused on scanning the photographs, of which there were a few thousand, and as many documents as I could.

But the United States and Indonesia were not the only sites with materials relevant to our family, as I have detailed in previous chapters. Hence, two months later in 2018, my mother, aunt, uncle, and I were reunited once again, but this time on the other side of the world in Europe to investigate the records and photographs of the Toba Batak at Leiden University Libraries in the Netherlands and the AMS der VEM in Wuppertal, Germany.

In 2019, we again crossed the Atlantic Ocean to the Netherlands, and then the Pacific Ocean to Indonesia, to continue to pursue the historical trail. In the Netherlands, we conducted research to find out further details about my grandfather's death, in order to honor his memory. A few months later, we visited Indonesia once more, as my mother wanted to travel to the village while she still was physically mobile, and go to the ancestral graves and other sites.

Having traced these routes—now multiple times—I am more fully cognizant of what it means to pursue the past, and why memorykeeping is such a precious task. Now that I am in my middle age, I am better able to appreciate the difficulties and challenges of what return means for family members who live away from the home village, whether in another part of the country or in another site in the diaspora. In 1985 when I had just graduated from Yale and was embarking upon adulthood, I was new to the past. Now, I understand more fully at this point that returning home is a fraught process for others in my family who have grown up during the colonial and revolutionary era in Indonesia, and experienced the 1930s, 1940s, and 1950s. For my elders, returning home also means recalling loss and absence, and assessing the costs of migration—the people left behind, the lifestyles distant in memory, the ruptures in time and space. My mother, too, contends with these processes. But I credit her for her determination as a leader, advisor, and multilingual researcher in this project, in terms of both its conceptualization and its implementation.

The chapters that follow offer my grandmother's and mother's memories. Chapter 5 presents my grandmother's personal narrative, and then my mother's autobiographical account is relayed in Chapter 6. Their stories focus on the tumultuous 20th century in which they lived, and illuminate the impact of the Dutch, German, Japanese, and United States empires on their lives. In doing so, their memories offer us rare insight into what it meant to be Toba Batak women in Indonesia and the United States during this period. By sharing their memories, both women wanted to convey their historical experience, and they were careful in how they discussed the past, and the people they encountered and knew. Both saw that the narratives they shared were their own historical truth. As they navigated the terrain of personal memory, they tried their best to be considerate of other people, even as they strove to retain the integrity of their perspectives so that they could communicate the history they experienced. Their primary goal for relating these stories was to tell the past as they knew it so that younger generations might have it as a legacy.

In addition, I should mention that their narratives have very different styles, as my grandmother's narrative was produced as a series of memories she related in 1985, and my mother's autobiography was written as a more integrated narrative from 2017 to 2019. I have used brackets to convey explanatory information for both narratives, and in the case of my grandmother's narrative, to assist in the transition between topics as well. Lastly, I also want to acknowledge that both these narratives were conducted primarily in their fourth fluent language, English. I have chosen to keep the narratives close to their original voices, and to their own personal phrasing.

It is time now to enter the past, as presented by H.L. Tobing and Minar T. Rony.

CHAPTER 5

Across Empires
The Narrative of H.L. Tobing

1   Raja Pontas

[Tobing began by explaining the history of the family.] There were four sons of Ompu [the honorific title used for the rank of grandparent] Sotaronggal. And then the four sons were Manahan Laut, Raja Pontas, Ompu Batu Hasak, and Ompu Raja Ingan. They lived first in Sumur and Huta Baginda, Sosor Pardomuan [in Silindung Valley]. Raja Pontas [her husband's grandfather] was very strong and wise. According to the legend, when a mad buffalo came running to him, he was able to catch the buffalo by its horns, and turn the head around so that the buffalo died, was killed. He was the second son of the Raja Ompu Sotaronggal. So he became here the Raja. The oldest one, Manahan Laut went to Pagar Batu. The other two remained in Sumur and Huta Baginda, Ompu Boksa and Raja Ingan. At that time, the one that is strong and wise can give advice, he becomes the chief or the ruler. If you say royal family, there is in the Batak language "*Rajanami*," it means "my raja," everybody who is well behaved is raja. That is why I said we are very democratic.

[Tobing also explained the early arrival of outsiders to the region.] The American missionaries Munson and Lyman first came in 1834 from Boston. But they were killed. They were white with blue eyes and looked like ghosts. They didn't know the language, they only had an interpreter. They were not prepared. They couldn't tell the people what they wanted.

And at that time in 1834, Nommensen was born in Nordstrand, [now] north Germany. And then in the 1860s, Nommensen came to work with the Toba Batak. The first converted Batak was about that time then. Nommensen lived there in Sait Nihuta, close to the river. Every time the river was flooded, his house was almost drowned and so on. He had too many difficulties. After that, he wanted to make it in Huta Dame. Then later from there he moved to Pearaja because that was the land that your grandfather's grandfather, Raja Pontas, let him [use to] start his mission. Raja Pontas was the chief here, he was the raja from this area. According to the notes that we could find, he was the founder of this village. That is why we have the rice fields there, on the left if you go to the market. He worked very hard to plant rice on it. The whole piece of land is still ours.

2   The Old Times

I had an aunt, an old aunt from Lintong Nihuta. And she said, "When I was a child, maybe seven, eight years old, people would come with a *tabanan*, that means a person that they caught in the war [who became a prisoner or slave]. I have never seen that they ate the person. But I remembered that I played with the fingers cut from the person. Because the hands were what did the evil-doing, not the feet or the mouth. So the hands were cut off. And so I played in the yard with the fingers for a time. That is all I remembered." She was about forty years older than I was, so around 1870 this happened then.

In the old times, if one village fights against another village and they have women and children captured from the defeated village, they will use these women and children as slaves. They have to work for nothing. The slaves ate rice, maybe with a little fish, but they wouldn't use plates like the masters had. They ate from the coconut shells. I myself have never seen it, but I heard about that. I also heard that in the Situmorang area if they had the slaves, they treated the captured people almost inhumanly because they were not allowed even to talk to their masters. They had to meow to ask for some food. They had to work hard. In Southern Tapanuli in the Angkola and Mandailing areas, they said that if you belong to these slaves or *hatoban* families, the steps to the house have to be even. Then, because of that, they know immediately that is the descendant of a slave. It is not only the father who is a slave, but also the children, and the grandchildren, the descendants. But nowadays you can't even know who are the master's [descendants], who are the slave's descendants. Because the slaves' descendants have moved themselves up by hard work and studying. Now you get the opportunity as long as you have the money to pay your school fee, you can go study in other areas. It was not like the slaves in the United States, for instance. I saw the film *Roots*, how bad it was.[1] Well, we didn't have it as bad as that, I think. And besides, they abolished that kind of situation with the coming of Christianity. Christianity came here in the 1860s. So it was recently here. Everything is recently here! Like I told you, my mother-in-law couldn't read or write. Her son managed to get the highest education. He studied medicine in a university in Leiden, in Holland!

---

1   Tobing was referring to *Roots*, a popular television miniseries in the 1970s that portrayed the intergenerational history of an African American family.

3   Family

I was born 1911 in Bekala on the east coast of Sumatra, close to Arnhemia. Arnhemia is now called Pancur Batu, not too far from Medan. My father was working at the railroad station. He was not yet the *"chef,"* the "station master." He had only his elementary school in the Batak language with a little Indonesian. But then he came to the east coast of Sumatra with his uncle, that is his mother's brother, in the Batak language, it is called his *"tulang."* He got his job at the railroad station, and he tried to study Dutch because in the old times, if you don't speak Dutch, you don't get much salary. Later on, he did his *Klein Ambtenaars Examen*, it means a small civil exam, I think it was equal to having a diploma of an elementary school with Dutch. So then, I was born there.

I could only remember when I was young, we didn't have much. You could say that we were poor. Not that we asked people for food, but my mother was very industrious. She collected banana leaves and sold them in the morning to the people who came to the market. And then she could buy some food. My father of course got his salary, but it was maybe very little, let us say five or seven *guilders* [Dutch currency] per month, I don't know. I only could remember that when I was seven years old, when we lived in Rampah and he was the railroad station master, he had it much better because he could send me to Tarutung, to school.

In Bekala, there were no Christian families. I don't remember that we ever went to a church there. We had our service in a school. I think it was a Chinese Methodist School, in a place like a shop. They used it as a school, but on Sundays they used it for service for maybe about eight, ten Christian families, Chinese and Batak Christians. On big events like Christmas, we went to a church about eighty kilometers from there in Tebing Tinggi. My father tried to educate us, to teach us how to pray and to sing some Indonesian and Batak Christian songs. That was all.

My father, I respected him very much. Whatever he said, we said "yes and amen." My mother was very like a friend. My mother was sixteen or seventeen years older than me. She was only nine years old when her parents died, both of them. After the death of her parents, she went to Siantar to stay with her brother and sister-in-law. She was married very young. My father maybe came there and saw her, and asked for her hand.

When I was five years old, we moved to Rampah. Then my father's father, my grandpa came. I thought he was very old, but actually at that time he was maybe only about sixty years old. But he was already senile. He went to

FIGURE 43   "Simorangkir mission stasion" [Simorangkir Mission Station]
AMS DER VEM. ARCHIVE NUMBER: 203–583

the railroad. He played with us, with the pebbles. Later on, he went back to Tarutung and died. I was not at his funeral ceremony.

They told me that when my brother was one year old and I was two and a half years old, they took us home to Simorangkir to give my brother one of the names of the great-great-great-grandparents. He was baptized Johan. But then he got named Namora Sojoangon. It is a big name because it is one of the great-great-great-grandparents. You have to have a ceremony with killing a buffalo.

The oldest relative that I knew, that was the uncle, the *tulang* of my father. He took my father to Kabanjahe on the east coast of Sumatra to get a job there. My father studied here in Sipoholon at elementary school, but he didn't pass to be admitted for entering the Normal School to become a teacher. Then he went away, looked for some job there. He got that job at the railroad station.

I was the eldest, and I have ten siblings. The youngest is Tagor. After me comes Johan Namora Sojoangon, that was the one who had the ceremony for his name about 1913. And then number three was Costan Gunung Solindungon. He became a policeman in Siantar. Three years later, Siti Zubaidah. She married a Simanjuntak and has thirteen children. After her comes Jan Henneri Hamonangan. He died when the Japanese occupied Indonesia 1942 to 1945 because he became a *hei-ho*, a soldier of the Japanese. Every young man was just taken away, you know. After him was my brother Wilmar Maruhum in Holland, an engineer on a ship, and then my sister Loide of Pasar Tiga, married to a Tobing. And then my sister Hulda Melani at Perumnas married to a Purba, and then my brother Arifin who has a physical education diploma, and then James, he died at nineteen of liver disease, and then Tagor, a plantation administrator.

4   The *Adat*

[Tobing discussed the important of the Batak *adat*, a cultural and legal code for life and spirituality which shapes the social relationships among the clans. She began with the importance of marriages.] If you marry, you get a wife by paying a certain amount. That is called the bride price. To this party, the *hula hula* [wife-givers], you have to be very respectful and talk to them in a certain way, you just can't talk to them as to your brothers or your cousins. And then the wife-taking party, that is your *boru*, which means "daughter". So then the whole clan or family is your *boru*. They have to help you in case there is something that is necessary to be helped, while you are helping the *hula hula*. And the *hula hula* of course has *hula hula* again, so that is why they called that the *dalihan na tolu* [a metaphor for social structure and connection among clans]. *Dalihan* is the cooking stones [in the fireplace], *na tolu*, the three, like in our kitchen you see the three stones. Everyone is related to the other. *Hula hula, boru, dongan sabutuha* [males of the same father's clan]. *Dongan sabutuha*, that means of the same father, so of the same name. For instance, the whole Tobing family is my *dongan sabutuha*. Simorangkir, because I am a *boru* Simorangkir [daughter of the Simorangkirs], is our *hula hula*, Not only mine, but my husband's and my relatives and all of the Tobings related to us, they have to respect the Simorangkir as the *hula hula*.

    There are many rules [in the *adat*], yes. [Tobing explained the rules around childbirth.] Before the birth of a child, the expecting mother will go with her husband and with some relatives of the same clan and bring some food to her parents in the form of pig and rice. And then the parents will prepare the food in the form of fish, and they will give the daughter an *ulos* [woven ceremonial and spiritual Toba Batak cloth] that is called *ulos ni tondi*, that means the soul's *ulos* [kind of *ulos* given to a pregnant woman]. The daughter and her husband get the *ulos* over [wrapped around] their shoulders so that they will get [spiritual] protection. Once the baby is born, the parents bring food to the *boru* [daughter] again in the form of fish and cooked *bangun-bangun*. *Bangun-bangun*, that is the kind of leafy vegetable we have next to the windows in the garden. *Bangun-bangun* also means alive. In the old days, they say if it is a boy, "*Taho ma i.*" "*Taho ma i*" means "very fortunate, very lucky." And if it is a girl, they would say "*Ngoluna i ma.*" "*Ngoluna i ma*" means "As long as it lives." A son is worth more than a girl. But nowadays, I never hear it anymore. Well, I think they are done with that idea.

If someone wants to get married, there are rules too [according to the *adat*]. The boy should come first to the girl's parents with his friends. He talks to the parents so that they know who his relatives are, his situation, his position. And then later, somebody would go to the bride-to-be's house and arrange how much the bride's price should be. And then officially, they will come with food, and the bride's parents have to cook food too. And with all the talk, talk, talk, they will arrange the day, arrange what to have for the wedding, what kind of food, is it a pig or a cow or a buffalo for the ceremony. Often the girl just obeys the parents because the *adat* says you have to obey your parents.

[Tobing also described the rituals around someone's death.] In death, there are two kinds of ceremonies, whether you die while you are still young, or whether you die at an old age. If you have already grandchildren from your son and also from your daughter, then you are old enough to get the full ceremony. [Having grandchildren is a mark of your stature in the community.] Usually they have a buffalo for the [full] ceremony and then all the different parents of the daughter-giving side [*hula hula*] come. So for instance, when my husband died, the Simorangkir [Tobing's family clan] came, his mother's family the Sihombing [a family clan] came, his grandmother's family, the Tampubolon [a family clan] came, and so on. Sometimes it is as far back as five generations. And then they bring rice, cooked rice or uncooked rice with the husk, the *padi*. For your grandfather, we had a ceremony when we took him from Tanjung Morawa [to inter him] here in Tarutung to the military cemetery. [Traditionally,] he couldn't have a buffalo killed [because he died young], but it was a big ceremony [anyway] because he was buried as a warrior or hero. The highest honor was allowed, otherwise it would be just with a pig. When he died, then I got from my own parents an *ulos* over my shoulders because I became a widow. It was a black *ulos* with white stripes [the *ulos tujung*]. And the Sihombings, his mother's family's clan, also brought an *ulos*. I think the Tampubolon, the grandmother's family, also brought rice and *ulos*.

See, that is the *adat*. The Batak don't dare to omit [what they are supposed to do], not to do as traditionally as possible. Because once you did it wrong, people could stand up and just walk away. If you are ignorant or conceited or too proud to do the custom, they don't like it. They won't even touch the food. If you don't do the *adat*, it is because you don't care. That brings the animosity [from other people]. You are not friendly then with your clan, with your family.

So unless you really want to hurt them and live your own life, you can't get out of the customs [of the *adat*]. And I'd like to be socially engaged with them, I don't want to live alone.

All the ties with the *adat*, as long as it is not combined with love, it is nothing actually. It is just the rules. It is just words. You don't like each other, what is the use of that? If I am trying to be good with a person, it is not just because of the *adat*, it is because I feel it too. Deep in the hearts of the Batak, they love their *adat* because of the identity. Because with the *adat*, they can know who their great-great-grandparents were, and who are their closest relatives, and how to do it [according to the rules and the customs], it is all written down. So then, I think they are proud of their identity and they don't want to lose it.

5   Christianity

[The role of Christianity and its relationship to the *adat* was an important subject for Tobing.] The Christianity is brought into the *adat* and the *adat* brought into the Christianity. You are one because of the culture, you can't separate it. I think my whole life I believe that there is a God and that He will provide you with whatever you need. Even the flowers, the birds they don't work, and they still get food. I was very young when I could see that you had to have a stronghold in religion. When I was about ten years old, I saw a woman on the east coast of Sumatra, a Muslim woman. She was maybe twenty-one years old, already five times divorced because with the Muslims at that time, you could just be divorced if you got a letter from the *qadi* [Muslim judge].

[Tobing also discussed the role of Christianity in the community when she was young.] In Tarutung, if you don't go to church, one of the German missionaries, the pastor Tuan [Mister] O. Marks went out to see what you are doing. If you dry rice, the pastor would tell you, "You don't do that on Sunday. Instead of the blessings from God, if you do this, you get punishment." And if he would see people gambling, playing cards on a Sunday behind a bamboo stool or wherever, he would chase them! And they were afraid of him, you see. So he would just go around and make sure that everybody did their duty, i.e. go to church. That was Tuan Marks.

In church, we always began with a prayer and we ended with a prayer. And maybe in between they had songs. It hasn't changed, it is the same. Only it is now more elaborate. Like everything, before you could walk, now you can go by car to church. The same with religion. Before it was just one song, maybe now more, three, four. Before it was just the elder who came, now with the *pendeta*, the minister.

The Batak [also] learned to sing in church from the German missionaries. So they replaced the [Batak] musical instruments with the [German] brass instruments [in church]. For [traditional] Batak music, they have their own instruments that are a little different [from instruments available in the US and Europe]. The Bataks have a gong, and they have a kind of guitar but then only with two strings. They had seven special melodies for the *gondang debata* or godly music [special music with drumming for the gods]. And someone would play on the flute, and then you would hear some melody, some tune. And there were seven different dances. And the last dance, they would have the scarf with the dancer weaving the ends towards herself, it means they ask the blessing from the deceased. They would dance around the deceased, if it was an old relative for instance. That is then the biggest honor that you can do, along with the killing of the buffalo, you know. You dance more at ceremonial funerals.

I know that the missionaries abolished all kinds of dances or *tortor* [a kind of dance] or music because they were afraid that we would go back to the old traditions and believe again in the spirits. There are now more Batak musical instruments abroad, for instance, in Germany and Holland, than even here in the Batak area. [Tobing discussed how the missionaries tried to stop Batak practices.] I remember at one time, they missed an old man three, four, five days, they couldn't find him. Then they went to a *dukun* [indigenous healer], to a *datu* [also an indigenous healer] and then they found this man in a hole about four kilometers from here. How he could walk at night, I don't know. He went down to do this usual thing. But then suddenly they couldn't find him [where he was supposed to be]. He was maybe just traveling and traveling [away from home]. They said he was carried away by dwarves, *homang* [a magical dwarf]. And when they found him, they gave him some *gondang* [spiritual music with the drum] because he was dazed and confused. They gave *gondang* for a week to drive away the bad spirits, to make him conscious again. But I heard this family who did it was banned by the church until they confessed their sins because they believed in the spirits.

Actually, as a Christian, I do not believe that there is black magic. See, we were educated as Christians, right? But the magicians, we were scared of them because they have the black magic. If you are naughty or if you are not doing what they want, then they say they will put a spell on you. Us young girls, we tried to avoid them because they [the magicians] were around. But it was said that if the magicians did not continue their magic spell, the magic worked on them. And that is true because some magicians died without any descendants, quite young, sickly, and thin. Everybody avoided them and no one really was friends with them. It was a hard life for them.

As girls, we were scared to walk past a certain fir tree because they said a demon, a ghost lived in the tree. Every time we had to pass the tree at night after the sun set, we would sing Christian hymns loudly to chase away our fear. We were then ten or twelve years old at that time. And up to now, decades later, the tree is still there and it is not growing, just the same size as before. This was at Sigompulon, the place where I was at school before [when Tobing was in sixth grade].

6   Tarutung

When I was seven years old, my father's mother's brother, my father's *tulang* [uncle], a Simatupang [family clan], came to Rampah. I called him Ompung, grandfather. He was the one that took my father to the east coast of Sumatra. This *ompung* took me by train from Rampah to Siantar, and then the next morning, from Siantar by bus to Panahatan or Sibaganding and Tigaras. Arriving there, you went down by foot about 300 meters to the lake. And then when I saw the boat from above, it looked as small as a bird. I didn't feel any fear because the *ompung* was with me, he helped me in the boat. I was so happy when I went in the boat with my white dress sewn by my mother. But soon, not even half an hour later, I was throwing up everything. So nowadays, if someone says "Let us go by boat," I immediately remember how it was. I mean, I don't want to be reminded of my trips by boat. The trip took us about two or three hours by motorboat. And then, sleep again in Balige, the next day by bus to Tarutung. It took two nights and three days before I came to the place where I went to school in Sigompulon. It was very difficult. Imagine, now by cab it takes only six to seven hours from Medan to Tarutung. Anyhow, we came to Tarutung, and Ompung put me in Harean, the village where I stayed for a whole year. Every vacation, he would pick me up and then we went again to Rampah. I think he was the guard. So during vacation, I would see my parents, two brothers, and a baby sister.

I remember the first time that I came into Harean, the village. I didn't understand the Batak language and the first thing was that the Batak boys shouted at me, scolding me , but I didn't understand. And I asked my uncle what it meant, and he said, "Oh you don't say that. That is a bad word!" "But that is the first word I heard," I said. "Well, forget it," he said. I was not even seven years old.

The only person who spoke Indonesian was my uncle. The rest of the family couldn't speak a word of Indonesian. So then if he was not at home, I felt lost.

I had a wooden bed with my parents in the east coast of Sumatra with a mattress, with a pillow, with sheets, everything. But then in the village, you sleep on the wooden floor with a mat only. And I had with me a blanket from Medan. And before I slept at that time, I would spread the blanket on the floor, roll myself up in the blanket like a mummy, and then there I slept. The people were still talking and talking [in the evening]. At night after they slept, about three o'clock in the morning then, I would wake up. And I would feel a mat over me to keep warm. They didn't have a blanket, they would just spread a mat over themselves. I would kick the mat off myself and then I would scream, "*Tidak mau tikar!*", "I don't want a mat!" and then everybody would be awake, my uncle too. And then he [my uncle] would soothe me and he would say, "Well, well, you can use your blanket. Don't put the mat on her." Every night, we had the same ritual. But then anyhow, I gave up [with that routine] because finally I could fall asleep.

And the funny thing is that at this time, we had [water] buffaloes under the house. It was a traditional [Batak] house on stilts. If you don't have buffaloes, you are not rich. So this uncle of mine is not really rich, but he has some buffaloes. In the morning, my cousin of about my age would wake up, let the buffaloes out from under the house. And then if they make some dirt, you put a stick on top of that. It means that it is already owned. They were fighting about this dung for fertilizer, very different from nowadays. Nowadays, no one will care because they have chemical fertilizer. But at that time, they would put it in a basket and carry it on their heads to the fields. That was remarkable.

Now about taking a bath. Because the young people like me, a stranger who couldn't speak the Batak language, the girls were very tolerant, very nice to me. If they went to the river, they would take me. They had a sarong [length of cloth wrapped around the lower part of the body and fastened at waist], they make a bubble, and then I could put my head down on there, and then I could move my feet, make movements as if I was swimming, I could just float on their sarong. It was nice, taking a bath in that way. I didn't know then about the dirt or whatever. I didn't care because no one cared. And they took home the water on their heads in a clay pot and let the sediment sink, and that is the drinking water. You didn't boil the water at that time. Now, I am amazed that no one got cholera or whatever. But that was the life in the village.

In the morning, that was again some event. In the morning, if I already saw the sun coming up, I would say, "I will be late! I will be late!" And everybody would have to hurry to leave the house soon. I knew that I had to go to school and I liked the school. So every morning at seven, or a little bit earlier than seven, I would go on the bike of my uncle together with him to Sigompulon. He would go to the *pasar* [market] to town. He was a salesman for Singer sewing machines. I went to school in Sigompulon then, and after school I would go to his office. And together we would go home again. For one whole year I did it.

The first day of school, I had my shoes on, my socks, everything like other children in the east coast of Sumatra had. I didn't know that you could go to school with bare feet. The boys would walk behind me and chant, "*Jaga par sipatu i,*" it means "Beware of the shoe wearer," something like that. Sure enough, five days later, I had no shoes on. I think that you try really hard to be the same as your friends, your peers. And my clothes were nicer because we [Tobing's immediate family] were in the east coast of Sumatra. Then later, I had my mother make dresses like they had. Usually I had white ones. But because of the water in the village, the dresses soon enough became a little yellowish.

My parents still were on the east coast of Sumatra. Every vacation, my father's uncle would take me by bus, by boat, by cab, by train to the place where my parents lived. Four vacations per year. You have plenty of schools on the east coast of Sumatra. Other people send their children just there to school. But not my father. He said that I should learn the Batak language, the Batak *adat*, the Christian religion. I think he was very farsighted. My father never let me feel that I am lacking something. He never told me, "You are a girl, you don't know any arithmetic." I was treated like my own brothers. I mean if he had problems for us in arithmetic, he never let me feel that I wouldn't know it because I was a girl. I didn't feel the insecurity of being a girl. So I think that my father was very far ahead of his peers. Like this, for instance. If I was not put in the village when I was seven years old, I guarantee I wouldn't come now to Tarutung. I wouldn't have all the love. I wouldn't value this as much as I do now because I knew the village from when I was seven years old.

7   Living in the Village

[Tobing explained how people lived and worked in the village.] People eat three times a day. Usually here, they eat dried fish and vegetables. The vegetables are usually the *daun singkong* [tapioca leaves], *daun ubi* [sweet potato leaves]. It [one's diet] depends on where you are, you know. Like in Siborongborong for instance, they eat sweet potatoes before they eat rice. They say they then can eat more. I don't think we have here too much malnutrition. You don't see people who don't eat enough.

FIGURE 44   *Ulos* in Minar T. Rony's personal collection. *Ulos* are given at ceremonies or on
             special occasions, and represent both spirituality and connection
             PHOTOGRAPH BY AUTHOR

Most people are farmers, and they work in the rice fields. They would like very
much to be the white-collar people, to work at the offices even if it doesn't pay
too much. At the time [when Tobing was young], the wages of most people was
twenty-five cents a day. The teacher at the missionary school got seven guilders
and fifty cents a month, that is all from the school fees of the children. And
I remember my father got more because he was the station master and he
could speak Dutch. It was a big difference. But then these teachers, we would
call them "blessed by God." If they have, let us say, less than ten by five meters soil, they would have so many vegetables from there which they could sell
every week. They [the teachers] got the money for the rice and everything.

For the women, either you work in the fields or you weave. The weavers,
once they begin to weave, they weave, they weave, they weave, ten hours,
twelve hours a day, from six to six and then sometimes to eight o'clock with
light. Now they have electricity in the villages, so at night they work too. Before,
when they didn't have the electricity, they would put a lit piece of pine needles
stick [with resin] in a hole in the wall. It gives some light, and then they weave.
They didn't earn too much unless they are very skilled. In 1970, the beginners
earned maybe three thousand rupiah [Indonesian currency] a week, equal to
two dollars. The best, maybe twenty thousand a week, equal to ten American
dollars for a whole week!

Long ago, the weavers here made their own dye, the blue indigo and the red,
so they had blue, red, and white of course, and they make their own thread by
spinning. The textiles came together with the colonizers. They brought good,

good stuff from London, also the *tobralco* [kind of cloth] from Holland. It [the quality of material] depends on how much you want to spend. Otherwise we had materials from Japan.

They [the people in the community] said if you have more children, you have more blessings. Some people have four, some people have five, some people have ten. There was no talk of family planning at that time because especially in the villages, the more children they had, the more help they would have on the land. The same was true in the United States. In the 1930s, some poor families couldn't support their children or wanted to buy something so that they will get a better life, maybe buy a buffalo or a piece of ground. Then they let their daughters work for another family [as indentured labor] for, let us say, fifty guilders for five years. And then after those five years, the girl would go back to the family or maybe she would marry. She could meet someone who would support her, or who was better off than her own family. It [this practice] started long, long ago, I don't know how long ago. But it stopped after the Japanese came in 1942 because then the social life was so different. The indentured servants were usually girls. We had at one time a boy because he could work in the garden. The boys are not so domestic, they would run away.

[Tobing commented on what it was like to be a woman during those times.] In the 1920s, I saw the suffering of the women in the east coast of Sumatra, that they had to have a man to be able to survive. When the woman was married, she had a protected life because there was enough to live on with the children. But when the husband got another wife, she had to leave and she had to take care of the children, usually because the stepmother wouldn't take care of the children and she didn't have the *marga* [clan system] like the Batak had. For the Batak, it would be shame if the children of their own class go to another clan or accept another clan's name. The whole clan would be ashamed.

8   Dutch Rule

I never thought about the rule or the conquering of the Dutch because it began when I was small, we already were under Dutch colonization. If you ask here, the Dutch didn't dare to do anything about the construction of the *adat* here because it was strong. We use their committee for criminals, but if it is for land dispute, we have our own government. The chief was called *chef*, then the *Raja Ihutan*, and later on it was *Kepala Negeri*. *Kepala Negeri* means "ruler," head of the district or land.

When the Dutch were in Indonesia, they had the plantations. Their wealth originally came from here, the east coast of Sumatra. They had the [plantation] contract for, let us say, seventy-five years or something like that. After they left, the Indonesian government took it over. It is now a national plantation. On the east coast of Sumatra in 1930 at the time, there were rubber plantations, palm oil tree plantations. Now there are also cacao, coffee, and tea plantations. The supervisors or the heads, the principal directors, they would always be the Dutch. They got the money. The labor they brought from Java, or from China too. Usually at that time the laborers were called *kulis* [usually refers to Javanese laborers that the Dutch brought into Sumatra during colonial period, commonly considered pejorative term], mostly from Java, because there are so many inhabitants there. Java was very densely populated. I had a relative working as a white-collar person in the administration. Not in the plantation, not as a laborer, no. The transportation system in the east coast of Sumatra was from the Deli Maatschappij as this was the company that had the contract with the plantations [Deli was a sultanate on the east coast of Sumatra]. The trains are still there, and the railroad is the same.

There were very few Dutch people here. In Tarutung, for instance, you have the *controleur* [comptroller], you have the *gezaghebber* maybe, that means the assistant civil servant [like a lieutenant governor], and then finally you have the police inspector, the doctor. If you don't speak Dutch, you get a salary very minimal, very little. Let me tell you this. A person who graduates from Malay Normal School, with Malay language only, would get forty guilders monthly for nine years of study. But the Dutch-educated would get seventy-five guilders for eleven years of study, so almost twice that amount. The same with doctors. A doctor who went to the STOVIA [School tot Opleiding voor Indische Artsen, a school to educate natives becoming medical doctors in Indonesia] in Jakarta will get 250 guilders, while when your grandfather was finished [with his advanced studies] in Holland, Leiden, he got 470 guilders. So, of course you try to get the highest education.

9   Elementary School

In Tarutung, the first Dutch school, the Hollandsche-Bataksche school [Dutch Batak school], was established in 1911, and it was seven years. The Malay-language school was started earlier, and it was five years. And the Batak schools, they were done by the German missionaries after they came, so it might be after 1860.[2] Elementary school with the Batak language but also with

---

2 See Jan S. Aritonang, *Mission Schools in Batakland (Indonesia), 1861–1940* (Leiden: E.J. Brill, 1994) for a discussion of the formation of the Batak mission schools in the region, 111–112.

FIGURE 45   "[Area below] Pearaja"
AMS DER VEM. ARCHIVES NUMBER: 203–766

a little Indonesian was only three years. At the time, there were other elementary schools with Dutch language like in Balige and Narumonda, in Sibolga, and in other places. It depends on where you are located. There were many more schools in Java. They are very advanced [in Java] because, don't forget, [in the 1600s] Jan Pieterszoon Coen already came there, so the Dutch schools were started there earlier.

In 1911, before you were admitted to that school in Sigompulon, Tarutung, you had to have 600 guilders. But then the whole seven years that you were at school, you didn't need to pay school fees, that was supposed to be the interest of the 600 guilders. And after I left school, we got the money back, the 600 guilders. And my uncle, that was the son of my father's aunt in Harean, could buy a piece of rice field, "sawah," with that money.

Mynheer [Mr.] Ydens, he was the principal of our Hollandsche-Bataksche school, the HBS, the Dutch-Batak School. I remember in my class there were about forty students, and there were seven grades. So there were at least 250 students at the school. In the old days, there were not too many girls who went to school. The last year, when I was at that elementary school, there were four girls and thirty-five boys in our class. The regular pattern for girls was they go to their elementary school with or without Dutch [as the medium for language instruction]. They married when they were seventeen, eighteen, nineteen years old. If you marry when you are twenty, then you were already too old.

When I first came to school, I was in Harean. Then I was with my aunt, my mother's sister. And when I was in sixth grade I went to Sigompulon as the girls' dormitory was opened. We had school from seven to one o'clock. Seven to seven thirty we had Bible Study. Other government schools began at 7:30.

I don't use too much Dutch now, but the expressions of Dutch are hammered into my head. One can't forget it anymore. In 1919, my first year in school, we had to be perfect in speaking it. Otherwise, the teacher would be so angry, and would just slap us [students] in the face. Not me because I was a girl maybe, or I was too tiny to get a slap from him.

In 1922, we had a German *mutter* [mother], German missionary Zuster [Sister] Frieda Lau in charge of the dormitory. Zuster Frieda Lau was very religious. She was a Bible woman. She drilled us to become Christians, to do the Good Work. If we did something wrong, or if someone lied, or someone didn't do her job, she wouldn't talk to this girl until this girl came asking for forgiveness. That was what she taught us. Before you go to bed, if you did something wrong, you have to ask forgiveness so that you could sleep well.

Sister Frieda Lau taught us how to clean the house, clean the bathroom, of course sanitary everything. She also taught us sewing, cross-stitch and simple stitches, and the sewing machine. I liked it immediately. We began by sewing our nightgowns, and then for twenty-five cents you could buy [the materials] and sew your own dress. So I learned how to sew my own dress from Sister Frieda Lau. I think I had it [the skill] from my mother because my mother was really handy in everything. She could embroider on a sewing machine, which was not easy. With one hand you have to drag the wheel, with the other hand you held what you were sewing, keeping the needle and the stitches in the right place. My mother got sewing lessons from the Singer Company. And if you say "Singer," that means the sewing machine. Like toothpaste, if you say "*pebeco*," then it means the toothpaste.

When we were in seventh grade every Saturday night, four of us girls would go to Zuster [Sister] Frieda Lau's room for half an hour or an hour to talk. I remember what she taught us about boys: "Girls are like butterflies. A butterfly, if someone holds the wings, then the glittering thing will stay on the fingers." Well, I took it literally. So when I was in Java [where Tobing later was a student], if a boy held my hands too long when he shook my hand, I would snatch my hands away! I was so naïve. I was then fourteen years old.

In 1925, we had our exam from Jakarta when I was in seventh grade and thirteen years old. A *controleur* [comptroller], that is the highest civil servant of this place, came to the school to supervise us. And the *demang* [government official], that is now called the *bupati*, supervised us too. Our exam papers were corrected in Jakarta because there were not too many students like today. From our school, only about fifteen persons took the exam. We were tested in translating a piece of a story, translating from the Dutch to the Indonesian, and from the Indonesian again to the Batak language. After seven years' study we had to know three languages and mathematics. The translation was one test, then another test on reading, and then you answer fill-in questions, and then a composition. I think we had four days for the exam!

After the written part, after three weeks, we were called to Medan. From the fifteen, there were only eight left. To have that oral exam, we had to travel from Tarutung to Medan, imagine how far it was at that time. We went by bus from Tarutung to Siantar for about twelve hours, the next day by train to Medan. In the oral exams, we had to read a piece in Arabic script and I couldn't do that because we were not as advanced as students from the east coast of Sumatra. There they were mostly Muslims, some were used to reading the Koran. And besides this Arabic script, we had our own Batak script too, so then we were far behind [those students who studied Arabic]. And we hadn't had too many oral exercises in Dutch. When they had me speak in the Dutch language in Medan, I couldn't do that. I passed for my written, but not for my oral. Since I didn't pass my exam to go to the teachers' training school in Salatiga, I went to Sigompulon for another year because I wanted to try again to take the test for the Meisjeskweekschool voor Inlandsche Onderwijzeressen, MKS, the school for educating native women teachers for four years with the Dutch language as the medium of instruction in Salatiga. Or, I wanted to become a midwife because I thought you could be a midwife even if you are married. As a midwife, you don't have to have a hospital or whatever, you are just called if they need you. But then the following year, I passed because it was only a written exam, no oral exam.

10   Salatiga

Then, my father took me to Salatiga [so that Tobing could attend the teachers's training school]. At that time, you went by boat three nights and four days to go from Belawan to Tanjung Priok, Jakarta's harbor. Then you stay the night in Jakarta, and go by train from Jakarta to Salatiga. I think it took us the whole day to get to Salatiga. We left at seven o'clock in the morning, and arrived at five in the afternoon in Salatiga. When my father was taking me to Salatiga on the train, he pointed out to me that Sumatra looked much better than Java. "Look," he said, "all of the grasses are yellow-brown because of the dry season."

My father took me to the dormitory and there I met with ninety-five other girls in four classes. The school was called the MKS. At the time I went to Salatiga, there were 60 million people in Indonesia. From all of Indonesia, there were only twenty-four girls admitted each year at this schools. We came there from all over Indonesia. That was an education for me because I learned the special attitudes of the Achehnese, the Ambonese, the Menadonese, the Minangkabau, the Javanese. Those were the ethnic groups represented.

We lived in a square dorm with a courtyard in the middle, and a place for a teacher to guard us in each corner. The rooms in the front part were class-rooms. On the sides were the dorms. In the middle of the back were the bath-rooms and the place for the wash or ironing because we did some of our wash ourselves. We gave a kimono and a towel every ten days to the laundry, as well as the mosquito net, the bedsheets, and the pillowcases, as those were their responsibility too.

We were not allowed to go outside the campus. And the funny thing was that the campus was quite far from the road, maybe 200 meters or something like that. We could only walk fifteen meters from the front of the porch towards the street, up to the second electric pole. We were not allowed to walk the rest of the way. And when we went shopping once a week for two hours with one of the teachers, we had to walk in a row, four by four. Coming back too. We would have to sing so people would look up and say, "Who are they?" And soon they would know. Two classes went on Friday, and the other two classes went on Saturday.

We learned all kinds of subjects at this teachers' school: sewing, batiking, cooking. Even ironing, we had to have an exam in that too at the end. They wanted to know whether we learned how to fold the clothes. We also had Dutch and the Malay language. The Javanese had Javanese, the Sundanese had the Sundanese language too. But no Batak anymore as there were only two Batak girls among the ninety-six girls. I learned batik for four years, but I think that all I did was one triangle piece for making a corner of a desk pad, and later on a square thing just thirty centimeters by thirty centimeters, and then at the end, a fifty-centimeter square for making a cushion. We couldn't do much because it was only two hours a week. What can you do in two hours a week? My favorite subject was mathematics because you don't need to memorize it. If you know it, you know it. While other things you have to memorize, like geography and biology.

I liked school. It was fun because there is always something going on. Sometimes you had jokers, sometimes someone is nasty. You just choose the best girls that you want to get along with. I had very many good friends. Up to now, once a month, they have the gathering in Jakarta of the girls from the MKS Salatiga.

When I was young, when I was at school in the 1930s, we didn't want to have the bride price. Because we thought we were "sold out," something like that. We thought we were bought by the husband's family. We, the first girls who went to school in Java, wrote something about that. But when we married, we did the same. It was the same with all the ceremony and so on. No one dared to go outside that. So they wanted to have the *adat* too. And so, even now we do it.

During vacation, the boys would visit us. We had our organization, the School Union or whatever you call that in Salatiga. The boys were in Solo and we would go there for a conference, a trip of two hours by train. So then we'd meet boys, of course and sometimes they would write us. At that time in the dormitory, our letters were censored by the principal. You would be called to her room, "Who is this? Do your parents know about him?" If you say "No," then [the principal would say], "I'll keep the letter. You don't need to answer it." Well, she was very strict.

In 1934, the school became a six-year program. The four-year program was not enough. So my sister was one of the last there. So it existed maybe twenty years only. Many of the girls I went to school with are gone. In Medan I have one classmate, in Jakarta I have another one.

11   Early Marriage

I was eighteen years old when I finished. And then three weeks later, I married. I think I met him [her future husband Gerhard L. Tobing] at school in Sigompulon because he was the brother of one of my good friends. Later when I was in my third year at Salatiga, he came over with his sister and we made acquaintance then. His sister was in Solo at another school, a Christian girls' school. And then when I was on the boat from Jakarta going to Medan, I met him again but I didn't talk to him.

My husband was the third child in his family, but the other two died when they were infants. He was born here in this house, the only son of his father. His father died when he was only six months old.[3] His mother was very prominent, good looking. She was the daughter of Si Singamangaraja's sister. Si Singamangaraja was the king of the Batak clan. My husband got the desire for education from his mother because he was always sickly when he was

---

3 Gerhard L. Tobing's father was Raja Aris, who died at a young age when Tobing was an infant.

FIGURE 46   Gerhard L. Tobing, ca. 1930
             TOBING FAMILY COLLECTION

small. So she said, "You have to be a doctor." And he became one. She really had
a strong character.

He grew up here in Pearaja and lived with his grandmother after his mother
remarried. He went to that school in Sigompulon, the HBS, I think around 1911,
and was one of the first graduates from this school. And when he was in sixth
grade, he went to Jakarta to go to the Dutch elementary school, a *Europeesche
Lagere School,* so that he could be admitted a year later to the STOVIA for
medical school because only children from a European-educated school were
admitted to the STOVIA. The STOVIA was a ten-year education. He got the
money for the STOVIA from the government, sixty *guilders* [Dutch currency]
a month, as he was looked upon as a son of a chief, Raja Aris, and grandson of
a chief, Raja Pontas. Sixty guilders was enough for the school fees, the dorm,
and everything.

I think we liked each other, that's why we began to write letters. By that
time, my husband already was a doctor as he was nine years older than me. His
first post as a doctor was in Semarang in 1928, and later he was transferred to
Amuntai, Kalimantan.

When we decided to get married in 1930, my husband made the arrangements with his family and with mine. We got married in Surabaya as my

husband said if we go to Sumatra, it would cost a lot. And it was true. At that time, it was twenty-five guilders by boat in second class, Tanjung Priok to Belawan. First class was fifty. Third class was maybe seven guilders and fifty cents.

He was a good catch, but I was a good catch too. Mutual, ya? Because at that time, how many Batak girls had graduated from the teachers' school? Later on, twenty years after that, there were a lot. But not at that time. And how many doctors? There were not many.

Our families approved of our marriage and my father came to the wedding. My father knew the family of Serefinus Tobing who was there, so he stayed with them. Serefinus Tobing's wife was my classmate in the sixth year in Sigompulon. The wedding was very simple because my mother was not there, his parents were not there. Maybe there were just fifty persons, that is all.

I thought my husband was good, otherwise we wouldn't have married. We had our education in common. He trusted me, he could see that I would be a companion in his life. We were idealists, of course, in the letters we wrote before we got married. He thought that he would have a long life. He thought that his children would be better educated than he was. When he went to Holland for his Leiden diploma [in 1937], he told me that after the children finished high school, then I would take them to be educated in Holland. Well, his ideal came true. Even if it was not Holland, it was the United States. All the four children had the chance to study in the United States. And I am very grateful, I never expected them to go there.

After we were married in 1930, I was in Amuntai for about two years because that is where he was posted. In Amuntai, my husband worked from eight until five, that is all. He didn't go to the hospital unless there was an emergency as it was a general hospital. After you have your degree, you are not called unless you are already appointed to be on duty, except if there is surgery.

My husband thought that it was most important for me just to take care of the social life [in addition to the house and family], as that was needed for men with power and influence. But I said, "I want to become a teacher, because I have studied to become a teacher." So your grandpa said, "How much do you get [as a teacher]?" "Seventy-five guilders," I said. "Well, I'll give you the seventy-five," he said. "You can teach me."

[Although the Dutch were there,] you never think about mixing because they have one life, we have another life. At school we didn't have any Dutch girls. It was only for the natives. When I married, then I had to mix because you have there the Dutch civil servants and the police inspector. Occasionally, we will come together. For instance, two or three weeks after I arrived in Amuntai, I had to invite the elite to our place. I had just married, and then we had

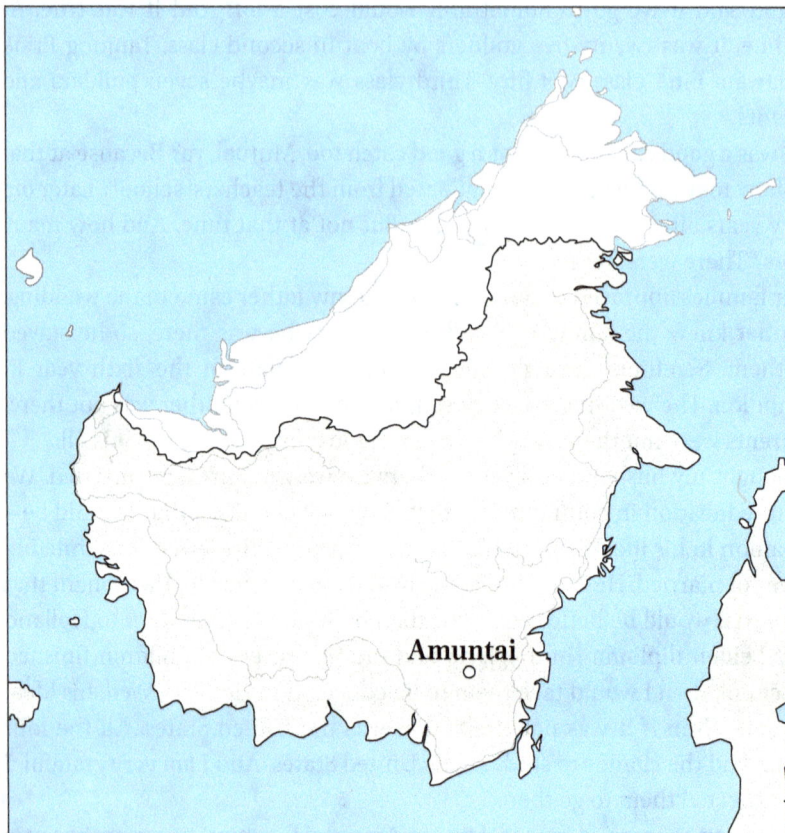

MAP 7   Kalimantan (formerly Borneo), with site of Amuntai noted

immediately sixteen guests in the house. My husband said, "We have to invite
them so I can introduce you as my wife." So then all the elite of that little place
came, the *controleur* [comptroller], the *gezaghebber* [lieutenant governor], the
Police Inspector, the *opzichter* or the postmaster, the *kiai* [mystical leader], the
griffier [registrar] all with their wives. Only three were Dutch: the *controleur*,
the *gezaghebber*, and the police inspector. The rest were Indonesians.

There I was, not even nineteen years old then. It was so difficult. To do the
right thing, I had to read books because I never had so many guests before.
I prepared myself and looked in cookbooks because I wanted to make a good
impression. I also asked Mrs. Hetharia, the *griffier*'s wife for advice. Mr. and
Mrs. Heiharni were Ambonese. She helped me a lot, cooking and so on, making cookies and cakes because there was no baking shop. Mrs. Soemarto, the
postmaster's wife, helped too. You couldn't buy anything as you have to prepare everything from scratch. Like a chicken for instance, you have to kill the

chicken and prepare it from beginning to the end. I didn't even have the tools. I had to buy them, like the baking pan or whatever, for the making of the dough. You should have seen me, if it was bad, I would throw the whole thing in the fire! I had never done it before, so I didn't know what to do. Even though we had learned cooking at school for a whole year, there were four in a group, So I could just do the chopping or the very least responsible job. But now, it was up to me.

Three weeks it took me to prepare. And afterwards they said to my husband, "Well, you have a good, charming wife." I didn't care for that, as long as they didn't have any remarks about my cooking or my attitude. Because after all, I had a good education from my school. I didn't want to give a bad image of my school or of myself as an Indonesian doctor's wife.

I think we lived in two worlds at once. I knew that the Dutch looked down upon us. We were called *Inlanders*. *Inlanders*, that means natives in a more humiliating sense. So you have to know how to live like a Dutch person while with the Dutch. If you still act like a full *Inlander* or Indonesian among them, they would think you are strange. So you do like they do. Without thinking, you do it automatically. Some people, because they are going on more with Europeans, they look down on their own people. But I never did that, I hope. I don't know whether people feel I am ignoring them or looking down upon them, but on purpose I wouldn't do that. Once you are among your own people, you are just like one of them. I want to respect my own people too.

My husband was a doctor, and he was a doctor both of the rich people and the poor people. The poor people, they paid, let us say, twenty-five cents for the government, not for him. The rich people they paid five guilders for one visit. My husband was used to getting along with his own people and with the Dutch. He would charge the Dutch or the Chinese, as they had more money. But not the Indonesians if he doesn't feel like the Indonesians have enough money to pay him. He wouldn't want their money, let me say that.

12   Semarang

My husband became a general practitioner in 1932 when my daughter Minar was just a baby of one month. Then we moved from Amuntai to his third post of Semarang. And in Semarang he specialized in surgery and gynecology, under Dr. Soekario. I wonder if Dr. Soekario is still alive now.

To go to Semarang, it was 200 kilometers from Amuntai to Banjarmasin. It took us about six hours in our Fiat. The Fiat was the best car at that time because if you have a flood, the car was so small that it could kind of swim on the road. It also was a little high so the water didn't come to the seat. Once in a while, you would have a flood in Amuntai. And so many mosquitoes. The land, left and right from the road, was all planted with rubber trees. If I waited for my husband in the car, within a couple of minutes I could rub my hands and I would have four or five mosquitoes in my hands, so terrible it was. The land was swampy, the best place for mosquitoes to lay their eggs.

When we left for Semarang, a city in Java, Minar was only one month. Imagine, traveling with a baby at that time. Then I thought, "How could I hold her, traveling with a one-month-old baby?" I read in books, in magazines, you put the baby in a basket. But then I couldn't find a rattan basket in Amuntai. I just used a big pail with an oval form. I covered it with thick flannel, all the way around outside and inside, and then I put a rattan bow on top so you could hold it, and I sewed a mosquito net over it. Of course, I held the baby in my arms if we went out, or the maid held her in her arms.

We had a maid then. The maid went with us to Surabaya with the promise that she would stay with me for at least two months because she wanted to go to Java. But then, when we were in the boat for only one or two nights, she was seasick, I was seasick, my husband was seasick, and no one took care of the two children. My son was not even two years old, and he was crawling up and down all the steps in the boat. When I saw that, I was so scared that he would fall, but fortunately the captain helped us. When we arrived in Surabaya, this helper asked us permission to go see her family, and she never came back.

In Surabaya we stayed with Dr. Ferdinand Tobing, a colleague of my husband. He had graduated one year earlier than my husband from the STOVIA. I stayed in Surabaya for one week and went to auctions to buy furniture for the house in Semarang. After my husband came back from Semarang [as he had gone ahead], the furniture was sent by trucks to Semarang and we traveled there by train.

We got a house in Kalisari No. 8, close to the Burgerlijke Ziekeninrichting, the hospital for the public, the general hospital. From the house, it was only about a five-minute walk to the central general hospital. We didn't need a car because the hospital was so close by. To go shopping or somewhere else, then you just take a *chitney*, the little buses, or the *sado* [horse cart], cars. *Chitney* is the Singapore name.

I liked this place because it was very clean with deep ditches so you don't see the dirty water. The place was higher [in elevation] than the town of Semarang, so the temperature was a little cooler. In Semarang, we had easy access to helpers for the house. We stayed in Semarang from 1932 to 1934.

13   Magetan

From Semarang, we were transferred to Magetan from 1935 to 1937. The hospital's name was Mardi Doyo. My husband wanted to enlarge the hospital and trained about twenty nurses and nurses' aides. He was hard-working and not just at the hospital. He had to take care of a big area, the hospital and six other clinics, and went to other places to give injections, help the midwife there, and so on.

In Magetan, we had a large house with a big yard. The house was owned by the brother of the regent, the highest of Indonesian officials in Java. When we got there, they said the house was haunted. But then I didn't believe in that kind of situation. When we went in, I saw that the windows were too small, so we enlarged the windows so that you could get more air. And in front, I saw some plants like the sugarcane, with many shoots and many leaves. Of course, the mosquitoes were laying all their eggs in the leaves of the plants

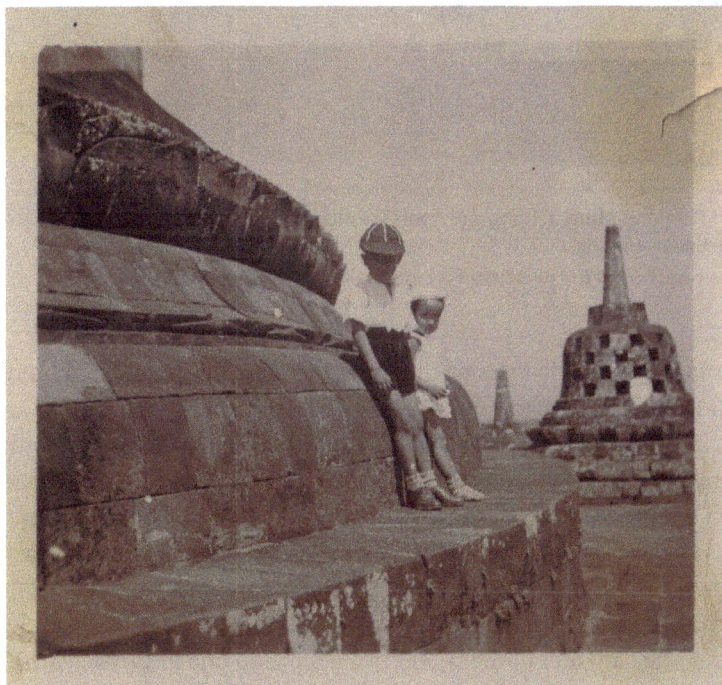

FIGURE 47   Family photographs in the early years show the family engaged in
leisure pursuits. Here, Apoel Loembantobing and Minar T. Rony are
visiting Borobudur with their family, ca. 1935
TOBING FAMILY COLLECTION

FIGURE 48 H.L. Tobing, Minar T. Rony, and Apoel Loembantobing waving
goodbye, ca. 1935
MINAR T. RONY COLLECTION

so we cut it down. And then the next day our helper came to me. She said,
"*Nyonya* [Ma'am], the occupant of that bush talked to me last night. It was an
old woman, and she said, 'Oh, this *nyonya* didn't have any compassion with
me because she cut my bush, now I have to leave.'" And then I said, "Well, she
doesn't need to stay there because maybe she was the one who haunted the
house. So it is okay. Now you don't need to be afraid of anyone." At that time,
we had enough help in the house. We had a driver, a gardener, a maid to wash
the clothes, one to cook the food, one to take care of the children. Five people.

In Magetan, the daughter of the regent had almost no one to socialize with.
I was still a young mother, so she asked me to play tennis. So, we played tennis, the two of us, along with the Dutch wife of the civil servant, Mrs. Ably.
There were only two or three of us women in Amuntai playing tennis. And
you know how we played tennis? In our sarongs, with the pleated skirt. I think
I tore about seven while playing because how can you run while wearing such
tight sarongs? I liked tennis very much because it makes you healthy.

When I was in Magetan from 1935 until 1937, I took midwifery lessons with the *wedana*'s wife, Mrs. Utomo. Nowadays, the *wedana* would be called *camat* or civil servant. She was my friend, Mrs. Utomo. She was a very bright and progressive woman and had gone to high school. Her children already were in school.

Mrs. Utomo was very far-sighted because she said that if there was no doctor and there was no midwife, then I could always be of help if a midwife was needed. With me actually, my daughter was only three years old, my son four and a half, so I didn't have too much time. But I went with her to learn to be a midwife in the hospital for a whole year. I went to the hospital two or three nights a week, and sometimes in the morning with the student nurses. We had lessons in the lab, and in anatomy, and so on.

I think we went about eighteen times to the villages helping these poor women, either by car or by walking. We went to the villages with the midwife, Mrs. Joyo, a very nice, middle-aged woman. Dermatol, the medicine at that time, was a powder, and we would bring that for the baby. Because the village people were so poor, they might only have their own sarong. And I would bring some old sarongs for the mother. We believed at that time that you have to bandage the stomach tightly so the muscles could come back, and I would bring the *gurita* [special girdle] for them too. Nowadays, they just exercise. I also sewed girdles for after the umbilical cord fell off. Then, the navel had to be covered with a little piece of cloth sewn with bands which they tied around the whole stomach. We also would bring some shirts that opened up in the front, and some diapers. If the woman doesn't need them after two or three weeks, she could give them back to the hospital so other women could use them later.

In that way, we tried to help the women in the villages. It was not easy. You might come to the mountains after three hours walk to find the woman on the floor in her own blood. The baby is already dead one day, and the woman is also dying. You can't do anything, you know. You just try with the midwife to clean her out so that the afterbirth and everything comes out to prevent infection.

14   Pearaja

From there, my husband went to Europe on our own expense to study in Leiden. He didn't have any scholarship grant from the government. He was gone for twenty months exactly. By boat, I think it takes three weeks before you arrive in Amsterdam. My husband studied in Leiden because he wanted to have the same rights as the Dutch. The Dutch were the colonial conquerors. From when we were born, we were told that we were inferior to the Dutch.

Of course, deep in our heart, we wanted to be like them too, and that is why we studied so hard. We wanted to be equal, have equal rights, equal standards. We didn't want to stay on the level that they treated us, as second-class citizens. That's why we tried so hard to save money so that he could study in Holland. After my husband got his degree in Leiden, he felt much more able to stand up against the Dutch. According to him, he didn't learn much more there than he learned at the STOVIA, because the knowledge they learned was taught by the Dutch doctors too. But [at that time,] he had to go to Holland to have the same diploma as the Dutch doctors, as the Dutch diploma was required for him to move up in his career. Sometimes the Dutch women who came to Indonesia only finished elementary school, and they came to Indonesia. But they spoke Dutch and they looked white, so they were the superior nation, right? But I had my education too.

While my husband was gone, I lived in Pearaja in the family home with my mother-in-law, my brother-in-law, and his wife. First, we had two helpers from Java, one who could clean the house named Mangun, and one who could cook and do the wash named Minah. But then they left and I was alone to take care of the house. This education in the village, that was the hardest education. Harder than a university education because I had always to be in the same mold, doing what was expected because otherwise I wouldn't be accepted by the family. But, I couldn't work [on the rice fields] like my mother-in-law did. She could work on the rice field, she knew how to look for good laborers, and so on. I didn't know how to do that, even how to spread the rice grains on the mat to dry them. Because in the old times, the grains had very sharp points like needles. So if you touch them, they will hang on to your fingers. My mother-in-law said, "You have to touch them firmly! Otherwise you get the thorns in your fingers."

I tried helping out in the rice fields, but it was hard work for me because I was not used to it. I had never done that, so I didn't know how. I worked for half a day. The seedlings had to be about one foot from each other in the ground. And when I came home at night, my whole neck was aching because I had to bend and stoop. I didn't know the ways of the village. My mother-in-law would say to people, "Well, my first daughter-in-law's hoe is only her fountain pen. She can't even hoe the ground once. But my second daughter-in-law can have a plot of ground hoed as big as a winnow, about three yards square, with one hoe."

So, I had to cook around 4:30 or 5:00 AM for everyone. My mother-in-law with the four or five laborers that we hired from Dolok Sanggul would eat early in the morning around 5:30 or 6:00 AM, and I had to be ready here with the food, the rice, the vegetable dish, salted fish, or whatever. About that cooking, we had a high cooking place for the rice, and it was too high for me. You have the pot of rice on the tripod, and the pot can contain about four liters of rice. I had to climb on a chair to stir the rice. Otherwise, the rice will burn underneath at the bottom of the pan. Then, I had to spread the mat for them to sit as they had to eat early in the morning. Six, six-thirty, they already had to leave for the rice fields. And there I stayed, washing the dishes and cleaning the house. At that time, if you hire people to work in the fields, you are supposed to bring meals to the rice fields for them, and I had to deal with that too. I said to my mother-in-law, "Why don't we just let them pay for their own food, and we give them the money for expenses?" And then she said, "Oh, you want to begin another *adat*? A new *adat*? It is obvious that you don't know how to take care of the rice fields." But nowadays, many people do it that way.

And I also had to take care of the pigs, buying the ingredients for their food at the market, making their mash, and then giving it to them every day. I said [to my mother-in-law], "Instead of that [feeding the pigs] every day, why don't we just buy a pig if we want to eat a pig?" And then my mother-in-law said, "Oh, you don't know about that!" So then, it went on. But who takes care of the pigs? Me. Can you imagine? This happened in '38 so I was only twenty-seven years old. Oh, I cried. I cried sometimes while squeezing the mash: "Is this now a doctor's wife's job? Is this now a teacher's job?" I had my teaching diploma, and yet I had to take care of these pigs! Well, that was one of the hardest things, I think.

I was told that I was possessed because I didn't have many children like the villagers did. I had only two, and my youngest child Minar was already five years old. My mother-in-law thought I should be examined by a magician woman. And then the magician woman came, and all these other women let her see their palms, like a soothsayer. But I said, "No, I don't want it. I believe in God and I don't want anything to do with these kind of people." The next morning the magician woman said to me, "You really have a very tough soul." I said, "What do you mean?" "Well, I tried to call your husband [in a vision]. He came. But when I tried to call you, you just stayed away and you said 'No, no, no!'" I said, "Well, that is true." Because before I slept, I prayed to God that I would have nothing to do with a soothsayer. And whether it is true or not, believe me, I was scared by these people because they can harm you if you believe in that.

I wrote to [my husband in] Holland, "I want to leave the house, I want to go to Java." But then, what could my husband do? Choose between his mother and his wife? He wrote me a letter and said; "Whoever shall fight to the end, he or she will pluck the sweet fruit." For me it meant "You stay there, put." Then I stayed on, but it was really with heartbreak. That was the hardest schooling I ever had because I never said back any word to my mother-in-law even if she said this or that. So there are so many lessons from her that I would never have in school, you see, lessons of life. I never fought back because she was the mother of my husband. My husband was only six months old when his father died.

15   Bengkalis

When my husband came back after twenty months in Leiden, the children were both at school. Minar was at the Hollandsche Bataksche school in Sigompulon and Apoel was still in Tangsi at the Dutch [elementary] school. But then we were transferred to Bengkalis in 1939. And that was another life. Bengkalis was an island, so the road in the city of Bengkalis was maybe only one kilometer long. So we had to travel by motorboat or by *perahu* [boat]. My husband would go by a steamboat to Selat Panjang over the sea to one of the harbors there, and to Pekanbaru over the Siak Sri Indrapura river once a week. Once in a while, he

MAP 8   Island of Bengkalis (where the town of Bengkalis also is located), Bukit Batu (on Sumatra), and Singapore

also went to Bagansiapiapi. They say Bengkalis was a place where they had political exiles before, but I never saw one. I did know Bengkalis was important for being a place where all the boats stop before going on to Singapore.

In Bengkalis, there was a hospital and clinics, but no doctors except for my husband, only male nurses. The hospital had maybe a twenty-four-patient capacity. My husband was there because Bengkalis had an *Assistent Resident*, a quite high civil servant of the Dutch, so they needed a *Europees Dokter* to work with him, a doctor who was educated in Europe.

A doctor was very special at that time because there were very few doctors. We tried very hard to help everyone, to give aid to the less fortunate people. My husband would go by motorboat or *perahu* to all these clinics in the area to give them medical help and other advice. For instance, when we first came there, they didn't even know that there were germs in the river water and that you have to boil it. For them, it was normal to have some blood or pus in the feces. They would have dysentery without realizing that it was a disease. So that is why, the best thing I could do since I married a doctor was to help him, and to give some education and advice to other people. If he went to the villages, I usually went with him. I would tell the women in the kitchen about the drinking water and so on, whatever they needed to know.

[Tobing discussed her children's education.] First I tried to teach them *De Clerk Methode* [curriculum for 1st, 2nd, and 3rd grade ordered through the mail]. I think we did it for more than a year. But then their friends, the children of this *Assistent Resident*, the *controleur* [comptroller], they went to school in Berastagi, to the Dutch elementary school. We tried to have them admitted but had no success because they said that only Dutch children were accepted there. Then, we had to write to the *Resident* of Medan for approval so the children could go to the Dutch elementary school in Siantar, the *Europeesche Lagere* school, that means "European elementary school." We didn't have such a school in Bengkalis. We wanted them to go there so they could stay with family.

After they were accepted, they went to school in Siantar from 1940 till 1942. But when Minar and Apoel went to school in Siantar, they couldn't go to the dorm of the Dutch school because we were Indonesians, we were *Inlanders*. They were not allowed to even go swimming in the swimming pool. So I took the children to the highest civil servant there, that is the Assistent Resident Mynheer [Mr.] Dirks. I told him, "I think it is unfair, see." I said, "How come my children can't swim there? They are not allowed to go to the dorm. I have to find a place for them to stay at the boarding house. Even swimming. Do you feel that they are dirtier than the other Dutch children?" I said, "Unfair. How could you accept that children of educated *Inlanders*, educated natives, are not allowed to swim while a child born out of a Dutch and a *babu*, a maid, can swim there because it has the name of a Dutch?" I said. "My husband was Dutch-educated from Leiden. I had a Normal School, Dutch education too," I said. "And my children can't even go there!" "Well," he said, "what can I do? The one that donated the swimming pool, that was her restriction, the swimming pool was only meant for Dutch children."

Another time, I went to attend the Christmas service at their school. My daughter Minar played a role in the Nativity play. And then suddenly, a Dutch little girl nearby said, "Look, look Mama, a *babu* [maid]." Because I had my *kebaya* [blouse tunic] and sarong on. For the Dutch, you should have a gown, a dress like a European. Then you are a European. You are not supposed to wear native dress, for then they think you are only a *babu*, a maid. The mother said, "Pssssst ..."

Then in 1942, when the Japanese almost came, I got a letter from the sister who was in charge of the dorm that the children now were allowed in the dorm. I think I got it in March, and then by May the Japanese were in Indonesia. So maybe the Dutch felt that they had to be more friendly to the Indonesians.

16   Japanese Occupation and World War II

The Japanese were there by March 1942. They landed in Pantai Cermin by parachutes. Suddenly, the Japanese were here, we saw them around on bikes. The Indonesians didn't fight too much against the Japanese because we thought the Japanese would help us get rid of the Dutch. The Japanese called themselves the older brother, "*dai toa*" or something like that. "*Dai toa*" means the big country or something like that. So they would be like the big brother helping the Indonesians get rid of the colonizers. I was afraid of them because the first troops looked very rough, rude. We evacuated to Lintong Nihuta with the two children because my mother-in-law's brother lived there. Her brother was the chief of the village, the leader.

My husband stayed in Bengkalis. He was the doctor, so people needed him. After three or four months, I went with the children to Bengkalis from Tanjung Balai in a boat, two meters by six meters. We were accompanied by four relatives who also wanted to go to Bengkalis to try and get a job there. There were two seamen [to sail the boat], so there were nine people in that small *perahu* [boat]. It was difficult. We had water rations and bathed with sea water. The men tried to sail as close as possible to the land for four days. Then, thank God, we arrived in Bagansiapiapi on the fifth day, and saw my husband on the dock. We went with him to Bengkalis in a steamboat.

But it was very bad at that time. Many young boys were taken away to become Japanese soldiers, the *hei-ho*s [military worker for Japanese]. My own brother died as a *hei-ho*. I think he was only twenty years. Even Apoel at that time was almost taken because he was big for his age and like a grown-up boy already. So that is why I took the children to Bukit Batu on the mainland [of Sumatra across from Bengkalis]. I could work on a piece of land planting rice and vegetables, so that we could give the Japanese some rice after the harvest as the Japanese wanted you to have more produce. During that time, I was sometimes at home in Bengkalis, sometimes there in Bukit Batu. It is not very far, one or one and a half hours. You can go in the morning and come back in the afternoon. My husband was almost the whole time in Bengkalis because he was the doctor there. He couldn't leave. When the Japanese were there, he didn't travel too much anymore to the other hospitals. That was 1942 till 1944.

In Bukit Batu, we harvested rice, sweet potatoes, and vegetables [in a farm] that people could buy. At that time, we had around twenty workers on the land, Chinese and Javanese. Most of the people in the area were fishermen so they didn't know how to work on the rice fields. They planted the rice after they just burned the land [instead of waiting for the land to be ready], then they moved again to another piece of land. Sometimes they didn't even come to weed the plants. Then the harvest was very minimal, very little. We tried planting *sagu* [sago] too, a kind of palm tree, because my husband thought if we had a *sagu* field, we would have more income after he retired.

In Bukit Batu, I had about four young Chinese boys working there with us because they didn't want to go fight as a *hei-ho* with the Japanese. I was teaching them at night how to read and write because they only knew how to read the Chinese characters. They didn't speak Indonesian well, but you could understand it. Their parents had shops in Bengkalis or Bukit Batu and were rich people. Bengkalis was such a little town, everybody knew everybody, and my husband was the only doctor. Together with Apoel, the Chinese boys worked on the land. Whether the Japanese saw it or not [the young men being shielded from conscription], I don't know. As long as you worked and you delivered rice to them, as long you gave them something ... I once gave them sixty big kerosene cans [of rice], 600 liters, after the harvest. They liked it, that is our contribution. Then if the Japanese soldiers came to our land, we treated them richly so they wouldn't harm us. If they didn't get anything, they would just hit or kick people. They would come in groups of seven, eight, something like that, on a motorboat. To please them, you just cook plenty of food, because they could eat a lot. We killed chickens [for them], we gave noodles, rice, we gave them food.

I didn't feel any fright from them. You know why? Because at that time, I wore khaki pants, slacks, a blouse, and a hat. Just like in the jungle, you know? When they came, I sat on the other side in front of them so they were farther away. Because at that time, I was quite young right. In '42, I was thirty-one years old only.

Bukit Batu is on the mainland of Sumatra, on the other side of Bengkalis. Living in the jungle is quite scary because at night you could still hear the king of the jungle, the tiger. The sound is like this, "Knngg ... Knngg ..." They imitate the sound of the deer. And then the deer would come, and then the deer would be the prey. Once in a while, my husband came on a Saturday or Sunday. One time I thought I saw a tiger. I saw some gleaming eyes. Lights. And then my husband caught my hand and said, "Stand still," I didn't ask what it was about. I immediately felt it was the tiger. But see, if you are not afraid, you confront it, the tiger will leave. At least, that is what is believed there. I don't know whether it is true. This tiger then left us and didn't come towards us. But I felt the presence of this tiger because after the Japanese signed the [peace] treaty, one of our dogs might be taken away at night by the tiger. Our house was built on stilts, on posts, so the dogs would be on the veranda. Every night we would hear "PMMMMMMM!" and then one of the dogs would be taken away. The dogs didn't bark if they saw a tiger. They were just hypnotized, I think, maybe because of the hugeness.

The funny thing too, one time we were having a coffee on the veranda at back and I saw an animal with very tiny legs. That was the mouse deer. Very nice. But suddenly the dogs barked and the mouse deer fled. That is the only time I saw it. They were almost as big as a cat, very, very dainty, like a deer. They ate our *kangkong* [water spinach], which we had planted next to the house.

I didn't have any difficulty managing the plantation. I saw at one time someone cheating the scale, with the little pinkie going down on one side to help the weights and make it heavier. When I saw that, I said, "Don't do that with me." He replied, "Well, everybody does it." "You are fired," I then said. He was so surprised. He was a good man, actually. But if he cheated others, he would cheat me more, right. I also saw a woman drinking the blood of a snake. They killed a snake in the chicken house. My husband got out and shot the snake with a pistol. And when the snake was almost dead and didn't move anymore, this woman hung it up on a pole by the tail, cut off the head, and drank the blood. And then she said, "If you drink the blood of a snake, you get long life and you become stronger." That is not a story. I saw it!

When the Japanese came, Dutch was not taught in schools anymore, there were only the government school with Indonesian as the medium. My children couldn't go to Siantar anymore because of the Japanese Occupation.

So as soon as there was a school in Bengkalis, we sent them to the school there, the Indonesian school. At that time, Apoel would come home very often with some skin disease, the white one called *panu*. Minar would come home often with a headache because even in the midday sun, they had to hoe the soil, to work in the garden. She was at that time only eleven years old. The children also had to learn the Japanese script, *katakana*, and the Japanese language too, Japanese songs, Japanese dances. At one time, your Mom went with her classmates to Pekanbaru, on a boat, to perform a dance there. I think it was called the *Sakura* dance, the flower dance. The trip took at least ten hours and the principal of the school went with them. They wanted to perform the dance for the Japanese authorities because the school wanted to show that they learned something, and that they could be better than other schools. There was resentment, but you can't show that. Otherwise you could just be beaten or hung up until you tell them whatever is happening. Or you would be put in prison or even killed.

My husband was finished with his study in Leiden in 1939, so only three years after he got his European diploma, he had to be a doctor during the Japanese time. He did his best, but he saw that the Japanese didn't care sometimes, just hit people. One time he took a towel bar from the wash basin to his office. I said, "What are you going to do with that?" He said, "Well, I'll put this on my desk. If a Japanese tries to touch me, I'll kill him with this." I said, "Before you do it, you will be killed first." He said, "Well, anyhow I feel safer if I have this. This is my security." And every night he studied Japanese. For three months he really studied, until three o'clock in the morning. He said, "If I don't understand them, they could get angry." Because they didn't speak any other language than Japanese. He said, "I have to know Japanese. I don't want to be touched by them."

For three years, the Japanese would come into the house with heavy shoes pounding on the floor, then we know those were the Japanese coming. And our dog would bark madly. Then, I would go out. One afternoon, two Japanese were writing on a pad in our living room. I said, "What do you write?" They asked, "*Orandakah, Orandakah*?" "*Oranda*" means Dutch. [The soldiers were asking if she was Dutch.] I said, "No, Indonesia Mama." And I showed them our picture. I told them as well as possible that we were the ones who lived there. My husband didn't dare to go out of the bedroom because he knew they would just slap you if you made mistakes. But I don't know, I wasn't afraid of them. I just came out and said, "No, no, no. This is Indonesia. Me Indonesia Mama." "Oh, Mama, mama." Because the "mama" maybe, that word is international. The easiest word to pronounce as a baby. After that they left. Maybe they were just planning to take the furniture out to use it.

In Sumatra, we didn't have too many laborers. So, the Japanese imported them [from other places like Java]. On a boat maybe with a capacity for eighty people, you would have 200. It was overcrowded and they didn't have enough plates. The Japanese just threw the rice, and these passengers would catch the food, the rice, in their hands or with a hat. I heard that is what they did. And I know in Bengkalis that these poor people then got dysentery, and they would just die on the edge of the road. And the prisoners would be the ones who would bury them because they had no relatives. In war, they didn't care. A chicken's life had much more worth than a human life. A chicken, if you kill it, you can eat it.

There also was the devaluation of the money. For instance, in 1941, I bought a piece of ground for ninety guilders. That was a lot of money. But when the Japanese came, those guilders had no value. With ninety guilders, you can get a chicken. So, she [the person who had sold the land to Tobing] sold her chicken to the market, she got ninety guilders, she sent me the money, and the plot of ground was again hers. I didn't make an issue of it because I thought, "Well, that is my bad luck." And you know what my husband said: "Well, I didn't have you buy rice fields, so that is your luck!" Many people quarreled about these things, but I didn't. After all, maybe these people needed their rice fields back more than I did. During that time, I heard there were suicides. If you have five million guilders and suddenly it became nothing, maybe just [worth] ten cans of cigarettes, better to die, no suffering anymore.

One time, my husband was called by the *Kempeitai*, the [Japanese] military police service. Of course, I was very anxious, very worried. When my husband came back, he said, "Do you know what happened? They called me in the middle of the night just to see one of their wives who had dysentery. And I was so worried that if I made a mistake, they would accuse me." Because that is what happened. They would just beat a person if they didn't get the right answer to their thinking, they would just think you were lying. But like I said, it was wartime. Now I think you shouldn't have any animosity against them. You feel not happy if you still have some grudge against whole nations.

At another time a young officer came. We were scared. He was sitting there and he said, "I would like to have some ice cream." I said, "Well, I have a refrigerator. It is with kerosene." Electrolux was the brand at that time. "I can make you ice cream, but I don't have eggs, sugar, and milk." The next day, he brought the ingredients and I made the ice cream for him. He was so happy. He visited me maybe three, four times. Once he held his hands on his shirt. I said, "What do you do there?" He didn't speak Indonesian, so we just did it with gestures. I thought he meant, "Well here is a button loose. If my mama would see this, she would be upset. I have to sew it but I don't have a needle or thread." I guess he was one of the good Japanese boys. Among the Japanese of course, you have good and bad. Like anywhere, you have good people and you have bad people. Even in the war.

In 1945, the Japanese withdrew. They didn't stay. I was at that time in Siak Sri Indrapura, the palace of the Sultan of Siak. We stayed in the *pasanggrahan*, the place for the officials, like a hotel. On the other side of the river, we saw the Japanese burn all their papers from their office as the place for the police and the army was on the other side. They were shouting and screaming. We heard from somebody that the Japanese had capitulated. And then the 17th of August, that was when Sukarno proclaimed the independence of Indonesia. Poh An Tui, that is an organization of the Chinese, [the nature of its political affiliation,] I don't know [Pao An Tui, World War II-era political organization for Chinese Indonesians]. But this organization took over the whole government of the area there.

Later in Bengkalis, I saw someone being tortured and killed, because he had collaborated with the Japanese. He was from that island, Taiwan. During the Japanese time, if you didn't cooperate with the Japanese, they would torture you. He had no choice. I still remember how he was taken to the cemetery with his hands [tied] behind his back only with a little rope. I think he was the interpreter, so they hated him. And he had to walk between two men through the street. Many people shouted as they followed him. And the people would burn his hands and his back with cigarette butts. I saw that when I looked from the window, from behind the curtains. He got really tortured. And later I heard he was killed there. Just shot and put in a grave with some more people.

We fled from there too and went to Tarutung. Because when you feel there is no law, you better leave the area. It was a terrible time. Like when we were in Siantar in 1945, they came to the house and took whatever they liked. You can't protest because they have the guns, they have the power. Minar was then in junior high school in Tarutung, and Apoel was in senior high school in Siantar.

17   Kisaran

After the Japanese left, we first went to Tarutung and then my husband found a position in Kisaran in February 1946. Kisaran had a big hospital with about 200 patients. My husband went regularly to Tanjung Morawa, from '46 to '47 because the Indonesians were fighting against the return of the Dutch. The Dutch thought they could come back and take over Indonesia again. But Sukarno didn't want that. We already had our independence. The Indonesian troops were close to Medan, and the Dutch were in Medan in Hotel De Boer.

Around the 20th of July, 1947, they came with parachutes to Pantai Cermin. So the Dutch came here in 1947. And my husband was always going to Tanjung Morawa. He told the army that he shouldn't be going to Tanjung Morawa anymore, he should stay at the big hospital in Kisaran because he was a surgeon [and so had a specialty that was essential during wartime.]. He said the younger doctors should go there for first aid. [But they still wanted him to travel to Tanjung Morawa to administer to the wounded.]

And when he was going on the 29th of July [and while he was in Tebing Tinggi], he met the first troops of the Dutch going to Siantar and they shot his car with the machine gun. The car had a red cross on the front, but they didn't care, they said it could just be camouflage. My husband was shot on the road in his right leg, many shots there. There were three in the car. The driver was hit. The nurse was killed. Later on, the driver was taken with my husband to Tanjung Morawa. By then, the driver and my husband were already dead when they arrived at the operating table in Tanjung Morawa. So he was killed on July 29, 1947. A week later, one of the Red Cross people came to the house in Siantar. And the man said, *"Mana Ibu Tobing, Nyonya Tobing?"* ["Where is Mrs. Tobing?"] *"Saya,"* I replied. ["Me."] They said, *"Ibu, ada kabar kurang baik. Jadi, ibu isteri Dokter Tobing?"* ["Ma'am, there is bad news. So are you the wife of Dr. Tobing?"] *"Saya."* ["Yes."][4] *"Dokter Tobing sudah meninggal."* ["Doctor Tobing has died."] Just like that. I was still standing there. He said it so bluntly. Not even "Sit down first."

I went to other people to ask them to go to the Dutch bivouac post, the place where they were stationed, the Dutch army. But no one dared to go. So, I went with Apoel to the bivouac, to the post. And I asked them, "Is it true that my husband is already buried in Tanjung Morawa?" Then they brought me to the doctor who saw my husband on the operating table. He said, "Please sit down." Then he asked me the name of my husband's mother, the name of his father. And then he typed. Within the hour I got the statement that he was killed on the 29th by such and such. And he even gave the drawing of the place where he was buried, in the back of the hospital in Tanjung Morawa where he usually was working. And the Dutch doctor said, "We are sorry, but we didn't expect to find there a doctor. We thought it was one of the Army people." Because my husband had on Army dress too, not a doctor's, and he was on the road. My husband was buried in Tanjung Morawa until 1950. Then, we took him to the military cemetery here in Tarutung so he could be reburied with military honors at the *Makam Pahlawan* [veterans' or heroes' cemetery].

---

4   Literally, "I" but in context it means, "Yes."

18   Medan

Independence came in 1945, my husband was killed in 1947. It was like a dream. Everything was so fast, and you had no support from anybody. The Red Cross, yes. But since there were so many people, they could only give salted fish, some bad rice. If I needed money, I sold one of the sarongs or whatever I had to survive. There were so many saleswomen, the brokers. They would come to the house and ask if you had something to sell, jewelry, clothing, whatever. You don't need to go to the market. And once you sell something, they know they can come again, as long as you need the money, right?

My husband died in 1947, but I still went on with his name, the wife of Doctor Tobing. You are behind the husband, being the doctor's wife, even after his death. That is the way they think of you, it is always *inanta ni* [widow of] Dr. G. Tobing. *Nahinan* means "the former, the deceased." I tried to do my best to survive with the children. When I lost my husband, I was then at that time, thirty-six years old, my children four, the youngest one three months old. I could have come back home to Tarutung, but I knew that if I did, we only had the rice field to support us. Otherwise, nothing. And I would have to wait maybe one or two years before everything was settled with my husband's affairs, like a little pension for the widow and the children. So, I chose to live on my own in the city and not go back to Tarutung.

After six months I applied for a job teaching in Medan. They said to me, "You are a widow, you have children, do you guarantee not to miss school because we don't want to have teachers who don't come regularly, who will miss teaching." I said, "One guarantee, if I don't come, you can substitute me with another and my salary goes to her for the day." So then they accepted me. At that time, I was fighting for my job.

I don't think I am strong but again, God gave me the strength. The first years of being a widow in Medan were the hardest because at that time I was teaching two classes of elementary school at Josua Institut. I didn't ask to teach at a government school in 1947 because at that time, the Dutch were still there. Not everything was taken over by the Indonesians yet. I taught half the day, then in the afternoons I took classes to have a six-year teacher's schooling diploma [to earn more money to support the family]. The girls' teachers' school in Salatiga was only a four-year teachers' training school, so I needed to take other classes. I did the classes with other colleagues and office clerks, and did the work in one year instead of two.

At Josua Institut, I had seventy children in the morning, and seventy children later on [in the day] in second grade. I was always correcting their papers. It was very noisy because for three years during the Japanese Occupation, there was not enough school for the children, so their schooling was irregular. I got all kinds of children. In the second grade, there were twelve-year-old children who hadn't gone to school for three years, along with children of seven years, eight years. Once in a while we got a boy with a big voice, a low voice already, maybe thirteen years who hadn't gone to school during the Japanese time.

I also took Indonesian lessons from Pak [Mr.] Madong Lubis for about two years because my Indonesian was not so good. And I had to learn how to sing Indonesian songs too. It was difficult to have the children disciplined, so we sang a song almost every twenty minutes! I learned a song at night, for instance, and that was what I was teaching the next day. At that time, they said that they thought I had T.B. [tuberculosis] because I was very thin. Thirty-six kilos.

19   Progress

There were many changes happening during that time. The Indonesian Christian Women's Party began with President Sukarno. He said, "*Wanita adalah tiang negara.*" "The woman is the pole of the country." *Tiang* means the stronghold. He urged women to be strong, to assist their husbands. So President Sukarno encouraged the women's movement. Within these twenty years, really, there was so much progress among the women. We were invited to join all the activities in the government. Then, women's organizations rose up, like Perwari, which means Persatuan Wanita Republik Indonesia or the Indonesia's Women's Association; Gerwarni, the Gerakan Wanita Indonesia, which is the Indonesian Women's Movement; PWKI, the Persatuan Wanita Kristen Indonesia, the Indonesian Christian Women's Association. Many Batak friends encouraged me to join the Christian Women's Association. They came to the house, one by one. Having no husband, they thought that I would have more time for the organization, and they thought I had more experience. I had my schooling, my diploma. This was still when I was at the six-year [elementary] school. I didn't want it at all. But they said, "Don't you see, you have more schooling than we have. You are more fortunate, even if you lost your husband. We'll support you from the back." They meant support in terms of work and everything. So I joined the organization. We were together with the Indonesian Christian Party, whose leaders were in Jakarta. In Medan, the leader was Melanthon Siregar. So I was the chairman of the Christian Women's Association for North Sumatra at that time. I worked hard. But it was good.

In Medan, I was teaching at the elementary, junior high, and senior high school from 1948–1964, sixteen years. We also opened the SGTKPWKI [Sekolah Guru Taman Kanak-Kanak Persatuan Wanita Kristen Indonesia or the Training

School for Kindergarten Teachers] in January 1954. That teaching was the nicest thing that could happen to me because I had support from everyone. The first was my own sister's husband, R.M. Simanjuntak, and then there was Marcus Tobing, he always called me Ompung [honorific title for rank of grandparent] and Martin Siagian, he was at one time the inspector of the Department of Education in Medan. Mangara Manik, Melanthon Siregar, there were many who supported me. They were the ones who suggested that we have a woman principal for the teachers' training school for kindergarten. Because a girls' school, imagine with a man as a principal! That does not sound good. And they knew that I had my B-1 English, almost the same as a Bachelor's degree in English today. They trusted me wholly. If I had some questions or some difficulties, I came to them. They always were ready to help me. So I taught English and I was the principal of the training school for kindergarten teachers.

20   Opportunities

[At that time,] Professor Karl Pelzer from Yale University went to Nommensen University in Medan and asked for people who could interpret from the Batak language to English. My old teacher, I think his name was Suyck, was Dutch and at the teachers' training school. I had been there for one year, so Mr. Suyck knew me, and he knew my son Apoel. Mrs. Pelzer, Karl Pelzer's wife, came to my house, and she chose Apoel for their research, to go with her to Bakara, to Tarutung, to Lintong Nihuta, all those places, to interview people about matters like the *adat*. And when they came back, Mr. Pelzer asked Yale University for support to have a young man to go with him to America as an assistant to finish his book. So Pelzer interviewed people for the position. When he did, some boys would answer Pelzer's question, "What did he say?" with the response, "Oh, that is not so important." But with Apoel, Apoel could interpret because he liked to talk. Apoel knew English, Batak, Indonesian, Dutch, and a little German. And so they asked to have Apoel go to America. At that time, it was 1956. I said "No, he should marry." But then Apoel said, "What do you mean? I thought you were an emancipated woman. Now I have the chance, without any expense, to go to the United States to study, and you don't let me go?" On that, I couldn't say anything, so he went. He was twenty-five years old then. I thought he was old enough to marry and settle down. I didn't feel so secure being a widow with no married children with me.

And then after that, Minar had the chance to go to the United States too. Apoel helped her come over so that she could teach Indonesian at Yale University. So she went in 1958. In 1960, Minar earned some money by teaching

FIGURE 49   Demak Tobing Mark and Apoel Loembantobing in New Haven,
            shortly after Demak's arrival in the United States, 1960
            TOBING FAMILY COLLECTION

summer courses at Cornell University, and she had the money to let one of us
come, me or Demak. And I said, "Let Demak go." Because she was then seventeen years old. In fact, she celebrated her seventeenth birthday on the dateline.
Apoel found a place for her in Boston through his friend's father, Dr. Joslin. And
there she stayed for a year and went to Newton High School. She had finished
high school in Medan, the Methodist English school, but the extra year helped
her to enter a university in America. I was happy that they could go to America,
because so many people tried hard, but they couldn't go. While these three
children, God gave them the chance, right? I was grateful for them.

21   United States

Before I came to the United States, I said to my daughter and her husband,
"I would like to come but only under one condition, if you could find a job for

MAP 9   The United States, showing Los Angeles, California; Washington, DC; Ithaca,
New York; and New Haven, Connecticut

me. Otherwise, I think it is too much expense."[5] My youngest son Bistok was at
that time too young to come. He was still at the SMA [*Sekolah Menengah Atas*],
the Indonesian senior high school. At least, I thought, he should finish the SMA
before he goes to the United States.

I arrived in May. At the beginning of September around Labor Day, my
daughter and my granddaughters went with me to New Haven and we got a
place for me on Crown Street because there was a Javanese family there studying law at Yale. It was a one-room apartment, with a kitchen and a bathroom,
that was all, in a three-story building towards Howe Street. The next year
I moved to Trumbull Street. That place had two bedrooms, so I got a roommate,
an English woman from London.

I had two classes, undergraduates and graduates, and also at that time, students from the ROTC [Reserve Officers' Training Corps]. The Yale students were
all neatly dressed. The undergraduates had to have their ties on. The graduate
students, they didn't need that. Yale was only males. In 1968, Yale became co-
educational. I didn't have any problems teaching them.

---

5   My mother wrote this story differently, that she first tried to get my grandmother to visit and
then later found a job for her.

FIGURE 50
H.L. Tobing at
Minar T. Rony's home,
ca. 1964
MARK FAMILY
COLLECTION

FIGURE 51
Demak Tobing Mark and H.L. Tobing at
same visit, ca. 1964
MARK FAMILY COLLECTION

Professor Hendon [Rufus Hendon, Tobing's supervisor] asked on the first day that I came, "What should they call you?" I said, "Let them call me Ibu." And then he explained to the students that *Ibu* means mother, *Ibu* means teacher, *Ibu* means older lady, *Ibu* means a respected lady even if it is a young lady. So *Ibu* is very appropriate for Mrs. Tobing. At Yale, if they said, "Is Ibu in?" it was me as there was no other *Ibu* there in the whole university.

I think if you give a good impression the first day, it will remain. Do you know, the first time I taught the students, they were smoking in the class, and one had his feet on the desk. Unbelievable! There, I stood. Then I said, "Well, boys, if you are in my class, you may not smoke. If you want to smoke, you just ask permission to go out." "Yes, but with the other professors we smoke." "In this Indonesian course, you may not smoke. I don't allow you to smoke because if you smoke, I can't talk anymore. If my throat is not in perfect order, I can't speak, I can't say 'Repeat after me, repeat after me.' So, it is better not to smoke in the class." And then the one with the leg, I asked, "Are you used to doing that in class?" "It depends on the professor." I said, "This one doesn't like it." He put his leg immediately down. The first day that you are confronted with a person, you try to make a good impression. But if I were tolerant, I think they would just smoke and they would just sit nonchalantly at the desk.

The teaching of the American students at Yale, it was quite funny. The pronunciation and the intonation were so different than what they were used to. I tried very hard to let them imitate me because according to my boss Professor [Rufus] Hendon, they should try to imitate my pronunciation exactly. And only with one I didn't succeed.

I liked being at Yale, otherwise I wouldn't stay there so long, fifteen years, 1964 to 1979. In New Haven, I had my friends from the church. I also had fellow teachers, colleagues like Daw Tin Tin who taught Burmese. The Lutheran Church in New Haven also was quite active. Every Friday we had our potluck, and then had some crafts during winter. I became a member of the Women's Club, and once in a while we had conferences at different places.

I never thought that I would stay at Yale for so long as there was no contract, it was just extended by the year. I thought I would just stay there for a year, at the most two years. After the fifth year I thought, "Well, I should go back to Indonesia." So in 1969 I went back, and without knowing it, it happened that they dedicated the hospital of Tanjung Morawa to my husband while I was there. I also went to Holland in 1969, to teach during the summer for ten weeks in Oegstgeest as the Indonesian teacher happened to be sick. And in 1972 I came again to Indonesia. None of my siblings had told me that they would reinter my parents in Simorangkir, but I was able to be there.

22   Homecoming

I returned back to Indonesia in 1979. Here in Tarutung, most of the younger generation have gone off to Medan and Jakarta and other places because they can earn more money there working as a white-collar worker. They don't want to be a laborer on the land and live with whatever they have day to day. But usually, the parents don't want to stay with the children outside of their village because they love their village. They always go back there, especially because they don't want to die in a foreign area, in a strange environment. The older you get, you have the feeling that you have to be close to your loved ones who have already died. For instance, your parents are already buried in that village. So you want to go back there when you are older, because you think when you die, you want to be next to the family grave too.

When I first came to the village in 1918 at seven years old, I was like a creature they never saw. I was from Medan so the clothing was different. I had shoes on. The children in the village almost never wore shoes at that time, but I didn't know it. And I had the idea that sleeping under the mat was so bad. But they were used to that. So many things were so different. I think I live with conflicts my whole life. I never thought about that until now. But see, I was used to a bed, and suddenly, there I was on the floor on a mat, with only a mat over me at night. Well, that was a contradiction from what I was used to in my parents' home. But with me, it is just going forward.

FIGURE 52   The ancestral home in Pearaja, with the burial site of our ancestor Raja Pontas and the Huria Kristen Batak Protestan [HKBP, the Batak Christian Protestant Church] in the background
PHOTOGRAPH BY AUTHOR

Even though I could stay in Medan or Jakarta, I wanted to come back to the village because this is the inheritance of my husband's family. From 1937 to 1939, when my husband was in Holland to study, I was in Tarutung and my mother-in-law was in this house. And I had to respect her for all her teachings and wise remarks in the past. That was actually maybe the main reason that I came back. She planted in me the love, or the awe, the respect for our grandparents' effort to have this village established. So when I became older, I thought I should come here. I have to take care of my husband's property, to keep and preserve it for my own children. Because that is the custom according to my mother-in-law then. The twenty months that I was here was a good lesson for me.

For Those Who Follow

The Autobiography of Minar T. Rony

1   Beginnings

As a Batak, I am very conscious of my heritage, my customs and traditions, my genealogy. For Bataks, it is important to know a person's *marga*, which is comparable to a clan name or surname here in the United States. That way, they can know their connection to another person. In the US, I will say I am Indonesian if I introduce myself, and then I will say that my mother tongue is Batak. My father insisted that Batak be the first language in the home because no matter where we lived, he wanted us to know that we were Batak.

FIGURE 53   Minar T. Rony, ca. 1935
MINAR T. RONY COLLECTION

I first came to my father's village of Pearaja before my fifth birthday. I remember that when I was four years old, we moved from Magetan, Java to Pearaja in northern Sumatra in the town of Tarutung. The oldest relative I remember is Ompung Boru [Grandmother] Situmorang, the daughter-in-law of Si Singamangaraja [The Singamangaraja]. I knew Ompung Boru Situmorang best. She was married to the oldest son of Si Singamangaraja and was the wife of my grandmother's cousin. My grandmother's mother was the sister of Si Singamangaraja. She lived next door in the *rumah ganjang* or long house when I was growing up. The long house was given by Raja Pontas when Si Singamangaraja was taken in by the Dutch authorities in Tangsi Tarutung, and his family was kept under house arrest in Pearaja.

Every morning, the old people would come out of the house, sunning themselves in the yard, and they would tell stories. They were elderly, so they didn't have to go to work. There, I would hear stories. This *ompung* would tell stories about how Raja Si Singamangaraja [The King Singamangaraja] was trying to escape from the Dutch with his family. They were trying to avoid capture by the Dutch. So they hid in the woods, moving from place to place. Naturally, they had to find food in the forest, or rely on food from whomever was living near the forest. Because Raja Si Singamangaraja was the leader, other people were always ready to help and give whatever was available. My *ompung* told stories of how they lived in the forest, ate and slept there. This *ompung*'s husband, the oldest son of Si Singamangaraja, was killed by the Dutch, maybe it was in the battle or the detention center. They were detained in Tangsi, Tarutung by the Dutch. This *ompung* must have been very pretty when she was young. They didn't have children though.

Ompung Boru Hombing, my grandmother, was my dad's mom. She was tall and beautiful, and strong and strict to me. My grandfather passed away after she had three children. My father had an older brother and sister. I don't know their names. They died young. My father Gerhard L. Tobing was born in July 1902. He was given a German name, Gerhard, and the name Mangidotua. *Mangido* means to ask, and *tua* is blessing. He was given this name because two of his older siblings died young. So my father was the baby. He survived because he was always in a sling with my grandmother. She would carry him around all the time because if he was left behind, he might get sick and die. He wouldn't have survived. They wouldn't have known which disease it might be because there were no doctors around. I think this was why my grandmother wanted him to be a doctor.

My paternal grandmother, who was widowed when my dad's father Raja Aris passed away at age 31, must have been in her twenties when she had to remarry one of my dad's family members. That was the custom at that time.

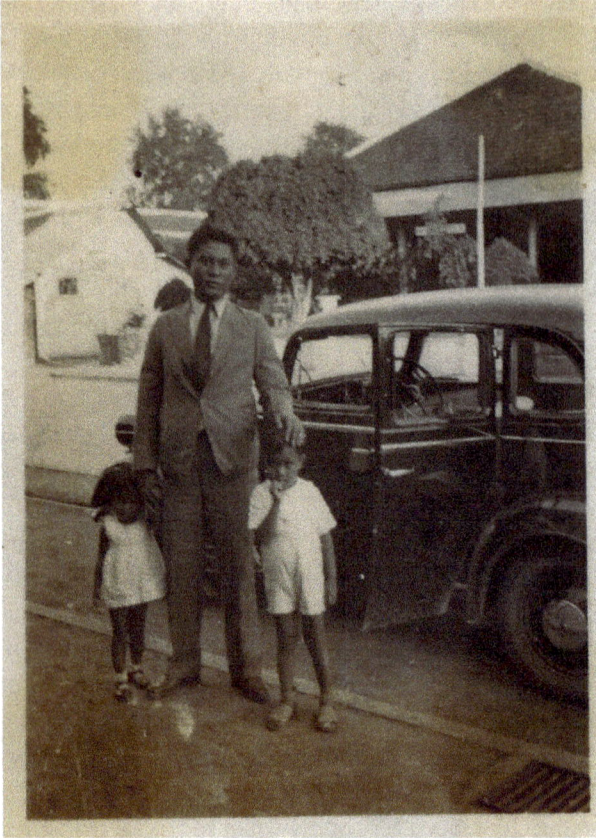

FIGURE 54
Gerhard L. Tobing with
Minar T. Rony and
Apoel Loembantobing,
ca. 1935
MINAR T. RONY
COLLECTION

Once you are a widow, you stay in the family or you go back to your family
and return everything that you got for the bride price when you got married.
Women had to stay in the family or go home. That's what the *adat* said.

My dad, her son, had a strict upbringing, and did become a doctor like his
mother wanted. The Dutch started the school in Tarutung in 1911, and I think
my dad was one of the first students. Later, I think he studied in Jakarta for ten
years and graduated from the medical school in 1928. My dad told me when he
was studying in Jakarta, there were only eight of forty students that passed the
exam when he was there.

My parents got married on May 16, 1930. My mother was born in 1911 in
Arnhemia. She was the oldest of eleven siblings. When her family was on the
east coast of Sumatra, she wanted to go to elementary school in Tarutung. My
grandfather really supported her education, even though she was a daughter
and not a son. Usually, the education of sons came first. To take her to school,
they took a horse cart, then a boat across Lake Toba, and continued with

FIGURE 55   Minar T. Rony and Apoel Loembantobing, ca. 1935
            MINAR T. RONY COLLECTION

another horse cart. She stayed in the village of Harean with her extended family. I think she graduated when she was fifteen from the HIS, the *Hollandsche
Inlandsche School* [Dutch Native School]. My mother wanted to go to a school
in Java, but she told me that she failed the entrance exam because there was a
portion where they needed to know Arabic, and they had not been taught to
write in Arabic script. But the following year, they changed that requirement,
so she was able to go to the school after all.

My mother got married after she graduated from the teachers' training
school, the *Meisjeskweekschool* [school for educating native teachers for four
years with the Dutch language as the medium for instruction] in Salatiga,
so she was eighteen when she got married, May 16, 1930. My brother Apoel
was born April 1931 and I was born November 1932. We differed about twenty
months in age. Both of us were born in Amuntai, Kalimantan, which was called
Borneo at that time. My family moved to Semarang and then Magetan because
of my father's posts as a government medical doctor. When I was maybe three
or four years old, my mother learned how to be a midwife. She went to the

hospital and learned how to deliver babies. But she never took the exam. I think it was in Magetan.

In 1937 when I was young, my father went to Holland for almost two years for further medical study. While we were waiting for my dad to return, my mother, brother, and I moved from Java to Pearaja, Tarutung, when my dad went to continue his study at Leiden University. The way I understood it then, my father's education in the Dutch East Indies medical school was not considered the same as the Dutch medical school. So his salary was less than the salary of the Dutch medical school graduate of his time. Later on they changed the system so the pay was more equitable. My father saved money in order to go to Holland, to go to Leiden University for medical school. He stayed there for almost two years, and passed the exam to be a medical doctor and also became an ear, nose, and throat specialist. Leiden is one of the oldest universities in the Netherlands. They have a lot of Indonesian collections in their library and museum.

In Tarutung I attended a few months of the HIS, where Dutch was taught as a language. When we were in Tarutung, my brother attended the first and second grade of the Dutch elementary school. At one time my brother was talking about fighting the native boys who lived near the school. I was about five or six years old, so my brother must have been about six or seven years old. My mother was shocked, and I was shocked too. I guess he didn't realize he was different from his Dutch classmates, that he was also not a white. My mother had to explain to him that he was one of the natives.

My grandmother Ompung Boru Hombing was of royalty. She was very strong, and knew how to work the rice fields, and how to cook. And she was very disciplined and strict. My mother tried to get along with her, but my mother was raised as a girl on the east coast of Sumatra and not in the Batak area, and then she went to school and was not expected to do the same kind of work that girls and women did in the village. My mother learned more about the Batak culture as an adult when she was staying in her mother-in-law's house. My mother worked hard to become more familiar about the way of life in Tarutung.

In Tarutung, my grandmother Ompung Boru Hombing organized and oversaw all of the work in the family's rice fields and hired and supervised the workers. They sowed the fields, planted the rice, weeded the rice, and then harvested the rice. Sometimes they had six or more people working in the rice fields. They would come early in the morning to the house for breakfast at 5 o'clock or 6 o'clock, and then go start working in the fields. By ten o'clock they would get a snack. At one time, I remember, my mother had to carry all that stuff on the fields on the *gadu gadu*, the path between the plants in the fields, carrying supplies for these workers. Once in a while, I would come along and help. My mom, the city girl, had a hard time doing all that and adjusting to that way of life.

I also remember how my grandmother would want me to act a certain way because I was a *boru ni raja* [daughter of royalty], and the daughter of her son. One time, my brother and all of my cousins were playing around outside. I remember that my grandmother made me sit in a chair while everyone else was having fun outside. She told me that I was a *boru ni raja*, so I was supposed to stay there, which I did. Later, I realized that my brother was allowed to run around outside because he was a boy, and my female cousins were allowed to play outside too because they were descendants of a daughter. But me, I had to sit in the chair and wait because I was descended from a son. I learned early on my place in the family, as I was the daughter of my grandmother's only son from her first marriage.

2   Bengkalis

At the beginning of 1939 when my dad came back from Holland, he was assigned by the government to work in Bengkalis. Bengkalis did not have a Dutch elementary school, so my brother Apoel and I were home schooled. My mom taught my brother Apoel second and third grade, and I got first and second grade from her. My brother was one year ahead of me. My mother got the curriculum through the mail, *De Clerk Methode* [curriculum for 1st, 2nd, and 3rd grade ordered by correspondence]. I think she got it from Holland. She was a teacher and a graduate of a Dutch school, so she could teach us Dutch. In the mornings, we had to learn through home schooling. In Bengkalis there was only a village school, *Sekolah Desa*, first to third grade. I remember for Sinterklaas, December 6, we went to the *Societeit*, the Society Club. It's all Dutch, all Europeans. There was a Batak community in Bengkalis, but it was very small. So we lived with the Dutch there. The Dutch buildings and homes were laid out in the square. Our social life, birthdays and so on, were with the Dutch children. The only exception was Sundays. They had a service for the Indonesian Christians in the local school. We would meet all the Indonesian Christians there, most of whom were Batak.

As a young boy in Bengkalis, my brother Apoel was into exploring. He liked football [soccer] and he liked flying a kite in Bengkalis. I would follow him, and then he would say, "You go home because you're a girl. You're not supposed to follow me with the boys." He liked being active, I don't think he could sit still and concentrate. He was taller than I, and very agile. I was kind of quiet, but he would make friends easily, he was outgoing.

My ambition to be a doctor must have started when we moved to Bengkalis because of my father's job. I was six and had been in the first grade in Tarutung. The head of that region, I think it was like a county, was called the *Assistent Resident* [high civil servant of the Dutch]. My father was the doctor in the region. He had clinics in the islands all around the island of Bengkalis, and he also trained his nurses at the clinics. I am sure he interviewed and tested them before he accepted them, so he knew who could do the work. He would recruit a class of young nurses. These nurses were people from all walks of life, like young people from the interior who came and looked for a job in the hospital. I noticed also that a cousin of mine was one of his students at one time.

I remember that he taught them the basic principles of nursing. There were no schools for nursing at that time, so he had to do everything himself. He would have classes during the week and teach them how to take care of the sick. All of them would meet at the same time in a room. So his nurses were all trained by him, and he knew who were the best ones, and where to place them in the hospital. Some of them got a desk job, some of them went through a test so they could be the ones to really nurse the people in the ward. Some of them were only there Fridays in the afternoon. After school, I would go around and watch him teach sometimes in Bengkalis. And I also know he did the same in Kisaran in 1945–1947. I never really asked questions or interrupted him though when I was there, I just watched and observed. My dad was a patient and fair instructor, and a good teacher. He would teach them systematically, give them examples, and make sure that they had hands-on training.

At one time, the Sultan of Siak was one of his patients. This was during the Dutch Occupation, so it was before December 1941. The Sultan of Siak was a good Muslim. He had his own group of people who advised him on his health and tried to treat him. But they were not successful at that time. His local medicine man couldn't heal him, and finally the Sultan had to ask my dad. He knew my dad was a Christian, while he himself was a Muslim, but he asked my father to treat him. My dad helped him and the Sultan was healed. And the Sultan was grateful and called my dad his great friend. He gave my dad a cigarette case and lighter made of gold. When my mother died, the cigarette case and the lighter came up in conversation with my brother and sister. And I said, "Since I remember all of the things that Dad did and when he got this set, can I please have it?" So the family gave it to me. As a daughter, I am allowed to ask and be given things that are removable and can be carried away.

At that time, I thought I should become a doctor just like my dad. Doctors heal the sick and help those in pain. I thought it would be good for me to learn and study and become a doctor like my dad, helping the sick. Later, during the struggle for independence from the Dutch in Sumatra, my dad also took care of the wounded during the military conflict. The Dutch tried to return to Indonesia after the Japanese left, and there were a lot of injured people on the battlefield.

My dad supported me in my dream of becoming a doctor. From what I saw, my dad was very calm, caring, loving, friendly, and studious too. He wanted all of his children to have education. And he wanted all of us to be treated equally.

As a young girl, I liked to go to the hospital and visit and see what my father was doing. I would come to his examining room, which had a curtain for privacy. I would say, "Pa, can I come in?" And he would answer, "Yes, but stay in the corner and sit on the chair." If it was all right for me to see the patient, he would draw the curtain so I could see the person whom he was examining and to whom he was talking. When he was making rounds, I would ask, "May I come along?" And he would say, "Sure, come along and listen." I usually didn't ask questions of my father. I just observed and listened and walked with him through the wards. And my mother never forbade me to go the hospital. She knew that my dad was there to watch over me.

Because he was a doctor, my father always was on call. When we were living in Bengkalis, I remember clearly, vividly, that people would come to the house even if it was midnight or early morning. They would knock at my dad's shutters and say things like, *"Lukun, bini goa mau beranak la!"* ["Doctor, my wife is in labor!"] So my dad would get up and go with the person to his home and deliver the baby. At one time during the Japanese Occupation, he delivered twin girls and the family asked my dad if he wanted the girls to raise. My dad had to refuse, saying that he could not provide milk to feed the babies. And when he came home, he told me the story. And I said, "Pa, why don't you at least take one, I will take care of it." He said, "Where are you going to get milk? The babies need milk to live and grow up." And then later on, I heard that the babies died. This was a Chinese Indonesian family that wanted to give him the babies. At that time, the Chinese preferred to have boys rather than girls because the boys would carry on the family line. It was sad. They didn't have any milk to drink. But how could we provide food for the babies? We didn't have milk at that time because there were no cows in Bengkalis. Even my sister Demak, when she was born in 1943, didn't have enough milk. So we had to get milk from our goats. Or, we had canned milk, or the sweet milk, *susu kaleng* [canned milk].

Since my dad was responsible for the medical care in the area, my father would go to visit all of the clinics in the other islands. Usually, they were each managed by a male nurse. If there was a seriously ill patient, my father would treat them and prescribe medication so the nurse could follow up afterwards.

If it was life-threatening, they usually tried to bring the patient to the hospital in Bengkalis by boat.

Sometimes I would go along when my father visited his clinics in the area. We went by motorboat in the morning with my mom to visit all of the clinics on all of the islands. I do not remember my brother Apoel coming, I guess he had different interests. It takes maybe half of a day. Sometimes if we visited a clinic during lunchtime, they would prepare lunch for us. My mother also would bring snacks. I remember her bringing boiled eggs, because I liked boiled eggs. I remember how we would eat these snacks on the boat.

My dad didn't have that much time for leisure because he spent seven days in the hospital. At that time, I was only six years old, and my brother was eight years old. In the afternoons and maybe on weekends, we might be able to sit down together for dinner. On Saturday evening, the family would play dominoes, or Chinese checkers, or checkers. My father's favorite food was *babi panggang*, roasted pork, and *babi kecap* also, soy sauce pork, and naturally always with the hot sauce, *sambal*. My dad sometimes would drink beer at the end of the day after work. Once he even let me have a taste because I was curious.

My mom and dad raised me by example. It's not a one-way street, you have to be generous and share. If someone gives you something, you have to give something back. It's not always money, sometimes it is help or attention. People are very grateful if you can help them. My dad was very compassionate and helped whomever needed aid. He accepted three young Chinese men into our house.[1] They stayed with us during the Japanese Occupation so they wouldn't be conscripted by the Japanese. My father had Chinese patients, so maybe he knew these people through a former patient, or a professional connection. He went out of his way to give everyone a chance to try to heal and make them well. Pang Foon was one of the people that my Dad helped. He was a *pang long* employee and worked in the logging company. He was partially paralyzed but was healed after my dad treated him. Pang Foon decided to dedicate his life to my dad and became a part of our household, became our cook. He was the one who took care of my dad's meals. He really watched what my dad was getting for his lunch and dinner. Pang Foon stayed with us for the rest of his life, even after my father's death and then later on in Medan until my mother's death. Pang Foon really cared for my brother Bistok and helped to raise him. Apoel was the one who buried him.

---

1 H.L. Tobing said "about four young Chinese boys" in her narrative, but Rony remembered that there were three who stayed with them.

3   Siantar

For my third grade, my parents decided that I should go to the Dutch school in Siantar. First, my parents tried to get us to the Dutch elementary school in Medan.[2] As students, we were supposed to stay in the school dorm. But we were not accepted at the dorm because of the discrimination, as we were natives. That's why we ended up in my father's sister's house in Siantar. Siantar is not too far from Medan. We stayed with the Sihombings, while attending the Dutch elementary school. I attended third and fourth grade. My brother Apoel was in the fourth and part of the fifth grade. We were accepted in that school because my father and mother were Dutch-educated parents. Most of the Indonesians were attending the HIS, including the children of the aunt with whom we were staying. They were not accepted in the Dutch school.

At this time as a little girl, I had my first experience of discrimination as an Indonesian in a Dutch elementary school and learned that we were second-class citizens in our own country. Eurasians and Chinese and also those Indonesians serving in the army were considered first-class citizens. I felt the discrimination clearly. Although the teacher didn't treat us differently because there were only two of us Indonesians in my third-grade class, the other students made it clear that there was a difference between the natives and first-class citizens. I remember the things that the other children said. There were only two natives in the class, and we were the star students. The other Indonesian was the son of a Batak Karo, local royalty. The two of us always competed in math, which was a subject I liked. Whenever we had math, the teacher would ask questions and you would have to raise your hand if you knew the answer. There were the two natives who usually were raising their hands. My brother, who was one grade higher than I, also was in a class with only a few Indonesians. In his class, there were two daughters of a medical doctor.

But the other children didn't really socialize with us. They were mostly Dutch and Eurasian children, children of those in the Dutch army. Only a few talked to me. And one Eurasian called me a dirty native for no reason. I never visited a Dutch classmate's home. I didn't have European friends because of the racial hierarchy, except for my friend Thea, a German girl. I was invited to her house, and I even know where the house still is. It is near the intersection there on the main street. Thea was not like the Dutch children. She didn't have that mentality of talking down to me, talking to a native. She was my classmate and we were friends. We talked and we compared notes. She could communicate

---

2   Tobing mentioned that she tried to enroll the children at Berastagi too.

with the Dutch and with me. But when the Second World War broke out, the Germans were interned by the Dutch. And then my friend was gone.

One time, my mother was wearing a *kebaya* [blouse tunic] and sarong and she went to a Dutch church with me in Siantar for the Christmas service. My Dutch schoolmates knew me from school but they were surprised to see my mother there. The Dutch girl from the elementary school I attended said to her mother, "What is the *babu* [maid] doing here?" I thought, this girl only knew one in *kebaya* as the help in the house, not as a person you socialized with. And the mom of my schoolmate said, "Shhh …" And I think they were one bench behind. The mother understood that this was my mother, not my nanny.

In Siantar, I had to bike to school. It was a long way from the house, about ten to fifteen minutes by bike, depending on the traffic. The school was located on the other side of the city near a golf course, which was behind the school. Apoel was less happy in Siantar as he didn't have the freedom to go around like he did in Bengkalis. It was not like home where he could go wherever he wanted. We also were away from our parents.

4　　　Return to Bengkalis

When World War II broke out, the Germans were interned by the Dutch. Later on, when the Japanese came, all the Dutch were taken away. The Japanese came halfway through the school year. I remember when the Japanese Occupation started in 1942. They occupied Singapore. We heard about it from the radio and then later on they had it in the newspaper, naturally.

When the Japanese came, we evacuated for safety. So my mother took Apoel and me to Lintong Nihuta, which was the village of my father's mom. We stayed with my dad's *tulang*, his uncle, my grandmother's brother, who was the *Kepala Negeri* [political leader, district head] there. We stayed there for about a month.

And then later on, after a month, we went back to Bengkalis in a big sailing boat. I remember, there were a few of us, including relatives. I was scared of sailing in the boat. There was wind and rain, a storm, and we were there for a few days. I remember praying that we get to our destination safe and sound. I also remember that the two crew members had to cook dinner on the boat. They had a little tray and a cooking tripod, just like they use in camping nowadays, and then whatever you could cook, rice, dried fish, salty fish. We didn't have much to eat, just rice and whatever.

On the trip, I was quiet and listening. I learned a lot from my mother. I didn't talk unless I was talked to. If I asked too many questions, I would know a lot that I didn't need to know. But I knew how to pray. I hoped and prayed that we would get home safe and sound. I think my brother Apoel was also quiet.

We went to Bagansiapiapi and happened to meet my dad, which was a happy surprise. My dad was on a medical tour, visiting his clinics. And then we all went together to Bengkalis by my dad's motorboat.

After we got to Bengkalis, both my brother and I started as students at the Malay school. It was called *Sekolah Sambungan* [two-year Malay-language school for fourth and fifth grade] I became friends with some of my classmates. This was a Malay school, so everyone was Indonesian, not Dutch. The Dutch had been interned. I didn't know where they went, but I didn't see them anymore during the Japanese Occupation. I went to school in Bengkalis for fourth and fifth grade.

There was a change when the Japanese came. I had to switch to learning in Malay and Japanese. We still had our regular teachers but then the Japanese soldiers, one or two of them, would come and teach us. During that time, I learned a lot of Japanese. I had to learn the Japanese language including the writing, *katakana*, *hiragana*, and *kanji* [kinds of Japanese script], everything Japanese. Also, we had *kinrohosi*, which I think is outdoor and agricultural activities. Every morning at seven all of us had to be in the green, the entire school including the teachers, staff, and government employees. We all gathered there to sing the Japanese anthem, greet and bow towards *Tenno Heika*, the Emperor of Japan, towards the rising sun. We also had to do some exercise, the *taiso* they called it, physical calisthenics with music. I still remember the music. I had two years of that, fourth and fifth grade. We went through those rituals every weekday morning before we would start school. There were two classes, one for fourth grade and one for fifth grade. I was not scared though. I was always happy to be in school and learning stuff. They had a small collection of Malay books that I liked to read, like *Layar Terkembang* [*Boat with Full Sail* by Sutan Takdir Alisjahbana*]*, *Si Tjebol Rindukan Bulan* [*Aiming for the Moon* by Aman Dt. Madjoindo]. I was only nine, ten, eleven, reading the grown-up Malay novels. It kept me busy. We didn't have any subjects but Japanese writing, language, singing, and dancing. All the other subjects were not taught.

The children were supposed to learn singing and dancing in Japanese so we could entertain the soldiers. We performed for the soldiers usually on certain occasions, or on weekends or holidays. We even had a competition of the play *Momotaro-san* [*Peach Boy*] singing and dancing with two other schools from that area. I was the grandmother, *obasan*, of *Momotaro-san*. On one competition with the other schools, we had to travel to Pekanbaru, and along the way, we stopped for the night in Siak. I don't know how the Sultan knew about me traveling there, but he sent someone to pick me up to stay in the castle where he lived as he had been a patient of my dad. When I got to the castle, they welcomed me and served me dinner, and they showed me a room where I could stay the night.

My parents realized though that during the Japanese Occupation, my brother and I didn't learn much about school subjects like geography, history, and math. Since we were taught a limited curriculum, mostly Japanese in school, my dad arranged to teach math and English to my brother and me. My dad also taught German to my brother Apoel. My dad knew the Dutch, German, and English languages—he knew everything. He used to teach us these subjects with books from 3:00 to 5:00 in the afternoon during the weekdays in the storage room near the kitchen. The storage room had a window with a curtain. Our dog Hector would warn us whenever a Japanese soldier was approaching the house because Hector would bark and jump out from wherever he was until one of us would come out to tell Hector to be quiet. He would be the first to hear the soldiers' boots. You know, dogs have very sharp hearing. And I think he was sensitive to our feelings and wanted to protect us.

My dad was educated and kept up with the field through his friends who were doctors. Doctors were usually stationed far apart, so he didn't see his friends too often. But whenever they were near, they would visit us. Or if my dad was traveling, he would visit them. My dad also kept up with his medical knowledge through reading books and magazines to which he had subscribed. He would read them in the early morning or late evening in the dining room when everyone else was asleep. So that was how he could keep up with the latest developments. And even during the Japanese Occupation, he would get up at three in the morning to study Japanese so he could communicate in Japanese. There was not always a translator around, so my father was learning medical terminology in Japanese so he could explain things to the Japanese. If he said something to the Japanese medical staff, the Japanese nurse might not know what he was talking about, and there might be problems. The Occupation was scary. At one time, he was taken by the Japanese for interrogation and kept there for a whole day. He was tortured by the Japanese, and he became very ill. My mom had to nurse him for about three weeks until he was back to normal. He never told me what happened to him then.

Still, there were many good memories. When we were in Bengkalis, I got to see my dad every day, and talk with him. My dad would give me advice regularly, and also let me try out different things that I wanted to do. When I was in fifth grade in *Sekolah Sambungan*, the students had a co-op to sell pineapples to other students during break time. And I helped in peeling the pineapple and slicing it, and selling it to my fellow students. From that experience, I realized that you could earn money by doing things. I talked to my dad because

I thought it might be a good idea to sell snacks. I asked, "Can I sell peanuts and sugarcane *di muka bioskop* [in front of the movie theater]?" And my father's answer was, "As long as you do all of the work and the preparation, it is okay with me. So do not get help from the cook, nor any help from the other servants we have. You can ask them how to do it, but you have to do the work yourself."

I decided to start my own business. I went on my bike to the countryside and bought some sugarcane in long stalks. I had to clean the sugarcane and cut the stalks into pieces about one foot in length, and I put them in a basket. As for the peanuts, our cook showed me how to roast them over the fire. Then I had a basket of peanuts and a basket of sugarcane. The movies started at six, so at about five o'clock, I went to the front of the movie house, and sat at the edge of the street with my sugarcane and my peanuts. A middle-aged man passed by and stopped when he saw me. The man said, "You are the daughter of the doctor." I replied, "Yes." And then he told me, "Well, I'm going to buy all of your stuff." So there I was, my sales had gone very fast. I thought, "It's still afternoon, the sun is still out." And I thought, "Well, why should I go home? I will see what movie they are showing." When I went to the door of the movie house, the movie attendant also knew that I was the daughter of the doctor. He said, "*Noni* [Miss], come in, I'll show you a seat." And I got a seat. But then it got dark, and my dad apparently didn't see me at home, and he asked Ludin, the houseboy, to find me at the movie house. My dad didn't get angry. He asked me, "How did you do?" I told him the story. I don't think he expected that someone would recognize me and buy me out.

I always wanted to be a doctor like my dad. He encouraged me in this dream. During this time period, from 1942 to 1945, during the Japanese Occupation, I often went to the hospital because the hospital was diagonally located across the street from my school. After school, I could go and see my dad in his examining room helping patients. And I would watch him do his work if he said it was all right to come into the room. And I would see him examining and talking to the patient about the medical problems and what they needed to do.

In the hospital, they had two wards and towards the end of each ward they had one or two private rooms. At that time, there were no electric tools. My father had a stethoscope and the nurse would always accompany him. They all had their white coats.

If he had his rounds when I was at the hospital, I also followed him again. Again, if it was not intrusive, I would stay and listen to what he needed to say to the patient and watched his bedside manner to grown-ups and children. As long as it was appropriate and they didn't open up their clothing, he would allow me to stay. The patients he saw had all kinds of situations, such as a broken arm or whatever problems that required them to be hospitalized. The issues usually had to be major or long-term to be dealt with in the hospital, like a broken leg in a cast. But he also treated less serious cases too. Fridays were his day for operating on people. And if it was not a serious operation, I could sit in the corner on a high chair and watch him while he operated on people. I remember one patient had a growth on the neck that my father had to remove. I sat in the room on a stool in the corner and watched the entire procedure. At that time, I was eleven years old.

Bengkalis is the major island in the area, and he was the only doctor in residence at the hospital. If it was a significant illness, the people in the other islands close to us had to send the patient to Bengkalis for the hospital. In addition, my father was responsible for clinics in the other nearby islands. If I'm not mistaken, he took a weekly trip to the other clinics. All these other places were clinics managed by male nurses. They had some training either in a hospital, or from my dad when he had classes in the hospital. Whenever there was no emergency, my father had a scheduled morning class to train the personnel.

I also remember that there was a *kempeitai*, a military policeman for the Japanese, who was sick and treated by my dad. I think his family was originally from Taiwan. I was a young girl at the time, but I remember that the man told my dad that the Japanese planned to kill all the Dutch-educated people, including my dad and mom. And so my dad arranged everything for the children in case this might happen. As it turned out, it actually didn't happen because the list of those who were to be killed was lost. I heard they lost the list somewhere in central Sumatra, I don't know which city. Then the Japanese didn't have the new list ready when the bomb was dropped in Hiroshima and Japan had to surrender. We heard later on that after the Japanese surrendered, the Chinese in Bengkalis caught this man, tortured him, and took him to the Chinese cemetery. He died after being tortured there. I guess the Chinese wanted to take revenge on him because of what the Japanese did to the Chinese, the torture and killing of the Chinese in Bengkalis.

5   Bukit Batu

When I finished fifth grade in 1944, I graduated from the *Sekolah Sambungan*. So, that was the end of elementary school for me as the school only went up to the fifth grade. Then, I went to stay in the plantation with my family in Bukit Batu. Before that time, I would just vacation there, but after fifth grade, I lived there the entire year. I didn't go to sixth grade because of the war. So on my twelfth birthday, I was not in school anymore. Bukit Batu is on the island of Sumatra across from the island of Bengkalis. You have to go there by boat because it is across the straits. We got there by a *perahu*, a boat, to cross the straits.

We went to Bukit Batu because my mother was there, and she was running a plantation. I think she bought land with a rubber plantation first, and then she bought more land to add to the plantation. On the land, we planted rice on dry rice fields. And then later on, we planted fruit trees, tropical fruits like papaya, *rambutan* [lychee], some mango trees, jackfruit trees. Following that, she bought a sago palm tree area. We planted vegetables to eat and sell too. My mother kept buying land and expanding. She was very enterprising. She put her heart into the plantation and that's how she took care of the family. I stayed about a year in Bukit Batu.

Apoel, who was a grade ahead of me, was already in the plantation with my mom because he had finished fifth grade. Apoel was working with her, doing whatever work had to be done with the three Chinese teenagers who stayed with my family there. Their families knew my dad, that's how they asked my dad to give their boys something to do so their boys wouldn't be conscripted by the Japanese. The Chinese boys were very nice boys from prosperous, well-to-do families. I assume they were sons in merchant families. These boys were knowledgeable and adventurous. They knew how to sail, they knew how to work the land, and they knew how to do business. The Chinese boys stayed with us in Bukit Batu in the house, and they helped my mother with whatever she needed, like planting and harvesting. They also took some of our crops like vegetables and hot peppers, and maybe some fruits and tomatoes as well to sell in Singapore. I remember the hot peppers because I had to pick hot peppers for them while I was there in Bukit Batu. They went by a regular sailboat, maybe it was about five yards long, to cross the Straits of Malacca. If there was wind, they could get there in perhaps less than one day. If there was no wind, they would have to row the boat and it would take longer. There were four of them who would go, including my brother Apoel. They would sell the vegetables, and then they would come back with the money and produce or other goods that we needed in the plantation to give to my mother. Apoel was young, he was only thirteen, fourteen years old, but he was tall for his age. They were all good friends.

Apoel had all this training with his Chinese friends and learned a lot from them, not just sailing, but hunting too. The boys would hunt wild boar with our dogs. We had four dogs at that time. They would go out into the woods and the dogs would bark when they saw or smelled the wild boar. The four of them would kill the wild boar with spears, they didn't have a gun. And that's how we had meat. Some of the meat would be cooked and preserved in oil. My mother would keep the meat in big petroleum cans. This was wartime, so they used whatever containers they had. Then we had meat all year round.

At that time we had a Chinese cook, Kwan Sui. Kwan Sui would get river turtles and snakes, and he would cook them, monkey, squirrels, at that time whatever moves, Kwan Sui would cook it. And my brother would eat all of these kinds of animals in the kitchen. I tasted the turtle because it's from the river, but I didn't want to taste the monkey, snake, or the squirrel. Apoel though would taste everything. Apoel was adventurous: he liked to go places, he liked many kinds of people, and he tried different things. Also, he was able to do more of these things because he was a boy and he had different chores than me. His Chinese friends were his buddies, and they did everything together.

In Bukit Batu, I was the babysitter. My sister Demak was born in 1943. I had to watch my sister Demak and bathe her in the afternoon. In the afternoon, I could take her out and do things because she was in a sling, so sometimes I went fishing. There was a small stream in front of the house and I liked fishing. Once in a while, I caught shrimp. I went with another boy who was a friend, a younger boy, the son of one of the staff. I followed him and learned how to set fish traps in the afternoon by using a basket, how to check the traps in the following morning, and how to collect the fish. I also went rowing in the river. This was a real change in my life. I didn't have school for one year, and I was responsible for taking care of Demak in the afternoon. I had to do sewing too. I was learning elementary sewing, so I sewed sheets for my sister, and pillow-cases, as well as a long pillow, a *guling*, for my sister. I also did special embroidery. The Dutch word for this embroidery is *open naaiwerk*, you take the thread out, and you make patterns in between the open spaces. So after I sewed her pillowcase and her *guling*, I would embroider them as well.

Since we were on an estate, I was expected to help in all areas of the plantation. For example, we had a small grocery store for everybody there. I helped to serve customers when I only was eleven or twelve years old, getting things for them like rice and sugar. I would weigh and measure foodstuffs like rice, sugar, flour, and also frying oils. Also, I learned how to harvest red pepper, cassava, and sweet potatoes, and other vegetables which they took to sell in Singapore. When the women were processing the *padi* [uncooked rice with husk], I followed them too. I learned how to process dry *padi*, and to use a mill to separate the husk from the kernel. There always were many workers performing tasks, and I watched and learned from them. I kept myself busy that way. Whatever, they do, I follow and learn. There were lots of different jobs to do for the men and women. They were Javanese laborers that the Dutch brought in to Sumatra.

Then in August 1945 after the bomb, Japan was defeated and surrendered. It was my parents who told me that the Japanese had surrendered. My dad usually didn't talk politics to me because I was only twelve years. My parents tried to shelter Apoel and me from the war and other politics. I don't have a lot of memories about when the war ended, but it was August and I know that I had been out of school for one year and was twelve years old. Now we had a newly proclaimed republic with Sukarno as president and Hatta as vice-president.

At that time, my dad told me that both Apoel and I would have to go to Pearaja, Tarutung, to attend junior high. They didn't have that level of school in Bengkalis, so my dad suggested that we go to Tarutung because he knew that they would have schools there. If we went there, we also would be with family as that was my dad's hometown. My grandmother was there and the family house was there.

6   Pearaja

So in 1945, my mother took my brother Apoel and me to Pearaja, my dad's home in Tarutung. First we went by boat to Pekanbaru, and then by bus through Bukittingi and then past Padangsidempuan, to Pearaja, Tarutung. It took us three days and nights to get there. We spent one night at Bukittingi at the house of my father's colleague.

In Pearaja, Apoel and I attended the junior high, *Sekolah Menengah Pertama*, which was located next to the church in Pearaja. The school was later moved to Sigompulon. It was the first middle school. My mother took us there and enrolled us, then she went back to Bengkalis as she had to manage the plantation. Although Apoel and I only had finished fifth grade, they admitted us to the first year of junior high. I was so glad I could go back to school. I learned all of the regular subjects, as well as Batak as a subject in school. Of course, everyone spoke Batak in the community. That first year, Apoel stayed in Tarutung with me. But then he asked to be moved to Siantar, and he attended school there. I never asked him why he wanted to go to Siantar. But I think Apoel was used to the city, and there were more things to do in the big city of Siantar than in Tarutung.

I stayed with my grandmother in Tarutung. She had a stroke many years back and didn't even recognize me or know who I was part of the time. I washed her clothes and sometimes, once in a while, I cooked for her. Most of the time, my grandmother usually went down to eat her meals at her younger son's house, which was located on the way to the street down below our house.

I remember that when my parents were in Kisaran, they took into the household an orphan boy named Kasirin of Javanese descent. My mother took

Kasirin to Tarutung when he was about eight or nine years old. He was younger than me. He attended the school in Pearaja, and was very ambitious, and
studious. He worked really hard and finished all six grades in three years and
learned how to speak Batak well. He also attended church. Kasirin was very
strong and very industrious and did all kinds of work in the village, including
working in the rice fields. He also went to the market sometimes in my place.
Later, he went back to Kisaran. The last thing I heard from my mother, Kasiran
got married and had ten children. When he came to visit Apoel, who worked
in Kisaran at that time, he called Apoel, Abang [meaning older brother] Apoel.
When my mother returned from the United States, he visited her. He brought
her a chicken and she gave him a bible.

When the Japanese surrendered in 1945, my father was in Siak where he had
been posted. When they proclaimed Indonesian independence, the people in
Siak didn't want to have the old system, the Sultan, and they didn't want to
have any Dutch-trained officials. So my father had to flee Siak. He walked with
two young Batak who helped him to travel all the way to Pearaja, Tarutung. The
young men had been trained as soldiers by the Japanese.

My father was in Tarutung for a few months, and then he looked for a job.
He went to Siantar and Medan and then he heard that there was work on the
east coast of Sumatra in Kisaran. Finally, he found a job at Katarina Hospital
in Kisaran in 1945.[3] It used to be the hospital of the plantation, of the HAPM,
Hollandsche Amerikaans Petroleum Maatschappij [Holland American Oil
Company], which later became Uniroyal. And he stayed there until the Dutch
tried to come back in July of 1947. He was the only doctor in the hospital and
trained medical staff. He lived in a large two-story house up on a hill that was
like a mansion. I went to visit the house in 2015, but it is not there anymore.

The last time I saw my father was during Easter vacation in 1947 on my
final day in Kisaran before I had to go back to school. I think it was in April.
My father, mother, and I and all of the family had tea on the veranda on the
second floor of the house. My father said to me that I should always pursue my education as that was the one thing that no one could take from
me. That was my *senjata hidup*, the most important thing in life [your live-
lihood]. He also said that I should be twenty-five before I got married, because that was when I would be mature, physically as well as mentally. The
man that I chose should not smoke, drink, or gamble. And then he turned to
my sister Demak who was at that time three-and-a-half years old. He said to

---

3   James W. Gould refers to the Catherina Hospital, which opened in 1913, in James W. Gould,
    Americans in Sumatra (Leiden: Martinus Nijhoff, 1961), 89.

me, "This sister of yours is not going to wait until she is twenty-five". She was very pretty. I think my father might have had a feeling that this would be our last meeting. Before that conversation, my parents never really had talked to me about what I should do with my life in that way. And my dad never had talked about marriage either—the first time was in our last meeting. I was only fourteen years old at the time. But I knew that my father really thought about us children and wanted all four of his children to get the best education that they could, and be supported in the same way.

In 1947, the Dutch tried to come back to north Sumatra because that's where the former Dutch estates were located, the vast estates with rubber, tea, coffee, palm oil, cocoa, and oil. The hospital where he worked was the HAPM, so there were many Dutch and American estates around there. With the Dutch trying to retake Indonesia, there were many Indonesian nationalist forces protecting the battlefield. But there were only three doctors in the Medan area at that time. So my father and the other two doctors took turns going to the front and treating the wounded Indonesians, the Indonesian Republic soldiers in the battlefield. On my father's last trip, he had been giving medical care to soldiers on the battlefield. My father, a nurse, and a driver were on their way home from the front in a wagon marked with a red cross on top to show it was a medical vehicle. When they reached Tebing Tinggi, my father's vehicle was shot at the gate of the front entrance of Tebing Tinggi's hospital, and he was wounded in his right thigh. His nurse and driver were killed. Dutch forces that were advancing from Medan found my father still alive, but he had lost too much blood to be saved. They didn't have blood transfusions at that time. They tried to rush him back to the Tanjung Morawa hospital, but before he got there, my father passed away. He was buried behind the hospital. The hospital was named for him afterwards, it had been one of the hospitals that he oversaw.

My mom was in Siantar at that time with Apoel, on her way to Tarutung because I was going to be confirmed in the Pearaja church in Tarutung. But she was not able to go to Tarutung because of the Dutch invasion. So the doctor that treated my dad found her after a week and sent someone to tell her, because he had news that she was there. He brought her my father's wedding ring, his watch, his pen, and his doctor's pin, and notified her about the way her husband had passed away and where they buried him. My youngest brother Bistok didn't even get a chance to know our dad because he was born a few months before our father's death. My brother Bistok was born in Kisaran, in April 1947. Not long after that, my dad was killed by the Dutch in July.

My mother wrote me a letter about what had happened. I could see that tear drops had been flowing on the letter, and I could see the places where her tears had dried. When I got her letter about my father passing away, I was on my way to go shopping. I was walking to the market after school, when I was stopped by a relative. She asked me to come in the house so her mother could show me my mother's letter. She urged us to go back to Pearaja to tell my grandmother what happened. So, we went. My *ompung* sat on a mat in the front room when she was told about it. My grandmother didn't say a word for maybe about five minutes. The news was repeated. And then my grandmother started grieving, she called out her son's name again and again and said things to him. Then when other people heard the sad news, they came to the house to give their condolences.

Later, in July 1950, they had a burial for my father in *Makam Pahlawan* [heroes' or veterans' cemetery] in Tarutung. His remains were dug out from the grave behind the hospital of Tanjung Morawa where he had been buried by the Dutch in July 1947, and taken to Tangsi Tarutung. I was on vacation in Medan as my school in Jakarta had the month-long intersession vacation, so I was able to be there.

At the time of my father's death, I was alone in Tarutung with my grandmother. I was only fourteen years old. My brother Apoel was in Siantar, and afterwards my mother and he went to Medan. My mother had to find a way to support us children. I heard that a relative got a work order to make nurse uniforms for the hospital in Medan. She was able to have my mother help her sew these uniforms, so my mother could have some income to support four children. Although we are not closely related, they tried to help us. We were very poor and had just enough to eat.

In the meantime, I was still in Pearaja. My mother thought that there would be people around, and she thought they would take care of me. But this didn't really happen. When my dad was alive, there were many who would talk to me, but once he was dead, it was as if I didn't exist anymore. Some people did not acknowledge me, even when I met them on the street. They would not talk to me. They would turn their heads away so they wouldn't have to look at me. The only ones who would come to see me would be two distant uncles from Sumur. So these two would come and walk to the house and talk to me. They knew that my dad had passed away. They would say, "Have you heard from your mom?" I would say, "No." Then they would say, "Well, how are you doing in school?" They would say, "You have to continue in school," and they would try to give good words to me. To see me, they came all the way from their village, and they used their time to give kind, loving words. It meant so much to me.

My maternal grandmother and my mother's siblings also lived nearby. During that time, I would walk four kilometers alone to the village of Simorangkir to visit my maternal grandmother. My grandmother was small and slender, and from the Siahaan clan. My mother looks more like her dad.

My grandmother was sixteen when she got married, she was a teenager, and then she had eleven children. The eldest was my mother, she was born 1911, and the youngest was my Tulang [Uncle] Tagor, he was born 1937.

My maternal grandmother took care of the family and the home in Simorangkir. Before that, they lived in central Tarutung, but she moved back to the village after my grandfather died. She cooked, went to the market, and raised the three youngest children. My grandmother had to do a lot, especially because they did not have running water and it was kind of hilly. You have to go down to the rice fields to the *pancur* [walled water source] to get it. Then, she had to carry the water back on her head for cooking and washing dishes. My grandmother cooked rice with whatever fish and vegetables she had, using firewood and building a fire. I never saw her working in the rice fields, but she had rice fields too and helped there as well. Even after they harvested the rice, they made the field into a pond and raised fish for sale. And all other times, she was weaving too. She wove the *ulos* [woven ceremonial Toba Batak cloth], and once a week on Saturday mornings, she walked to and from the market and would sell the *ulos*. So that's how she had the money to buy meat, oil, salt, and other necessities. And she learned a lot of things by watching people. That was how she knew macramé and sewing, and I think she also painted silk. Whatever people were doing around her, she copied, and learned by observing and doing. She didn't have a formal education and she didn't talk a lot. She was a quiet person. But she was very industrious, hard-working, and smart.

My maternal grandmother in Simorangkir also was very loving and caring. She took care of eleven children. If she saw that something needed to be done, she did it. And she was loving to me too. She knew what I needed. For example, sometimes I needed to take a bath in the *pancur* among the rice fields. Everyone from the village used it. It was a big room, a walled bathing place. Water flowed down continuously from the mountain and came out in a pipe in an enclosed area. There was no running water, so they had to get all the water from the *pancur*: drinking water, cooking water, washing and bathing water. And they carried the water from there to their house for cooking and cleaning. So everyone does everything there. People wash their clothing, and people also bathe. One side was for the men and the other side was for the women. The whole family, adults and children, everyone goes there to take a shower. Usually the women, they have a sarong while they bathe, so you don't see their bodies, and their chest is covered. And that's how they take a shower. So I told my grandma, "I don't know how to use a sarong while I take a shower." So she was nice enough to take me when it was dark. We had to walk down the hill to the *pancur* in the dark, about one hundred meters.

Once in a while, I walked to Simorangkir in the afternoon after school. At that time of the day, my grandmother usually would be cooking. Then we had supper, and she washed the dishes. I had three uncles in the house at that time. The oldest was two years older than I, Tulang [Uncle] Arifin, then Tulang James, a year younger than I, and thirdly Tulang Tagor, four-and-a-half years younger than I. The next morning, I would get up and I would have breakfast with my uncles. Then we had to walk the four kilometers to school and we would talk to each other. They were very loving, very kind to me.

Saturday afternoons, since I never had any communication from my mom, I would just go to the market with an empty basket. School was only a half day on Saturdays, so I went after school. I would go to the place where my maternal grandmother sat and sold her *ulos*, and some *ulos* of her friends because she helps her friends that way too. I would come to her place and say, "Hello Ompung, how are you today?" And she would say, "Hello, have you heard from your mom." And I would say, "No." And then she would say, "Watch my *ulos*, I will be back in a few minutes." She would leave, and when she came back she would have money for me to do my weekly shopping needs. Usually, I bought salted fish, oil, and a little meat, like half a kilo of beef, then I bought myself a *cendol* [a kind of drink with tapioca droplets in palm sugar and coconut milk] as a treat. Then I walked home. I didn't know how she got the money. She must have borrowed it from someone to give it to me for my groceries. It must have been 100 *rupiahs* [Indonesian currency] to buy all that stuff. After I got back to Medan about six months later and met my mom, I told her how I managed. I told her that every Saturday afternoon I would go to see my grandmother so I would have the money to buy my groceries. My mother was amazed, naturally. I thought I should tell her. That was how I got my weekly salt, oil, and a little meat. I didn't have to buy any rice, vegetables, nor did I buy any fruits. Vegetables, we had in the village, like the tapioca leaves were grown in the back of the house. We also had *pisang* [bananas], all the banana trees in the back. I bought just the basics. After the meat was gone, I had salted fish. And I didn't buy sugar. That was how I survived.

While I stayed in Pearaja, I learned a lot about the Batak culture. My grandmother had someone put up a loom in the house, in the front room. If you entered the house, it was on the left side. My grandmother wanted me to learn how to weave *ulos*. I was in junior high and in school full-time, so I wasn't able to do much weaving. But I did weave two *ulos*. The first one was all blank, all white. The second one had stripes. I enjoyed weaving, I always welcomed learning something new. After school, I would sit there and weave. I think my teacher must have been one of those ladies from the village who knew how to weave.

It was all arranged for me and I'm sure my mom paid for all of that. Because you have to pay for the supplies for them to teach you.

I started to learn things about Batak culture by observing. No one really told me what was going on. They were all busy. But as a little girl and then as a young teenager when I lived there, I often was present at the ceremonies. If there was a family wedding, naturally I was there with my mother or another family member. Over there, people would just say "Let's go, let's go," and you go there in a group and after everything, you go home as a group too. Since I was in school, I wasn't able to participate a lot. It was only after school and early evening that I accompanied others from the family. If I happened to be there, I would follow them and attend the ceremony. Usually I went with the daughter-in-law of my uncle, the one whose house was close by in the back of the house. Sometimes we would walk to another village, if we needed to be at a family ceremony. There was no flashlight, so you walked together, holding hands in the dark.

And as close family or a daughter of the clan, you could not just observe, but you have to work and wash dishes and do whatever had to be done. I was trained always to help, especially if no one else was doing so. If there were not enough older people, they recruited the younger generation. During my uncle's funeral at the house nearby, for example, I stayed there and served coffee. They used firewood to heat the water, and I helped to boil water in the kitchen and give out coffee. There were two of us first, but the other girl left by midnight. I continued boiling water and serving coffee. The casket was in the house, so everyone had gathered there, and a few stayed till morning. Someone needed to be there to help, and I was the one who stayed. As a daughter of the clan, or the Tobing family, before I got married, I'm observing all of the customs and traditions. When you are not married though, you are not really counted in the *marga*, in the clan. But once you are married, you are considered part of the *marga*.

Even though my mother was in another city, I knew that I was in my mother's thoughts. My mother thought of her children and looked for possibilities. She had to figure out how to educate us. My mother was only an elementary school teacher at that time, so she didn't earn much. She had to be very enterprising because she knew that she was a single parent. So my mother went to the provincial office of education to ask for a scholarship for my brother Apoel. They said they didn't have one available for my brother, but they had a scholarship for her daughter to go to the home economics teacher training school. When my mom came home, she told me that she had accepted the scholarship for me and that it was a good opportunity for me to become a teacher. That way, I would be taken care of and have a future profession, and she could support my brother to attend the high school (AMS, *Algemene Middelbare School*) in Malang, Java.

I didn't say a thing when she told me that this was the best option for me. Later, I cried in private. I had finished junior high school, the IMS, *Inlandsche Middelbare School*. That was the four-year junior high at that time.[4] Actually, I already had applied to a senior high school, the VHO, *Voorbereidend Hoger Onderwijs School*. I wanted to go to the VHO in order to go to medical school. They had a medical school in Medan, North Sumatra University, Universitas Sumatra Utara, for the northern province. In fact, three of my classmates from junior high later became doctors. Once my mother told me about the scholarship though, I didn't say a thing. I didn't tell her of my ambitions for medical school because I knew that she had to give my brother, as the oldest, the first choice. She wanted him to continue. I am sure that she thought that he would go into medicine. So my dad was gone, and so were my dreams. I had to adjust as the second child and the daughter. My brother had to be given preference. And I knew that my mother also was working very hard. My mother was trying to get a better job so she could support the family. So my mother had to study in order to become a high school teacher, and go through all of her exams and pass them. She taught in the mornings, and she had to study in the evenings. She was always busy. My mother knew Dutch, but then she also had to learn English to be able to be qualified to teach in senior high school, so she took the *BI Inggeris* course for the English language. Her first teachers in English were a British lady and a Dutch lady.

7   Jakarta

And so I went to Jakarta to study at the Opleiding School voor Vak Onderwijzeressen (OSVO), the teachers' training school for home economics. Before my seventeenth birthday in August 1949, I left on a steamship from Belawan, the harbor of Medan, which is the capitol of North Sumatra Province. It took us about two days to get to Jakarta's harbor, which is Tanjung Priok.

I attended the OSVO for three years, 1949–1952. The school was there at least twenty years, since maybe the early 20th century. I knew that there were generations of teachers before us because my teachers were all graduates of the school. After students finished at the OSVO, they continued their education to get their certificates to teach in a teachers' training school. I was at the OSVO

---

4 Now, the school is three years.

during the fight for independence from 1945 to 1949. The Revolution didn't really affect me though because I already was in school.

The school had about a hundred students from all over Indonesia. My class consisted of three Dutch nuns, maybe around ten Chinese Indonesians, some Indos [Dutch Indonesians], and about eight native Indonesians.

I stayed in the school's dormitory. The other girls were all nice and also older than me. I was the youngest of the group in the dorm, and they called me "Baby." The one called "Baby" before me was also a daughter of a doctor from Java and seventeen years old. So I took over her title. They told me, "It was her and now it is you!" It so happened there was another Batak girl whose mother was a Tobing too. She was a distant relative.

Every morning, we had to get up at six o'clock or earlier because there were not enough bathrooms for all the students. Many were Muslims so they prayed before sunrise. And then we had chores. For example, one chore was to be in a group of four to six people and slice bread, or prepare breakfast for about a hundred students. I think our breakfast was maybe at 6:30 AM. At 7:30 AM, school started. We had our own clothing as we didn't wear uniforms for this school.

In the beginning, we had to take transportation to get to the school because the school was not near the dormitory in Pegangsaan Timur. But after six months, we moved to a complex where the dorm was inside the compound with the classrooms. It was located near Pasar Baru, that is in the city near restaurants and a movie theater. The Schouwburg, a performing arts center where they had shows and music, was right across the street from us. Nearby, there also was the main post office, a cathedral, a Catholic girls' school, and a complex for the religious clergy, including a convent. My two classmates who were nuns stayed there. It was a nice area. The third classmate who was a nun commuted from Bogor.

The medium of instruction was Dutch at that time. I had come from the IMS where the medium of instruction was Indonesian. But luckily, I also had four years of elementary school during the Dutch colonial period with the Dutch language used for teaching. I had to compete with people much more advanced than me who had graduated from Dutch schools. But I managed, somehow. I didn't have any difficulties.

It was a three-year training program. The first six months of the program, they call it *Voorklas*, that is like the introductory class. We had to learn all of the subjects, like cooking, sewing, washing, and ironing. And then we had the theory for these skills as well. We had to learn about textiles, how to clean utensils and what you use for the floor. And the same with the washing, we had to learn about soap and the other things that were needed to do all of the work. We also had to study childcare, psychology, pedagogy, and the Indonesian language. My favorite subject was chemistry because it was the only subject in science.

After that, we had to choose one of two tracks, sewing and cooking. I knew how to sew already. At age fourteen, I had made a comment about a dress my mom had sewed me, and she said after that, "You have to do it yourself. From now on, you have to sew your own dresses." So she sent me to a course and I had to sew all of my dresses. As it turned out, sewing was fun for me. But I had never really cooked by myself. Before, we had a cook, and my mother was the one who prepared special dishes for parties or special days, like on Sundays or holidays. So my mother advised me to take the cooking track, which is what I chose.

The cooking track had two kinds of cooking, European and Asian. We had to learn all about food and its benefits, such as nutrition. I liked the theory, but the practice was a different story! The European cooking was Dutch and French cooking. So you learned how to make steak, how to make gravy, how to make two kinds of *croquettes* [patties usually with meat and vegetables], the *ragout* [seasoned meat dish with vegetables], and the potato. For Asian food, you had Indonesian and Chinese dishes. And we had different kinds of teachers. The teacher for European food was a Dutch lady, *Mevrouw* [Mrs.] Guillaume. I knew her well. She always pulled my two braids because I was very slow in the beginning, and she would tease me. In Asian cooking, we had two teachers, an Indonesian Chinese teacher *Juffrouw* [term of address for teacher] Tio and also *Ibu* [term of address for teacher] Dee.

When I had my final exam in cooking, we had to demonstrate our skills for the teachers. We had our own table with all of the ingredients, in front of the stove. It so happened that a good friend of mine who was two years my junior, was helping to assist me. As part of my test, I had to make fried wonton. To do so, we had to make the skin. You have to roll the dough of the wonton into the skin. And when it was almost finished, I was in trouble. The last part of the dough was already hard and tough because I had to add a little flour to roll it along. I didn't know what to do with it! So my friend put it in her pocket and went out to throw it away. I was afraid because the examiners were very strict: they held the wonton skin to the light to check for mistakes. At that time, I was nervous that I might fail my grade because I wasn't used to cooking. Luckily, I got a passing grade.

During my last year at OSVO in 1952, they switched the language of instruction from Dutch to Indonesian. For me, it was not difficult because I had studied Malay in Bengkalis, which later became Indonesian. But those students who were in a Dutch school before had a really hard time switching languages. The last six months is when we learned about teaching, and we had to do so in

Indonesian. My three classmates who were nuns had to drop out because of the language change, especially as they needed to be able to teach in Indonesian.

Looking back, the OSVO and my three years in Jakarta were the best time in my schooling. Since I was the youngest of the students in the dorm, I stayed in the dorm, and the other girls looked out for me. They always asked me whether I would like to go and accompany them to learn new activities. One activity was Balinese dancing. At that time there was no television, but there was a radio center where they had training for Balinese dancing. I think the course was in the afternoon, 4:00 to 5:00 PM. I was the one who had no training in dance, so I had a hard time trying to follow the instructor. This also was my first time to learn Balinese dancing, which has precise, specific hand and leg movements in time to the music. Later, I tried another kind of dancing in the evening, ballroom dancing, I think maybe from 7:00 to 8:00 PM. I went with some friends from the dorm. We walked to the class as a group, and then walked back home. This also was my first time learning these kinds of steps and this kind of dancing. In the beginning the instructor would show you how to hold your hands, and the steps you needed to do with music. Then we would partner with the other girls.

During that time, I also attended a course by myself in machine embroidery which meant using a sewing machine. I had to go to the place by myself by bus for the class, which was once a week, 3:00 to 5:00 PM. I thought it would be a good skill for when I returned home after graduation and started working, or I could even teach it. I liked sewing and learning additional techniques so I thought it could give me more expert, professional skills. We made samples, and then we also learned how to make machine-embroidered flowers. I practiced one pattern of flowers with leaves.

When I went to the OSVO, it was the first time I was on my own and not with family. My brother Apoel would come on weekends to visit me at the dorm. Apoel was a people's person. The girls used to love him. Whenever he came to my dorm in Jakarta, the girls would say, "Please introduce me to your brother." Apoel would invite them out, and he would socialize with them. He was very outgoing, charming, courteous, and gallant. We had been taught all of these courtesies and everything when we were growing up by our parents, especially the Western-style formal manners. If there was a door, he immediately would open the door for the women.

Our OSVO dorm had a gathering of students at least one weekend a month where people could dance. We would invite students from a dorm next to ours that belonged to the University of Indonesia. We were neighbors for the first year that I was there before the move to Pasar Baru. Even though I had learned some ballroom dancing, I never really participated in dancing on a social level.

I was quite shy. After all, I only was sixteen or seventeen years old. I would leave to do some reading.

I had male friends too. There were former classmates who would come to visit me on their way to and from Java. At the dorm, if we had visitors, we stayed in the living room. Some of them invited me out, but I made many excuses to avoid dating them. I never really went out except in groups, even if my male friends tried to take me out alone. I did correspond with a few male friends, and there was one friend to whom I was particularly close. But I was careful because my mother told me that it was better not to go out with one person, but instead to go out in a group.

I knew that I always had to be careful. If I had to go out in the evenings, I always biked fast because I didn't want anyone to follow me. Or if there was someone following me, I would pretend to visit a family, I would go into the house and say hello to the family. I had to take care and watch out, to be guarded and vigilant, because I was a young woman alone in the city. I remember that before during the wartime, a drunk Japanese soldier chased me once.

When I was in Jakarta, I also attended church on Sundays. Sometimes I went by myself, or sometimes I went with friends. It would take me fifteen or twenty minutes to go there by bike. There was a Batak church, the HKBP church in Gang [Lane] Kernolong where the whole service was given in Batak. I would see all the Bataks, and some family and friends too. Sometimes I also visited family after church, like I would visit my cousin in Jalan [Street] Baladewa, or my uncle in Jalan Surabaya, or my cousin in Gang Kernolong.

In 1952, my last year at OSVO, a good friend asked me to go with her to the hospital for a medical check-up. Even though I had an exam the following day, I accompanied her to the hospital. My other friends reminded me that this was the day before the exam, and that everybody in my class was frantically studying. The whole morning was spent waiting for her appointment, going through the examination, and then getting back to the OSVO dorm. But I thought it was more important to accompany my friend and give her support. Decades later, I still meet her when I go to Jakarta.

8 Return to Siantar

After I graduated, I worked three years in Siantar from 1952 to 1955 as a government teacher because of the conditions of my scholarship. My mother was busy at this time, working to support the family. She also was in a special program learning English for a few months in Jogjakarta with the help of government funding. At the time I started being a teacher, there were home economic

FIGURE 56 "Schule in Pematang Siantar" [School in Pematang Siantar] School from the complex where Minar T. Rony taught in Siantar, 1952–1955. AMS DER VEM. ARCHIVES. NUMBER: 203–483

schools all over Indonesia in the big cities. Previously, the Dutch had regular schools and then they had vocational schools for home economics, carpentry and building, business, furniture-making, agriculture, all kinds of schools. They also had schools for nursing. My aunt, the one I stayed with in Siantar, was a graduate of the Dutch midwifery school in Medan, *Sekolah Bidan*.

In the home economics schools, the expectation was that the girls would be introduced to modern ways, up-to-date living. I was required to teach the same subjects I learned in the OSVO at a home economics school for junior high students, seventh to ninth grade students. They found an assignment for me in a Christian school in Siantar, which was on the east coast of Sumatra and closer to home. It was called the SKP Kristen (Christian Home Economics School). The principal was a Dutch woman, a sister of a Dutch minister.

The first day when school started, all the teachers gathered in a large meeting place. They even asked me to give a speech. The school had a set curriculum because after the students graduated, they had to be eligible to continue on to the teachers' training school. We taught our own specialties, which were assigned. I was a graduate of the cooking department from the OSVO, and I taught all of the related subjects: nutrition, setting the table, figuring out a menu, food preparation, housecleaning, everything that has to do with the house, the tools you use. The students came from different backgrounds, some from Siantar, and some from the villages around that area. Some of them were poor and new to the way of life that we were teaching, while others were from educated families so they were already exposed to a Western way of life. The teachers rotated among the classes so I didn't have the same students all the time. I taught maybe about two classes for each grade. Each grade had about fifty to sixty students, and there usually were twenty to thirty students a class.

Teaching was a challenge. The other teachers all were senior to me. I was young, and my colleagues were older and most of them were married women. They were experienced teachers. Even though I had all of the new up-to-date information, this was my first job and I was away from home. I was given a room in the school for my stay there and I had just the basic furniture: a bed, table, a little cupboard, chairs, and a stove.

From 1954 to 1955, I also began teaching in a home economics teachers' training school called SGKP, *Sekolah Guru Kepandaian Puteri*. It was not like the OSVO because the medium of instruction was all in Indonesian. Since I had to switch from Dutch to Indonesian, I had to do further preparation because of the change in language.

Meanwhile, in the evenings, I started studying economics. A course was offered in Siantar to all of the teachers who were interested in more advanced studies, *Kursus BI Ekonomi*, so they could teach in a senior high school. That course was the equivalent of two years of university-level training in economics, and the only one offered in the evenings. I took the course because I remembered what my dad told me during the last time I saw him, "Remember if you study, and have all the knowledge, no one can steal it from you. You can use it for your future. You can be independent, you don't have to depend on anyone. Always study. That is your investment and security."

So, I worked during the day, and then I studied economics through night classes in the evening, 6:30 to 8:30 PM, twice a week. There were three of us from my area who biked there to class. In the class, there were about ten students, maybe three women teachers, and six or seven male teachers. I loved studying economics because it was not home economics. To me, it was a science that I could apply in my life where home economics was something that you used at home. But at the end when I was about to leave in 1955, they had an exam and I failed it. Only one of us passed the exam.

In 1955, before I finished my contract, I applied to continue my training in home economics in a more advanced program in Jakarta. As a graduate of the SKGP Jakarta, I could continue to *Bı Kepandaian Puteri* [two-year course comparable to junior college degree in home economics] and take two years of college-level classes to earn a home economics degree. It would qualify me to teach at the teachers' training school for home economics. I was accepted there, but then my mother again talked me into another path. She wanted me to study economics at the Universitas HKBP Nommensen [HKBP Nommensen University] so I could stay with her and my brother in Medan. My mother said that if I left, my brother might leave too.

Before I wanted to be a doctor, and then I went to the home economics school. And then, when I wanted to continue in home economics in Jakarta, I didn't because my mother asked me not to do so. I thought of my dad. Once the dad is gone, everyone should support each other.

9   Medan

So I attended the Fakultas Ekonomi Universitas HKBP Nommensen [Faculty of Economics, HKBP Nommensen University]. They accepted me because I had attended the *Kursus Bı Ekonomi* in Siantar, and had some background in economics even though I had failed the exam.

During that time, I lived at home with my mother and siblings. My mother was always strong and she worked very hard. Bistok and Demak were children and attended school. My mother gave them attention, but she was working two jobs, mornings and afternoons, and sometimes in the evening too. She taught in the morning, and she taught a second shift of school in the afternoon. My mother also studied to get her certificate for teaching high school education so she could earn more money, and was enrolled in an evening English-language course that was equivalent to two years of university study. I think because we had learned Dutch already, that helped us in learning English as a second Western language.

In addition, my mother became part of the Persatuan Wanita Kristen Indonesia (PWKI) [Indonesian Women's Christian Association]. She was active in the women's group in her church, and they elected her as the chairman of the PWKI Sumatra Utara, Indonesian Christian Women's Association, North Sumatra. On Sundays, she would have all these things going on because they were so busy. The whole family would help her by making phone calls to get people to attend the meetings, circulating agendas or flyers during the meeting, and then cleaning up the flowers and everything else afterwards. After

I left for the United States in August 1958, she also became a state representative to the provincial assembly for a while as a member of the PWKI, belonging to the Indonesian Christian Party, Partai Kristen Indonesia. The acronym is Parkindo. My mother was unusual in getting involved in politics. She was one of the first to get active and be involved. She was a good leader.

As a college student, I was studying and working part-time so I could get some pocket money. I didn't want to have to ask my mother for money to pay for books or whatever was needed to take courses. I did whatever I could to help my mother and the family. As a result, when I went back to Medan, I also taught part-time for my pocket money at the SGKP Katolik [Catholic Home Economics Teachers' Training School]. During that time, I stayed with my family and was given a bedroom by my mother. I also had chores such as the laundry or ironing, and I helped too with anyone who was visiting. We always had to serve and attend to the relatives. Even if it was the middle of the night, we had to make rice and cook supper. If someone is our guest, you have to give up your bed or whatever they needed, especially if they were older, as that was the way we were taught. Whoever needs it more, gets it. At one time, my mother's aunt came from the village so I gave up my bedroom for her use. After she left, I couldn't find my best sweater. I only used a sweater for parties or special occasions. I mentioned it to my mother. Her answer was, "She came from the mountains. It must be very cold there. She must have a better use for it than you."

Demak attended and completed the Methodist English School, so English was her first school language. My mother told me that when she was taking Demak to be enrolled in kindergarten at a Dutch school, Demak said to her, "Please, may I not go to a Dutch school because they killed Papa?" And so, my mother took her to the Methodist English School, where she studied English from kindergarten instead. I used to take her to school on a bike, and then to pick her up. We all had responsibility to do that, whoever was home. She had American teachers from the start, and she went to the school for twelve years.

10   Teacher and Guide

Karl Pelzer, a professor at Yale, and his wife came in early '56, or maybe late '55. My brother Apoel was one of three young students helping Karl Pelzer, and his wife do research in Sumatra. They were recruited from the Fakultas Ekonomi Universitas HKBP Nommensen. Apoel was very polite, very friendly, and soft-spoken. Actually, Apoel helped Mrs. Pelzer more than Mr. Pelzer.

I also went with an American academic couple, a husband and wife, as they were doing research on a Batak village and needed someone to help them with learning the language and assisting in their research, whatever they needed. I think Apoel might have recommended me to them. The couple came to meet me in Medan. They interviewed a few Batak girls who were kind of educated, university students, then they came back to me again and asked me whether I would like to help them do some research in a village. After I thought about it, I decided, "Okay, for a few months," because I had to miss my courses at Nommensen University in order to help them. I was a student at the Fakultas Ekonomi at Nommensen University at the time.

For my work, I would go with the wife in the mornings to certain places to meet the village women. She would practice whatever she learned from me in Batak, such as Batak phrases. Before we left in the morning, we also had maybe an hour of reading, questions and answers, and drilling. In the afternoons, we would attend the *adat* ceremonies, such as weddings. The husband would be there too with us. The three of us would go to different places to attend all the ceremonies. Because the couple were the white people, the Westerners, the Batak looked up to them, and they treated them with deference. They would give the couple good seats, and they would talk to them. My responsibility was to translate and explain things to them, and answer questions like, "What is that?" and "Why do they do that?"

The elder who rented the couple their house knew my mom and the whole family, and knew that I was a descendant of Raja Pontas. At one gathering, he came to me and said, "Everybody know who this girl is?" And then he said, "She is the daughter of Dr. Gerhard Tobing, and the great-granddaughter of Raja Pontas from Pearaja, Tarutung." All the people were surprised because they hadn't known my full background. I was kind of embarrassed. I guess he knew that I would not reveal who I was. Because I thought that if I did, the people in the village would change their attitude to me and I wouldn't get the information that the researchers needed. Whenever people in the village met me, they would ask the Batak question, *"Boru Tobing sian dia do hamu"* ["Tobing daughter from where are you?" It means, "Where are you from?"] And I always answered, "Well my cousin is Patuan Natigor, *anak ni amangtua* [son of an uncle]." That is enough, because they knew that Patuan Natigor was the acting resident of Tapanuli at one time and could place me in relation to him. But I didn't say I was the daughter of Dr. Gerhard Tobing. I didn't want them to know that I was from an educated and middle-class family. The couple knew something about my background, but they didn't know exactly where I was from as I had never really told them. I wanted them to accept me as I was. After that the villagers treated me differently.

I think it is hard for people from outside the village to fully understand Batak culture. Even I, sometimes, had to learn more about Batak culture by looking to others and following them, because I was born and brought up with a different background. I always tried to watch what was going on and try to understand it from the perspective of people in the village.

Then, there was the political turmoil with the PRRI [Pemerintah Revolusioner Republik Indonesia—Revolutionary Government of the Republic of Indonesia]. We ended up evacuating and the couple had to leave many things behind.

11   The United States

Yale University told Professor Pelzer that he could bring one student back with him, and Apoel was chosen and given a scholarship to be a sophomore there. He left for New Haven in '56 by boat via Europe. He sent me two pairs of earrings by mail from Rome when the boat stopped there. At Yale, he met his good friend John "Jack" Larkin. They were in Berkeley College, which is a residential college right next to Sterling Library. Later, when I came in '58, Jack was in the US Army in Germany, and Apoel had a room overlooking the green in front of the library.

Meanwhile, my mother started mentioning that it would be good for her to have a married daughter accompanying her to the *adat* ceremonies so she wouldn't be alone at the ceremonies anymore. And at that time, there was a young Batak man who came and visited me almost every weekend in Medan. It looked like his family was thinking of me as a possible wife for him. This started in 1955 when I was twenty-two years old and already back from Siantar. He came regularly with all kinds of sweets and fruits, including apples and grapes, which must have cost a lot of money at the time. My younger siblings loved the treats. They had a great time, and they welcomed him. He usually visited every weekend, because he had to travel out of town by train to be at work on Monday.

During the same period, Apoel wrote to me to see if a friend of mine could come and work in New Haven because there was a teaching job available. Maybe he was thinking that this person would be someone for him. I wrote back to Apoel and said that the good friends I had were working for the government, and they just could not leave without prior notice. They had to request a leave of at least three months before they could go. And that is when I told him about my situation, that I had a suitor who kept visiting. I wrote him, "Please get me out of here because Mama wants me to get married." Apoel was close to me, and he immediately felt that he had to help me. Apoel talked to Professor Dyen at Yale. As the Indonesian instructor had not asked for a renewal of the annual contract, they had an opening. Professor Dyen interviewed Apoel on my behalf, and accepted me. He gave me money for the ticket from Indonesia, and said I could work as an Indonesian instructor for a year.

I was relieved that I now had an opportunity to leave. I told my mother, "I want to go for a year." But then, the young Batak man wanted us to be engaged before I left, so my mother and I went to her brother-in-law for his advice. Luckily he said, "Let Minar go for one year, and see if this marriage is going to happen."

When it was time for me to leave, my mother naturally had a get-together, a farewell supper for family and friends. The living room was full. And one Ompung Siahaan, a *tulang* of my mom, gave me a special *ulos* with a golden thread. There also were some close family who gave me a large amount of money, which was so generous.

From Medan, I flew to Singapore and stayed overnight in a hotel. And the next day, by propeller plane, we flew to Saigon. We stayed a few hours there, I guess to refuel and to let passengers off and on. Next, we flew on to Manila. When we arrived there, we were bussed around town for sightseeing. And then we went on to Guam, Wake Island, and Honolulu, Hawai'i. And finally, after a change of planes, we made a stop overnight in San Francisco. When I woke up the next morning and looked out the window from my hotel in San Francisco, I saw a highway full of cars moving along in six lanes of traffic. I remember being so amazed by the number of cars that I timed them and counted how many cars passed by per minute. We then went on to Chicago where I had to change planes. There was a young man in Chicago who helped me with my heavy briefcase when we had to catch a connection at O'Hare Airport to Idlewild. He asked me where I was going, and I mentioned that I was traveling to New Haven. And he asked me what I was going to do in New Haven, and I said that I was going to teach a language at Yale. After that, he changed his manner to me and became more formal. We finally arrived in Idlewild Airport in New York, which is now JFK airport. Apoel and another friend, I think it was Sutan Hutagalung, met me at the airport.

When I arrived in the United States, many of the Batak community were in New York City. There were two relatives there to whom I was distantly related. They had worked on a boat from Indonesia, and when they got to America, they jumped ship and stayed in New York City. One relative was in the same generation as my dad. He told me that he had first met me when my family was in Bengkalis, as he was in Bengkalis as a teenager and worked at the *Boswezen* [Dutch Forestry Service] during the Dutch colonial period. After the Sunday Batak church service in Bengkalis, these young men would come to the house to eat and drink. Our house was open on Sundays for the Bataks, including the

FIGURE 57   Apoel Loembantobing at 35 Cave Street, New Haven, ca. 1960
MINAR T. RONY COLLECTION

Batak young single men, and they were always welcome. Batak hospitality was important for my dad. At the time, I was six or seven years old, and although I remember that there were many young men coming to the house, I didn't always know them individually. I am sure that the Batak men who jumped ship went into manual work, dishwashing or cleaning when they arrived in New York City. I knew of another distant relative, a cousin of my mother's cousin, who said he was washing dishes.

I was very glad to be in New Haven with Apoel, even though we did not have much money as students. I would cook in my dorm to save money, and sometimes Apoel and I went out to fast food places. In 1959, we lived on Cave Street together. Sometimes late at night, Apoel used to take me to Jimmie's in West Haven once in a while for an evening treat. In 1960, Jack Larkin also stayed at Cave Street when he was studying for his master's degree. By that time, Apoel had finished both his undergraduate degree and his master's degree. Apoel then was hired by Uniroyal, and they trained him in Naugatuck, Connecticut, I think for six or more months.

Then Apoel went back to Indonesia because Uniroyal sent him back to Kisaran. He had a big house with a nice garden. I am sure it was one of the Dutch former executive's homes. He had promised our mother that he would go back, so he returned to Indonesia. My mother hadn't made me promise to come back as I think we did not know that my future would be here.

I was able to support myself in the United States by teaching Indonesian. In 1960, Professor Dyen was going on sabbatical for a year to Bandung with his family. I think he was going to teach in Bandung. Before he left, I applied to the graduate school of home economics at Cornell. They accepted me into their program, and I was to teach Indonesian at Cornell to support myself. When Professor Dyen heard about the arrangement, he encouraged me to stay another year at Yale to teach Indonesian and work with Professor Hendon. He also suggested "Why don't you study for your master's degree in Southeast Asian Studies here? You can talk to Professor Pelzer." Dr. Pelzer was the director of Southeast Asian Studies then. And that is how Professor Dyen changed my life because I was ready to go to Cornell.

So, I became a graduate student in the Southeast Asian Studies master's program. At Yale, there were professors affiliated with different departments like Professor Paul Mus, who was a visiting scholar, and Professor Douglas Paauw. I took courses related to Southeast Asian Studies. I also studied Vietnamese from Huỳnh Sanh Thông for one year. They didn't count Indonesian as fulfilling a foreign language requirement because it was our national language. Graduate school was challenging, especially because I had learned English as my fourth language. If they asked me to write a paper, my paper was not that great because of my English language writing skills. But if they asked questions, they would pass me because I could explain it to them orally.

I met my husband Kohar when he came in 1960. Apoel told me that there was an Indonesian student living in the International Students' House. One day, I was cooking lunch, and lo and behold, Apoel brought him over and introduced Kohar to me. At that time, Apoel and I rented a house at 35 Cave Street. So that is how we started to get to know each other. Kohar and I were in the Southeast Asian Studies graduate program together, and the two of us took the Vietnamese language class three times a week. Only the two of us were in that Vietnamese class. Kohar also was enrolled in Professor Benda's history class. I think I usually got the same grades as Kohar for my graduate courses. Kohar said, "How did you get those grades? I never see you study." I said, "I guess whatever I read, I retain."

In October 1961, I had bronchitis, so I was in the infirmary on Hillhouse Avenue at Yale. My sister Demak, who was in East Orange, New Jersey, studying at Upsala College, wanted to come and see me one weekend as I was in the infirmary for about a week or so. Since Kohar was visiting me in the infirmary, I asked him to pick up Demak at the railway station. When Demak came, Kohar brought her to visit me. While Kohar was somewhere else, Demak told me an Indonesian saying, "*Berudang dibalik batu.*" Literally, it means a shrimp that is hiding behind a stone or rock, meaning that Kohar had ulterior motives. And I said, "No, that's impossible!" I didn't have any interest in anyone at that time. I was already set on not getting married.

But Kohar kept visiting me. Every Sunday, Kohar would take me to church in his old car to all of the different churches in New Haven. And I thought, "Well, since Kohar is around, maybe I should consider him." He wasn't a smoker, a gambler, or an alcoholic, which was what my dad had told me to think about if I was considering getting married. And Kohar seemed to be nice, as he was taking me to church every Sunday. And I was living here on my own in the United States so I didn't have to face the Batak family and their disapproval for not marrying a Batak. This was my chance at marriage, as I happened to be here, and he happened to be there. Later, Apoel said, "If I had been in New Haven, this would never happen, she would never have married Kohar."

So Kohar proposed. We were poor students and didn't have many resources, but we wanted to get married. When we went to Professor Pelzer's house, we mentioned our plans. Professor Pelzer offered to have the reception at his house, and Professor Dyen said that he would help as well. It so happened that my mother's brother-in-law was studying for his master's in education at SUNY [State University of New York] Oswego. My aunt and my cousin also were with him. Before my mother's letter, I asked my uncle to give me away at the ceremony. He was willing to do it. But then I received a letter from my mother, and she didn't approve of the marriage because Kohar was not Batak. I called my uncle and said, "Well, if you don't want to attend the wedding, Uncle, I will understand it because I just received a letter from Mama." His answer was, "Oh no, your mother wrote me a different letter, and said to make the best of the situation." I was surprised. Later on, I came to understand what happened. She could not approve of the marriage in public because she had to answer to the greater Tobing family. But my mother could speak differently to her brother-in-law. That is the *adat* again. She was a Mrs. Tobing and there was the greater Tobing family to whom she had to answer. I was marrying out to someone who was not a Batak.

Kohar and I got married in the afternoon, and we had the reception at Professor Pelzer's house that evening at supper time. Everybody helped in the ceremony. I invited my friends, and there were many of them, including Batak friends who were studying in SUNY. We had met them all at Cornell in the summer of 1960 as they had orientation there. And there also were the Tobings from New York, and friends from New Haven, and also a few Batak friends in Boston that came. There was a total of eighty people. One of the friends studying in New Haven, a lawyer, was studying international law at Yale Law School. His wife Iertje [Ierce in present-day spelling] lent us their clothing, which is what we wore. She also lent me her *songket* [material with pattern woven with gold and silver thread] and a headdress to use. The headdress was put in by my former teacher at the teachers' training school because they were in New York at the time, Ibu Dee, the mother of Arta Panggabean who later married my brother Bistok and became my sister-in-law. The Indonesian friends who studied at SUNY got together and cooked *gado gado* [salad with peanut sauce], and *satay* [grilled meat skewers] for the whole gathering.

After we got married, we lived near Pegnataro's grocery store in a studio apartment with a bathroom and a kitchen. We had a sofa bed in the main room, and another single bed in the kitchen. I still was working then in April. In May, we got our Master's degrees in Area Studies at Yale. That summer, Kohar worked as a translator, guide, and interpreter for a State Department man, an Indonesian who was a guest and needed an interpreter. First, Kohar took him to Washington, DC. Then Kohar flew to California with him and asked me to visit them in San Francisco. So I joined them for a few days. By then, I already knew I was pregnant as I had found out in July, before I took the trip to California. I told Professor Dyen naturally. At the time, Kohar wanted to travel and not have children.

Harry J. Benda was one of the professors at Yale in Southeast Asian Studies and Kohar's advisor. He taught the history of Indonesia and other classes. And when there was an opening for a Southeast Asian reference librarian at the Library of Congress, Benda recommended Kohar to Mr. Hobbs, the head of the Southern Asia section at the Library of Congress. Kohar started in October 1962 at the Library of Congress, the Southern Asia section of the Orientalia Division of the Reference Department. I think he began as a reference librarian and was trained by Cecil Hobbs. Kohar was a good fit for the job.

I went to visit Kohar in DC in his one-bedroom apartment before the birth of our daughter Fatimah. At that time, a distant cousin's family was there as the husband was working as an official at the Indonesian Embassy, so we visited them. And in fact, when they went back to Indonesia, they left me some of their bamboo furniture and other odds and ends that they wanted to give away. There were other Indonesians in the DC area already. There was one who I think worked for the Voice of America. There was another one, my friend's husband who jumped ship, just like my Batak relatives in New York City, so they must have come around the 1940s, I guess.

FIGURE 58   A. Kohar Rony, Minar T. Rony, and daughters, 1967
MINAR T. RONY COLLECTION

My daughter Fatimah was born in March, and then I still had to finish my annual contract at Yale, which ran until August. Afterwards, I moved permanent-
ly to Washington to join my husband Kohar. He had rented an apartment with
two bedrooms on Fifth Street. I liked Capitol Hill very much. It was nice there
and not very busy at that time. On the weekends, Kohar took us out to the park,
to the memorials, and to the Smithsonian.

Then, our second child Dorothy was born. Two days after she came, my
mother arrived from Indonesia. I was still in the hospital. I had thought of
bringing my mom to the United States to give her a chance to travel in another country. Originally, I thought that she might want to live with us in
Washington, DC. But then I thought that she might get bored staying at home
with me and the two girls, as she was so used to working and being busy all
the time. I called Professor Dyen about whether he needed someone to teach
Indonesian at Yale. Since he did, she was able to begin a one-year position to
teach Indonesian there. We took her up to New Haven and settled her into an
apartment. I think she really liked it. She enjoyed working with students, and
also was active in the Lutheran Church. She kept renewing her contract every
year, and in the end, she taught at Yale for fifteen years. Because she worked so

long in the United States, she was able to get more support, and have enough in her retirement to live comfortably in Indonesia and also travel annually back to visit us. I was glad that I could help my mother in this way.

I started working at the Library of Congress on February 13, 1967. There was an Indonesian cataloguer who had decided to go back for more graduate school at Indiana University. So her section head thought of me because she knew that I had been a teacher before, and would like to go back to work. She asked Kohar to make a phone call to the division office so I could come for an interview. I was interviewed by the Assistant Division Chief, and I was hired. The next Monday, I went through registration and orientation in the Miscellaneous Languages Section, which was for all of the other cataloguers who didn't have a section for their language. I remember we had a Persian cataloguer, three Hebrew cataloguers, three Arabic cataloguers, a Turkish cataloguer, and me. The Library of Congress was a big place then with about 5,000 employees. It was a federal agency located on Capitol Hill, near the US Senate, the House of Representatives, and the Supreme Court. It also was close to Union Station and the Smithsonian.

FIGURE 59   Fatimah Tobing Rony and Dorothy B. Fujita-Rony at American
University, Washington, D.C., 1966
MINAR T. RONY COLLECTION

FIGURE 60
Minar T. Rony and
daughters, ca. 1969
MINAR T. RONY
COLLECTION

FIGURE 61
H.L. Tobing and
granddaughters,
ca. 1969
MINAR T. RONY
COLLECTION

I had to learn searching and cataloguing since my background was not in library science. Luckily, the Library of Congress offered courses in cataloguing. My teacher, Ms. Scott, used to teach library science at a university as a professor, and I attended a class with her twice a week for one month. Ms. Scott taught us all of the rules of cataloguing. At that time, we still had to write and make cards for the card catalogue, because the cards were all in drawers. One of the senior cataloguers also trained us in searching for books every morning. We had sessions where he explained different processes, such as whether an author's name was a personal name or a corporate one. Afterwards, we had to go to the card catalogue and search for the books he assigned us.

In August of that year, I was joined by another Indonesian cataloguer, Oemi Schmidgall-Tellings, who became one of my best friends. She came from Indonesia with her husband Ed after he retired. He used to work for the American Embassy in Jakarta, and he also compiled a dictionary. Oemi used to catalogue in the Jakarta Library of Congress office. But when she was sent to the Division office of the Library of Congress office in Washington, DC, the Division chief told her that he did not have a job for her because they had just hired an Indonesian cataloguer a few months earlier, which was me. But then, they asked her to be a Dutch cataloguer. I think her section was called the German Languages section. After a week or so, they sent her to our section, and I had to train her in whatever I knew. About a year or two later, my good friend Sameha Kotb, I call her Sami, joined the Library of Congress to work in the Middle Eastern Languages Section.

I began as a descriptive cataloguer. Later on, they trained me to be a serial cataloguer and then as a subject cataloguer so I could complete the catalogue cards. Library of Congress cards are used all over the world. I would look for subjects for cataloguing books by going through and checking the contents, and then I would go to the book's index and get more subjects through that. . After assigning subject headings, I would input them into the computer. I catalogued books and publications in Indonesian and English from Indonesia, Malaysia, Singapore, the Sultanate of Brunei, depending on whatever unprocessed books needed cataloguing. Sometimes I also worked on books from the Philippines, Vietnam, and other parts of Southeast Asia. I liked my work, descriptive and subject cataloguing, because that was a chance for me to read books and analyze them for their content, and to use my specific knowledge and expertise. I got to read the books that came from Indonesia, and sometimes I got a book about the Batak, or an author who used to be my friend at school, or an acquaintance. And sometimes I would find books from Indonesia that mentioned my family.

FIGURE 62
A. Kohar Rony in Annapolis,
Maryland, ca. 1977
MINAR T. RONY COLLECTION

So that is how I ended up living so long in the Washington, DC, area. Kohar and I had many happy years at the Library of Congress. Eventually, Kohar retired in 2002, and I retired in 2004. After that, we moved to Los Angeles as our daughters were in Southern California. First we lived in Silver Lake, and then in 2011, we made our home in Hollenbeck Palms, a retirement community near downtown Los Angeles. Kohar passed away in 2014, and I continue to live in our apartment. I miss him very much, but all the people and staff at Hollenbeck are very nice and friendly. I am happy here and have many good friends.

I like my apartment a lot, and in it I have so many things that remind me of different parts of my life: beer mugs that represent the good times with my dad, a nice picture of my husband Kohar where he is smiling and happy, some Delft china that brings back memories of my childhood (I have purchased many of these items in our Hollenbeck community bazaar in the last few years), and our family clock which I originally bought in the United States because it looked like the clock we had when I was a little girl. I also have a betel nut set that I brought from a trip to Indonesia many years ago because it reminds me of my grandmother, who used to chew betel nut in the morning. I even have macramé pillows that my mother made when she was a teacher in New Haven. All of these things help me to think about the different parts of my life. A lot of them have meaning for me because they tell a story that I want to remember. For example, one time my sister Demak was visiting me with other family when we were still on the east coast, and we took a trip to the Smithsonian Institution. We were just about to leave the museum, and Demak said, "Wait a minute, *Kak*" [short for "Kakak" or "big sister"]. When Demak came back, she brought me a souvenir mug that she bought for me to recall our time together. When I look at the mug, I think of Demak and her thoughtfulness. It is really important to me to remember all of the blessings that I have received in my life, and all of the people that I love, even if some of them are no longer with me.

In the last few years, I also have been fortunate enough to travel to both Indonesia and the Netherlands with my family. When my mother still traveled back and forth from Indonesia to the United States, I always used to accompany her so that she would have a companion. Now I go with my daughter to Indonesia as well as the Netherlands, so I can visit family and remember the past. A few years ago, my daughter started helping me write down stories that I remembered about my father, and also assisted me in organizing the family photographs. After that, we traveled to Indonesia to care for my mother's papers and to find out more about my dad. We also have gone to the Netherlands twice and Germany once to research the family history for the younger generations. I especially want to make sure that my dad is remembered as I am the only one now who really remembers him. For me, it is crucial that people not be forgotten, and that my grandchildren know about the past and what it means to be Toba Batak. Whenever I am able to be with the oldest relatives now, I always ask them questions about the past and take notes about the family history. It is not so much for me as for the younger people, because I think it is important for them to know where they came from, and to learn about all the things that we have gone through as a family. I am so glad that I have been able to share these trips with my daughter, my brother Bistok, and my sister-in-law Arta. In the past two years, we also have taken my grandson Theodore to Indonesia to accompany us on these trips. The past is such a precious legacy.

Although I originally was to stay only a year, I have now been in the United States for more than six decades. When I look back and think about all of the different things I have seen and done in my lifetime, I am grateful for all of the blessings I have received.

Conclusion
The Urgency of Time

It is August 2019. My family is visiting the Veterans' Cemetery in Tarutung, which is where my grandfather is buried. Every time we return to Pearaja, we go to see the family graves, to make sure they are cared for, and to remember the ancestors with flowers from the garden. We make our prayers and ask for blessings from the spirits. Part of the importance of these trips is that we do so as an intergenerational group—with Rony being the oldest and my son the youngest—so the significance of that moment can be experienced and remembered across the generations. As we travel to these sites and visit the graves, we share stories with each other about the past. I know that my older relatives are glad that my son is with us, and that he also helps to care for the ancestors' graves by cleaning around the tombstones. I recognize that this is important to them because there is an implied promise that he will remember this legacy. We understand that visiting the memorials not only is about commemorating past relatives, but also is about taking the knowledge of these ancestors' lives into the future. Maintaining this spiritual connection to our ancestors is a foundational part of the Toba Batak culture, and dates back to before the time when the colonizers arrived.

It is different for me this time to be here, the third year in a row, on this journey of return and discovery. Unlike other relatives, I am not a traveler, and rarely go abroad. With each trip though, the path becomes more familiar. Using Pearaja as a base, we have visited the surrounding locations, including Bakara, where Rony remembers being taken by her mother to visit Si Singamangaraja's village when she was a little girl; Lintong Nihuta, where the family fled during World War II; Sigompulon, where she and other family members have gone to school, as well as nearby family sites such as my maternal family's village of Simorangkir; the village where Rony was a cultural informant to visiting American scholars in the 1950s; and even to Porsea, which is where the German Lutheran missionary Nommensen is buried.

At the family home, we gather in the dining room around the table, my family speaking in a combination of English, Batak, and Indonesian, and occasionally Dutch as well. Being here is like traveling through time, as we share different memories about family over the past several decades. With these stories, we remember the ancestors and make sense of the past, reconciling what has gone on before with our present realities. All of us have different memories of this site. Rony has the most extensive recollections, reaching back to the 1930s when she was a young girl, and then again to World War II and the Japanese Occupation, as can be seen in her autobiographical narrative. For me, sitting at the table reminds me of the many conversations that I had with my grandmother in 1985, and my extended stay in the village as a young woman.

In many ways, as I near the completion of this book, we have come full circle. The project originally began in Los Angeles because Rony, the only immediate family member left with direct memories of her father, wanted to write down stories of the past so that her father would be remembered. We had many resources at our disposal, including the ability to travel to Southeast Asia, Rony's knowledge of many languages and her expansive memory, and close relatives who would help us with our project.

But we no longer have the luxury of one important factor that we had in the past: time.

Rony has an indomitable spirit, but the physical reality of being in her late eighties is making it more difficult for her to take the long trips overseas. We know that each trip might be her last. But we decide that as long as we can do so, I would take my mother on these world trips, as traveling and preserving family history and collective memory is what she wanted to do the most.

Women's memorykeeping, I have argued, is a process of gendered labor. What differentiates women's memorykeeping from other forms of knowledge preservation is the awareness of the differential hierarchies due to gender which shape the kinds of memories that are made and how they are preserved. These issues are especially important for Rony because, as a daughter, she will not inherit the family land or the home back in her father's village, owing to the patrilineality of Toba Batak culture. For myself, as the daughter of a daughter, this line of inheritance is even more tenuous. In my mind, however, the stories are the real legacy. Today, when I go to Los Angeles to help my mother with administrative and household tasks, or when we are taking a long drive in the car, we tell stories constantly as part of our entertainment and socializing with each other. It is a way of having the family with us, even though we are far apart in distance or time.

The book explores these processes through its six chapters. In Chapter 1, I articulated the interimperial frame which propels my family history, and gave historical context to Rony and Tobing's migration to the United States during the Cold War. In Chapter 2, I argued about the multiple hierarchies which placed women in a secondary position, and how memorykeeping emerges as a political strategy of inheritance, integration, and knowledge. In the following two chapters, Chapters 3 and 4, I examined further the processes of telling and representing this history, particularly through stories and artifacts. Finally, in the last section, in Chapters 5 and 6, I introduced and then presented my grandmother's and mother's personal narratives, thus creating an immediate resource for Toba Batak women's history and Indonesian American history.

The past three years of accompanying Rony to Indonesia and to Europe have been illuminating for me. Perhaps one of the largest gains is that, in assisting my mother to collect and document her father's history, my grandfather Gerhard L. Tobing has become real to me as well. Although Rony has told stories about my grandfather all my life, it was difficult for me to know him, as I was separated from his memory through geography, time, and war. All my life, he was more of a shadowy figure in the family's story, having passed away in 1947. But, as we have pored over the papers and photographs in Indonesia, the Netherlands, and Germany, my grandfather has begun to emerge for me not just as a historical figure, but as a family member to whom I feel a real link. Stories and artifacts do that for us—they enable us to know people from the past in important ways, even if we do not have the same relationship with them that we have with people whom we know firsthand. Marianne Hirsch calls this "postmemory," where the knowledge of past people and events is so intimate that younger generations feel as if they have a direct connection.[1]

And so this brings me to the afternoon when we are honoring my grandfather at the Veterans' Cemetery in August 2019. Before this day, I never was the one to say the final prayers, leaving it to the oldest members there to bring us together as a group, honor the relatives, and make that connection across generation and time. Furthermore, the prayers usually were said in Batak and Indonesian. But on this occasion, it was my turn, as well as my responsibility. When it was time to say a prayer, I volunteered myself. Although I spoke in English, I told my grandfather that we honored his memory, and all that he had given us. I remembered his life as a doctor, his emphasis on education, and his duty to helping others. And I told him that even though we younger generations were spread across countries and continents, we thought of him and tried to live up to the standards he had set. I remember speaking from the heart to him, not only to honor him, but also my elders, especially my mother, who had so supported me in this journey of history and reclamation. In that moment, I stepped forward to be a memorykeeper, linking past, present, and future.

I know that one of the biggest gifts that my mother has given me is not just a connection to the past, but her willingness to accept that my relationship to the past is different, especially as someone who was born and whose life is on the other side of the world from the family village. I am careful not to make presumptions about my relationship to Batak culture: after now decades of

---

1 Marianne Hirsch, *The Generation of Postmemory: Writing and Visual Culture after the Holocaust*, Kindle ebook (New York: Columbia University Press, 2012), 34.

learning, I still feel very much a student in this regard. But being a daughter of a daughter for me still is a political identity, and a way of honoring not only my grandmother, mother, and other ancestors, but also the gendered knowledges which they have passed on to me.

This continuing relationship to the past is something that I also bring to other aspects of my life, namely my work as an Asian American Studies professor. As I watch my students navigate difficult family histories, often spread across oceans and continents like mine, I tell them I am descended from many generations on my mother's side, and that we remember the time before the colonizers came. I offer my family's history as a way to see the role of interimperialism, including the often overlooked role of the United States in Indonesia, and how it produced Indonesian migration to the United States in the Cold War. I ask them to consider the politics that shape our understandings of 'Southeast Asia' and 'Asian American,' and what this tells us about US culture. And I encourage them to value the stories and document the photographs, as family history is a precious legacy, however fraught it might be.

Perhaps, ultimately, this is the role of memorykeepers. We go forward into the future, retaining the past for upcoming generations, knowing they may not fully comprehend or value what we are offering them in that moment. Nevertheless, we continue, secure in the knowledge that the past is important, and that what lies ahead cannot be discerned without understanding previous times. It is challenging labor, but also fulfilling work that defines our sense of self, and our gendered ties to the past and future.

As I complete the writing of this book in Summer 2020, these issues have become all the more urgent with the onset of the Covid-19 pandemic. Overseas travel has become much more problematic with the present crisis, especially for older people like my mother. While the last few years of research and writing have been very challenging, I also recognize that the knowledge I gained regarding my family's history has been of significant worth. Had we waited until a more convenient time to travel, the possibility would have been irrevocably lost.

As an Indonesian American, I know that the children of the diaspora will have other connections to the culture of 'home'—we have other ways of being, we speak different languages, and learn the past from alternate positionalities. We will not be 'authentic' when we 'return' to cultures that we do not know and that must be learned. However, my grandmother and mother have taught me that our relationship to others endures, even if the stories that bind you to the past and connect you forward to the future are spoken by you in a different language. And when we are called to be memorykeepers, it is important to take up that labor too, balanced as we are in time among the stories we have learned, the stories we are keeping for others, and the stories that remain to be discovered.

Timeline

1902	R. Gerhard Mangidotua Lumban Tobing (RGLT) born June 30, 1902
1911	RGLT attended Hollands Batakse School, Sigompulon (1911–17);
	H.L. Tobing (HLT) born in Bekala on the east coast of Sumatra, close to Arnhemia (now Pancur Batu)
1916	(approximate) HLT's family moved to Rampah where her father is station master
1917	RGLT attended Europeesche Lagere School, Jakarta (1917–18)
1918	RGLT attended School Tot Opleiding Voor Indische Artsen, Jakarta (STOVIA) (1918–28);
	HLT lived with extended family in Harean, went to school in Sigompulon
1922	HLT moved to dormitory in Sigompulon
1926	HLT's Hollands-Inlandsche School graduation
	HLT attended Meisjeskweekschool voor Inlandsche Onderwijzeressen (MKS) (1926–30)
1928	RGLT posted in Semarang (1928–29)
1929	RGLT, Hospital Head, Amuntai, Kalimantan (1929–33)
1930	HLT finished school;
	RGLT and HLT marry
1931	Raja Apoel P. Loembantobing (RAPL) born
1932	Minar Tobing Rony (MTR) born
1933	RGLT posted to Semarang (1933–35)
1935	RGLT, Hospital Head, Mardi Dojo Hospital, Magetan (1935–37)
1937	RGLT at Leiden University (1937–39);
	HLT, RAPL, MTR in Pearaja (1937–39)
1939	RGLT, Hospital Head, Bengkalis, (1939–45)
1940	RAPL, MTR at school in Siantar (1940–42)
1942	Japanese Occupation (1942–45);
	HLT and RAPL (1943–45), MTR in Bukit Batu (1944–45)
1943	DTM (Demak Tobing Mark) born
1945	RGLT, Hospital Head, Siak Sri Indrapura
1946	RGLT, Hospital Head, Katarina Hospital, Kisaran;
	Kapten Dokter ALRI and Majoor Dokter TNI (Army and Navy titles) (1946–47)
1947	Bistok P.L. Tobing (BPLT) born;
	Dutch return to Indonesia in First Police Action;
	RGLT killed during battle on July 29

© KONINKLIJKE BRILL NV, LEIDEN, 2021 | DOI:10.1163/9789004436237_011

1948	HLT teaching in Medan (1948–64);
	HLT, Chairman, Women's Christian Association for the Province of North Sumatra (1948–57)
1956	RAPL to United States
1957	HLT Member of the Provincial Council representing the Women Christian Association of North Sumatra (1957–61)
1958	MTR to United States
1961	RAPL returns to Indonesia
1960	Demak Tobing Mark (DTM) to United States
1962	MTR and A. Kohar Rony (AKR) marry
1964	HLT begins teaching Indonesian at Yale University in New Haven (1964–79)
1970	BPLT in United States (1970–81)
1979	HLT, part-time teaching and retirement in United States and Indonesia
1985	Dorothy B. Fujita-Rony (DFR) stays in Pearaja after college graduation
1994	HLT passes away at home in Pearaja

Glossary

Please note that this glossary is specific to the book, as some of these terms may carry multiple meanings depending on use and context.

1 Batak

adat   cultural and legal code for life and spirituality
amang uda   uncle
anak ni amangtua   son of an uncle
bangun-bangun   leafy vegetable
boru   daughter, also bride-receiving clans
boru ni raja   daughter of a raja
demang   government official
dalihan na tolu   *dalihan* (cooking stones), *na tolu* (the three); metaphor for social structure consisting of alliances among clan (*marga*), bridegiving clans (*hula hula*), bridetaking clans (*boru*)
dongan sabutuha   of the same father, males of the same father's clan
gondang   drum
gondang debata   godly music, special music with drumming for the gods
hula hula   bridegiver's family, also bridegiving clans
inanta ni   widow
marga   clan system
nahinan   the former, the deceased
Ompu   title used for rank of grandparents, honorific
Ompung boru   grandmother
ompung   grandparent
raja   king
Rajanami   my *raja*, my lord, my king
Si Singamangaraja   The Singamangaraja
sopo   building structure used to store rice, also a meetingplace
tabanan   person caught in war who became a slave, prisoner
tulang   maternal uncle whether immediate or once or twice removed, such as mother's brother
tortor   a kind of dance
ulos   woven ceremonial Toba Batak cloth or blanket
ulos ni tondi   *ulos* given to a pregnant woman

2   Indonesian

abang   term meaning older brother, term of respect used with a name

Bı Kepandaian Puteri   two-year educational program comparable to junior college degree in home economics

BI Inggeris   two-year educational program comparable to junior college degree for the English language

babi panggang   roast pork

babi kecap   soy sauce pork

babu   maid

berudang dibalik batu   literally, shrimp that is hiding behind a stone or rock, meaning person who has ulterior motives

cendol   kind of drink with tapioca droplets in palm sugar and coconut milk

chitney   small buses

datu   indigenous healer

daun singkong   tapioca leaves

daun ubi   sweet potato leaves

Deli   sultanate on the east coast of Sumatra

demang   government official, now *bupati*

dukun   indigenous healer

Fakultas Ekonomi Universitas HKBP Nommensen   Faculty of Economics, HKBP Nommensen University

gado gado   salad with peanut sauce

gadu gadu   path between the plants in the field

gang   alley

Gerakan Wanita Indonesia (Gerwani)   Indonesian Women's Movement

guling   long pillow

gurita   special girdle

homang   magical dwarf

· *Ibu*   term of address for teacher, older lady, respected lady even if it is a young woman

jalan   street

kak   short for *kakak* or big sister

kangkong   water spinach

kebaya   blouse tunic worn by women

kepala negeri   political leader, district head

kiai   mystical leader

kuli   usually refers to Javanese laborers that the Dutch brought to Sumatra during colonial period, commonly considered perjorative term

Makam Pahlawan   veterans' or heroes' cemetery

mama   mother

nyonya   mrs., ma'am

padi   uncooked rice with the husk

pak   term of address, Mr

pancur   bathing and washing place

pang long   logging company

panu   white skin disease

pasanggrahan   guest house, hotel

Pemerintah Revolusioner Republik Indonesia (PRRI)   Revolutionary Government of the Republic of Indonesia

pendeta   minister

perahu   boat

Persatuan Wanita Republik Indonesia (Perwari)   Indonesia's Women's Association

Persatuan Wanita Kristen Indonesia (PWKI)   Indonesian Christian Women's Association

PWKI Sumatera Utara   Indonesian Christian Women's Association, North Sumatra

Poh An Tui   name refers to Pao An Tui, World War II political organization for Chinese Indonesians

Partai Kristen Indonesia (Parkindo)   Indonesian Christian Party

pisang   banana

pontianak   fairy (from legend that if a pregnant woman dies, she becomes this kind of fairy)

qadi   Muslim judge

rambutan   type of lychee

rupiah   currency of Indonesia

sado   horse cart

sagu   starch taken from the pith of sago palm trees

sambal   hot sauce

sarong   cloth wrapped around lower part of the body and fastened at waist

satay   grilled meat on skewers

sawah   rice field

Sekolah Bidan   midwifery school

Sekolah Guru Kepandaian Puteri (SGKP)   home economics teachers' training school with an Indonesian-language curriculum

Sekolah Guru Kepandaian Puteri Katolik (SGKP Katolik)   Catholic home economics teachers' training school

Sekolah Kepandaian Puteri Kristen (SKP Kristen)   Christian home economics school

Sekolah Menengah Pertama (SMP)   junior high

Sekolah Guru Taman Kanak-Kanak Persatuan Wanita Kristen Indonesia (SGTKPWKI)   training school for kindergarten teachers by PWKI, the Indonesian Christian Women's Association

Sekolah Menengah Atas (SMA)   senior high school

Sekolah Sambungan   Malay-language school, two-year fourth and fifth grade after three-year *Sekolah Desa*, village school

senjata hidup   your livelihood

songket   cloth woven with gold or silver thread in special pattern

susu kaleng   canned milk

Tuan   Mr

Universitas HKBP (Huria Kristen Batak Protestan) Nommensen   Nommensen University

Universitas Sumatra Utara   North Sumatra University

wedana   civil servant (*camat* in present day)

3   Dutch

Algemene Middelbare School (AMS)   senior high school

Assistent Resident   high civil servant of the Dutch, rank below *Resident*

Boswezen   Forestry Service

Burgerlijke Ziekeninrichting   general public hospital

chef   in this context, short for *station chef* or station master, as *chef* also can mean a cook

Clerk Methode   kind of curriculum program

Controleur   comptroller

Deli Maatschappij   name of railway company in Deli

Europeesche   European

Europeesche Lagere School (ELS)   European elementary school, Dutch elementary school in this context

Europees Dokter   doctor who was educated or trained in Europe

gezaghebber   lieutenant governor

griffier   registrar

guilder   Dutch currency

Hollandsche Amerikaans Petroleum Maatschappij (HAPM)   Holland American Oil Company, later became Uniroyal

Hollandsche-Bataksche school (HBS)   Dutch-Batak School

Hollands-Inlandsche School (HIS)   Dutch-Native school

Inlanders   natives, can be in a perjorative sense

Inlandsche Middelbare School (IMS)   four-year junior high school for natives

juffrouw   term of address for female teacher, Miss

Klein Ambtenaars Examen   small civil exam, like having a diploma from a Dutch elementary school

Meisjeskweekschool (MKS)   teachers' training school for women

Meisjeskweekschool voor Inlandsche Onderwijzeressen (also MKS)   school for educating native women teachers for four years with the Dutch language as the medium of instruction

Mevrouw   Mrs

Mynheer   Mr

Nederlands Koloniale Petroleum Maatschappij   subsidiary of Standard Oil

open naaiwerk   kind of embroidery where thread is removed and patterns are made in the open spaces

Opleiding School voor Vak Onderwijzeressen (OSVO)   teachers' training school for home economics

opzichter   postmaster

Residentie van Tapanuli   civil servant, local government area for a particular geographical area

School tot Opleiding van Inlandsche Artsen (STOVIA)   School for the Education of Native Doctors

Voorbereidend Hoger Onderwijs School (VHO)   senior high school

voorklas   introductory class.

zuster   sister

4   Japanese

dai toa   older brother, big country

hei-ho   military worker for Japanese, likely forcibly conscripted

hiragana   Japanese syllabary, component of writing system

kanji   Japanese syllabary, component of writing system

katakana   Japanese syllabary, component of writing system

kempetai   Japanese military intelligence service

kinrohosi   outdoor and agricultural activities

Momotaro-san   "Peach Boy," a famous children's story

obasan   grandmother

sakura   flower

taiso   exercise, the physical calisthenics with music

tenno heika   emperor of Japan

5   French

croquettes   patties usually with meat and/or vegetables
ragout   seasoned dish with vegetables made with butter, flour, and salt

6   German

mutter   mother

Bibliography

Adib, Faishol. "Living with Uncertainty: The Experience of Undocumented Indonesian Migrant Workers in Philadelphia, Pennsylvania." Master of Arts thesis, Center for International Studies, Ohio University, June 2010, https://etd.ohiolink.edu/.

Aritonang, Jan S. *Mission Schools in Batakland (Indonesia), 1861–1940*. Translated by Robert R. Boehlke. Leiden: E.J. Brill, 1994.

Ballantyne, Tony, and Antoinette Burton. *Empires and the Reach of the Global: 1870–1845*. Cambridge, MA: Belknap Press, An Imprint of Harvard University Press, 2014.

Ballantyne, Tony, and Antoinette Burton. "Empires and the Reach of the Global: 1870–1845." In *A World Connecting: 1870–1945 (A History of the World)*, edited by Emily S. Rosenberg, 285–434. Cambridge, MA: Belknap Press, an Imprint of Harvard University Press, 2012.

Bastian, Jeannette. "Documenting Communities through the Lens of Collective Memory." In *Identity Palimpsests: Archiving Ethnicity in the U.S. and Canada*, edited by Dominique Daniel and Amalia Levi, 15–33. Sacramento, CA: Litwin Books, 2014.

Bender, Daniel E., and Jana K. Lipman. *Making the Empire Work: Labor & United States Imperialism*. New York: New York University Press, 2015.

Bender, Daniel E. and Jana K. Lipman. "Introduction: Through the Looking Glass: U.S. Empire through the Lens of U.S. History." In *Making the Empire Work: Labor & United States Imperialism*, edited by Daniel E. Bender and Jana K. Lipman, 1–32. New York: New York University Press, 2015.

Benitez, J. Francisco, and Laurie J. Sears. "Passionate Attachments to Area Studies and Asian American Studies: Subjectivity and Diaspora in the Transpacific." In *Transpacific Studies: Framing an Emerging Field*, edited by Janet Hoskins and Viet Thanh Nguyen, Chapter 6. Honolulu: University of Hawai'i Press, 2014. Kindle ebook.

Bowen, John. "The Development of Southeast Asian Studies in the United States." In *The Politics of Knowledge: Area Studies and the Disciplines*, edited by David L. Szanton, 386–425. Berkeley: University of California Press, 2004.

Bui, Long T. *Returns of War: South Vietnam and the Price of Refugee Memory*. New York: New York University Press, 2018.

Burbank, Jane, and Frederick Cooper. *Empires in World History: Power and the Politics of Difference*. Princeton, NJ: Princeton University Press, 2010.

Burton, Antoinette, ed. *Archive Stories: Facts, Fictions, and the Writing of History*. Durham, NC: Duke University Press, 2005.

Byas, Trikartikaningsih. "Music and Indonesian American Experience: Gamelan, Angklung, and Dangdut." In *Southeast Asian Diaspora in the United States: Memories and Visions, Yesterday, Today, and Tomorrow*, edited by Jonathan H.X. Lee, 236–249. Newcastle upon Tyne: Cambridge Scholars Publishing, 2015.

Byl, Julia. *Antiphonal Histories: Resonant Pasts in the Toba Batak Musical Present.* Middletown, CT: Wesleyan University Press, 2014.

Byrd, Jodi A. *The Transit of Empire: Indigenous Critiques of Colonialism.* Minneapolis: University of Minnesota Press, 2011. Kindle ebook.

Camacho, Keith L. *Cultures of Commemoration: The Politics of War, Memory, and History in the Mariana Islands.* Honolulu, HI: University of Hawai'i Press, 2011.

Caswell, Michelle. *Archiving the Unspeakable: Silence, Memory, and the Photographic Record in Cambodia.* Madison: University of Wisconsin Press, 2014.

Caswell, Michelle. "Inventing New Archival Imaginaries: Theoretical Foundations for Identity-Based Community Archives." In *Identity Palimpsests: Archiving Ethnicity in the U.S. and Canada,* edited by Dominique Daniel and Amalia Levi, 35–55. Sacramento, CA: Litwin Books, 2014.

Chang, Jason Oliver. "Four Centuries of Imperial Succession in the Comprador Pacific," *Pacific Historical Review,* 86/2 (May 2017): 193–227. DOI: http://dx.doi.org/10.1525/phr.2017.86.2.193.

Chang, Queeny. *Memories of a Nonya.* Singapore: Marshall Cavendish International (Asia) Private Limited, 2016. Kindle ebook.

Cheng, Cindy I-Fen. *Citizens of Asian America: Democracy and Race during the Cold War.* New York: New York University Press, 2013. Kindle ebook.

Chi, Sang, and Emily Moberg Robinson. *Voices of the Asian American and Pacific Islander Experience* (2 vols.). Santa Barbara, CA: ABC-CLIO/Greenwood, 2012. Ebook.

Cho, Grace M. *Haunting the Korean Diaspora: Shame, Secrecy, and the Forgotten War.* Minneapolis: University of Minnesota Press, 2008.

Choy, Catherine Ceniza. *Empire of Care: Nursing and Migration in Filipino American History.* Durham, NC: Duke University Press, 2006.

Choy, Catherine Ceniza, and Judy Tzu-Chun Wu, eds. *Gendering the Trans-Pacific World.* Leiden: Brill, 2017.

Choy, Catherine Ceniza, and Judy Tzu-Chun Wu. "Gendering the Trans-Pacific World." In *Gendering the Trans-Pacific World,* edited by Catherine Ceniza Choy and Judy Tzu-Chun Wu, 3–9. Leiden: Brill, 2017.

Clancy-Smith, Julia, and Frances Gouda, eds. *Domesticating the Empire: Race, Gender, and Family Life in French and Dutch Colonialism.* Charlottesville: University Press of Virginia, 1988.

Cook, Terry, "Evidence, Memory, Identity, and Community: Four Shifting Archival Paradigms," *Archival Science,* 13/2 (2013): 104. DOI 10.1007/s10502-012-9180-7.

Coppel, Charles A. ed. *Violent Conflicts in Indonesia: Analysis, Representation, Resolution.* London: Routledge, Taylor & Francis Group, 2006. Kindle ebook.

Cordova, Fred. *Filipinos, Forgotten Asian Americans: A Pictorial Essay, 1763–circa 1963.* Dubuque, IA: Kendall/Hunt, 1983.

Cruz, Denise. "Notes on Trans-Pacific Archives." In *Gendering the Trans-Pacific World,* edited by Catherine Ceniza Choy and Judy Tzu-Chun Wu, 10–19. Leiden: Brill, 2017.

Cruz, Denise. *Transpacific Femininities: The Making of the Modern Filipina*. Durham, NC: Duke University Press, 2012.

Cunningham, Clark E. *The Postwar Migration of the Toba-Bataks to East Sumatra*. Cultural Report Series, No. 5. New Haven, CT: Yale University, Southeast Asia Studies, 1958.

Cunningham, Clark E. "Unity and Diversity among Indonesian Migrants to the United States." In *Emerging Voices: Experiences of Underrepresented Asian Americans*, edited by Huping Ling, 90–108. New Brunswick, NJ: Rutgers University Press, 2008. PDF ebook.

Danico, Mary Yu, ed. "Indonesian Americans." In *Asian American Society: An Encyclopedia*, Thousand Oaks, CA: SAGE, 2014, 518–520. http://dx.doi.org/10.4135/9781452281889.

Day, Iyko. *Alien Capital: Asian Racialization and the Logic of Settler Colonial Capitalism*. Durham, NC: Duke University Press, 2016. Kindle ebook.

Day, Tony. "Honored Guests: Indonesian-American Cultural Traffic, 1953–1957." In *Heirs to World Culture: Being Indonesian, 1950–1965*, edited by Jennifer Lindsay and Maya H.T. Liem, 119–141. Leiden: KITLV Press, 2012, http://dx.doi.org/10.26530/OAPEN_403204.

di Leonardo, Micaela. "The Female World of Cards and Holidays: Women, Families, and the Work of Kinship." *Signs*, 12/3 (Spring 1987): 440–453.

Diller, Tony. "Heritage Learning of Southeast Asian Languages." In *Southeast Asian Studies: Pacific Perspectives*, edited by Anthony Reid, 257–266. Tempe: Program for Southeast Asian Studies Monograph Series, Arizona State University, 2003.

Duong, Lan P. *Treacherous Subjects: Gender, Culture, and Trans-Vietnamese Feminism*. Philadelphia, PA: Temple University Press, 2012. Kindle ebook.

Errington, Joseph. *Linguistics in a Colonial World: A Story of Language, Meaning, and Power*. Malden, MA: Blackwell Publishing, 2008.

Espiritu, Augusto. "Inter-Imperial Relations, the Pacific, and Asian American History," *Pacific Historical Review*, 83/2 (May 2014): 238–254.

Espiritu, Augusto. "Inter-Imperial Relations, the Pacific, and Asian American History." In *Pacific America: Histories of Transoceanic Crossings*, edited by Lon Kurashige, 178–191. Honolulu: University of Hawai'i Press, 2017. Kindle ebook.

Espiritu, Yến Lê. *Body Counts: The Vietnam War and Militarized Refuge(es)* Berkeley: University of California Press, 2014.

Espiritu, Yến Lê. *Home Bound: Filipino American Lives across Cultures, Communities, and Countries*. Berkeley: University of California Press, 2003.

Espiritu, Yến Lê, Lisa Lowe, and Lisa Yoneyama, "Transpacific Entanglements." In *Flashpoints for Asian American Studies*, ed. Cathy J. Schlund-Vials, Chapter 10. New York: Fordham University Press, 2018. Kindlebook.

Finch, Aisha K. *Rethinking Slave Rebellion in Cuba: La Escalera and the Insurgencies of 1841–1844*. Chapel Hill: The University of North Carolina Press, 2015.

Foster, Anne L. *Projections of Power: The United States and Europe in Colonial Southeast Asia, 1919–1941.* Durham, NC: Duke University Press, 2010.

Gee, Emma, ed. *Counterpoint: Perspectives on Asian America.* Los Angeles: University of California, Los Angeles, Asian American Studies Center, 1976.

Genthe, Arnold, and John Kuo Wei Tchen. *Genthe's Photographs of San Francisco's Old Chinatown.* New York: Dover, 1984.

Gonzalez, Vernadette Vicuña. "Making Aloha: Lei and the Cultural Labor of Hospitality." In *Making the Empire Work: Labor & United States Imperialism,* edited by Daniel E. Bender and Jana K. Lipman, 161–181. New York: New York University Press, 2015.

Gordon, Avery F. *Ghostly Matters: Haunting and the Sociological Imagination.* Minneapolis: University of Minnesota Press, 2008. Kindle ebook.

Gouda, Frances. "Good Mothers, Medeas, or Jezebels: Feminine Imagery in Colonial and Anticolonial Rhetoric in the Dutch East Indies, 1900–1942." In *Domesticating the Empire: Race, Gender, and Family Life in French and Dutch Colonialism,* edited by Julia Clancy-Smith and Frances Gouda, 236–254. Charlottesville: University Press of Virginia, 1988.

Gouda, Frances. *Dutch Culture Overseas: Colonial Practice in the Netherlands Indies, 1900–1942.* Amsterdam: Amsterdam University Press, 1995.

Gouda, Frances, with Thijs Brocades Zaalberg. *American Visions of the Netherlands East Indies/Indonesia: U.S. Foreign Policy and Indonesian Nationalism, 1920–1949.* Amsterdam: Amsterdam University Press, 2002. PDF ebook. https://www.jstor.org/stable/j.ctt45kf5g.

Gouda, Frances, and Julia Clancy-Smith. "Introduction." In *Domesticating the Empire: Race, Gender, and Family Life in French and Dutch Colonialism,* edited by Julia Clancy-Smith and Frances Gouda, 1–20. Charlottesville: University Press of Virginia, 1988.

Gould, James W. *Americans in Sumatra.* Leiden: Martinus Nijhoff, 1961.

Groeneboer, Kees. *Gateway to the West: The Dutch Language in Colonial Indonesia, 1600–1950: A History of Language Policy.* Amsterdam: Amsterdam University Press, 1998.

Herod, Andrew. *Labor Geographies: Workers and the Landscapes of Capitalism.* New York: The Guilford Press, 2001.

Heryanto, Ariel. "Can There Be Southeast Asians in Southeast Asian Studies?" In *Knowing Southeast Asian Subjects,* edited by Laurie J. Sears, 75–108. Seattle: University of Washington Press, in association with Singapore: NUS Press, 2007.

Hesselink, Liesbeth. *Healers on the Colonial Market: Native Doctors and Midwives in the Dutch East Indies.* Leiden: KITLV Press, 2011. PDF ebook, DOI: 10.26530/OAPEN_400271.

Hirsch, Marianne. *The Generation of Postmemory: Writing and Visual Culture after the Holocaust*. New York: Columbia University Press, 2012. Kindle ebook.

Hirshberg, Lauren. "Home Land (In)security: The Labor of U.S. Cold War Military Empire in the Marshall Islands." In *Making the Empire Work: Labor & United States Imperialism*, edited by Daniel E. Bender and Jana K. Lipman, 335–355. New York: New York University Press, 2015.

Hoskins, Janet and Viet Thanh Nguyen. *Transpacific Studies: Framing an Emerging Field*. Honolulu: University of Hawai'i Press, 2014. Kindle ebook.

Hsu, Madeline Y. *The Good Immigrants: How the Yellow Peril Became the Model Minority*. Princeton, NJ: Princeton University Press, 2015. Kindle ebook.

Imada, Adria L. *Aloha America: Hula Circuits through the U.S. Empire*. Durham, NC: Duke University Press, 2012.

Ingersoll, Earl G., ed. *Breaking the Alabaster Jar: Conversations with Li-Young Lee*. Rochester, NY: BOA Editions Ltd., 2006. Kindle ebook.

Kahin, Audrey R. and George McT. Kahin. *Subversion as Foreign Policy: The Secret Eisenhower and Dulles Debacle in Indonesia*. New York: The New Press, 1995.

Ketelaar, Eric. "Cultivating Archives: Meanings and Identities," *Archival Science*, 12 (2012): 19–33. DOI: 10.1007/s10502-011-9142-5.

Kim, Jodi. *Ends of Empire: Asian American Critique and the Cold War*. Minneapolis: University of Minnesota Press, 2010.

Kim, Junyoung Verónica. "Asia—Latin America as Method: The Global South Project and the Dislocation of the West," *Verge: Studies in Global Asia*, 3/2 (Fall 2017): 97–117. DOI: 10.5749/vergstudglobasia.3.2.0097.

Kipp, Rita Smith. "Emancipating Each Other: Dutch Colonial Missionaries' Encounter with Karo Women in Sumatra, 1900–1942". In *Domesticating the Empire: Race, Gender, and Family Life in French and Dutch Colonialism*, edited by Julia Clancy-Smith and Frances Gouda, 211–235. Charlottesville: University Press of Virginia, 1988.

Klein, Christina. *Cold War Orientalism: Asia in the Middlebrow Imagination, 1945–1961*. Berkeley: University of California Press, 2003.

Koo, Hui-Lan. *An Autobiography as Told to Mary Van Renssalaer Thayer*, 2nd edn. N.p.: Planbridge Editions, 2017. Kindle ebook.

Kurashige, Lon, ed. *Pacific America: Histories of Transoceanic Crossings*. Honolulu: University of Hawai'i Press, 2017. Kindle ebook.

Kwik, Greta. *The Indos in Southern California*. New York: AMS Press, Inc., 1989.

Kwon, Heonik. "The Transpacific Cold War." In *Transpacific Studies: Framing an Emerging Field*, edited by Janet Hoskins and Viet Thanh Nguyen, Chapter 2. Honolulu: University of Hawai'i Press, 2014. Kindle ebook.

Lai, Him Mark, Genny Lim, and Judy Yung. *Island: Poetry and History of Chinese Immigrants on Angel Island, 1910–1940*. San Francisco, CA: Chinese Culture Foundation, 1980.

Lam, Mariam. "Foreword." In *Southeast Asian Diaspora in the United States: Memories and Visions, Yesterday, Today, and Tomorrow*, edited by Jonathan H.X. Lee, xxii–xxvi. Newcastle upon Tyne: Cambridge Scholars Publishing, 2015.

Lee, Doreen. *Activist Archives: Youth Culture and the Political Past in Indonesia*. Durham, NC: Duke University Press, 2016.

Lee, Jonathan H.X., Fumitaka Matsuoka, Edmond Yee, and Ronald Y. Nakasone, eds. *Asian American Religious Cultures* (2 vols). Santa Barbara, CA: ABC-CLIO, 2015. Ebook.

Lee, Jonathan H.X., ed. *Southeast Asian Diaspora in the United States: Memories and Visions, Yesterday, Today, and Tomorrow*. Newcastle upon Tyne: Cambridge Scholars Publishing, 2015.

Lee, Li-Young. *The Winged Seed: A Remembrance*. Rochester, NY: BOA Editions, Ltd., 2013.

Lindsay, Jennifer and Maya H.T. Liem, eds. *Heirs to World Culture: Being Indonesian, 1950–1965*. Leiden: KITLV Press, 2012. DOI: 10.26530/OAPEN_403204.

Locher-Scholten, Elsbeth. "So Close and Yet So Far: The Ambivalence of Dutch Colonial Rhetoric on Javanese Servants in Indonesia, 1900–1942." In *Domesticating the Empire: Race, Gender, and Family Life in French and Dutch Colonialism*, edited by Julia Clancy-Smith and Frances Gouda, 131–153. Charlottesville: University Press of Virginia, 1988.

Locher-Scholten, Elsbeth. *Women and the Colonial State: Essays on Gender and Modernity in the Netherlands Indies, 1900–1942*. Amsterdam: Amsterdam University Press, 2000.

Long, David F. "'Martial Thunder': The First Official American Armed Intervention in Asia," *Pacific Historical Review*, 42/2 (January 1, 1973): 143–162.

Lowe, Lisa. *The Intimacies of Four Continents*. Durham, NC: Duke University Press, 2015. Kindle ebook.

Mabalon, Dawn Bohulano. *Little Manila Is in the Heart: The Making of the Filipina/o American Community in Stockton, California*. Durham, NC: Duke University Press, 2013.

Maekawa, Kaori. "The *Heiho* during the Japanese Occupation of Indonesia." In *Asian Labor in the Wartime Japanese Empire: Unknown Histories*, edited by Paul K. Kratoska, 179–195. London: Routledge, 2015. Kindle ebook.

Man, Simeon. *Soldiering through Empire: Race and the Making of the Decolonizing Pacific*. Berkeley: University of California Press, 2018. Kindle ebook.

Manalansan IV, Martin F., and Augusto F. Espiritu. "The Field: Dialogues, Visions, Tensions, and Aspirations." In *Filipino Studies: Palimpsests of Nation and Diaspora*, edited by Martin F. Manalansan IV and Augusto F. Espiritu, 1–11. New York: New York University Press, 2016.

Martínez, Julia, and Adrian Vickers. "Indonesians Overseas: Deep Histories and the View from Below," *Indonesia and the Malay World*, 40/117 (July 2012): 111–121. DOI: 10.1080/13639811.2012.683667.

Matsuda, Matt K. *Pacific Worlds: A History of Seas, Peoples, and Cultures*. Cambridge: Cambridge University Press, 2012.

Matsumoto, Valerie J. *City Girls: The Nisei Social World in Los Angeles, 1920–1950*. Oxford: Oxford University Press, 2014. Kindle ebook.

McCoy, Alfred W. *In the Shadows of the American Century: The Rise and Decline of US Global Power*. Chicago, IL: Haymarket Books, 2017. Print and Kindle ebook.

Missbach, Antje. "Moral Comforts from Remaining in Exile: Snapshots from Conflict-Driven Indonesian Exiles." In *Routledge Handbook of Diasporic Studies*, edited by Robin Cohen and Carolin Fischer, 197–205. London: Routledge, 2018. PDF ebook. https://doi.org/10.4324/9781315209050.

Munson, Samuel, William Thompson, and Henry Lyman. *Memoirs of the Rev. Samuel Munson, and the Rev. Henry Lyman: Late Missionaries to the Indian Archipelago, with the Journal of their Exploring Tour*. New York: D. Appleton & Co., 1839, electronic reproduction. [S.l.]: HathiTrust Digital Library, 2011. https://babel.hathitrust.org/cgi/pt?id=coo.31924068350697&view=1up&seq=7.

Nguyen, Mimi Thi. *The Gift of Freedom: War, Debt, and Other Refugee Passages*. Durham, NC: Duke University Press, 2012.

Nguyen, Viet Thanh, and Janet Hoskins. "Introduction: Transpacific Studies: Critical Perspectives on an Emerging Field." In *Transpacific Studies: Framing an Emerging Field*, edited by Janet Hoskins and Viet Thanh Nguyen. Honolulu: University of Hawai'i Press, 2014. Kindle ebook.

Ninh, Erin Khue. *Ingratitude: The Debt-Bound Daughter in Asian American Literature*. New York: New York University Press, 2011. Kindle ebook.

Obama, Barack. *The Audacity of Hope: Thoughts on Reclaiming the American Dream*. New York: Crown, 2006.

Padoongpatt, Mark. *Flavors of Empire: Food and the Making of Thai America*. Berkeley: University of California Press, 2017. Kindle ebook.

Pattynama, P., "Secrets and Danger: Interracial Sexuality in Louis Couperus's *The Hidden Force* and Dutch Colonial Culture around 1900." In *Domesticating the Empire: Race, Gender, and Family Life in French and Dutch Colonialism*, edited by Julia Clancy-Smith and Frances Gouda, 84–107. Charlottesville: University Press of Virginia, 1988.

Pearson, Stuart. *Bittersweet: The Memoir of a Chinese Indonesian Family in the Twentieth Century*. Research in International Studies, Southeast Asia Series No. 117. Athens: Ohio University Press, 2008.

Pedersen, Paul B. *Batak Blood and Protestant Soul: The Development of National Batak Churches in North Sumatra*. Grand Rapids, MI: William B. Eerdmans Publishing Company, 1970.

Phwan, Peter. "Game of Chance: Chinese Indonesians Play Asylum Roulette in the United States," 2009 article. In *Voices of the Asian American and Pacific Islander Experience*, edited by Sang Chi and Emily Moberg Robinson, 370–371 (2 vols). Santa Barbara, CA: ABC-CLIO, LLC Greenwood, 2012. Ebook.

Punzalan, Ricardo L. "Archival Diasporas: A Framework for Understanding the Complexities and Challenges of Dispersed Photographic Collections," *The American Archivist*, 77/2 (Fall/Winter, 2014): 326–349.

Rafael, Vicente L. "Southeast Asian Studies in the Age of Asian America." In *Southeast Asian Studies: Pacific Perspectives*, edited by Anthony Reid, 257–266. Tempe: Program for Southeast Asian Studies Monograph Series, Arizona State University, 2003.

Raymundo, Rizaline R., ed. *Tomorrow's Memories, A Diary, 1924–1928*. Honolulu: University of Hawai'i Press, in association with UCLA Asian American Studies Center Los Angeles.

Reid, Anthony. "Island of the Dead. Why Do Bataks Erect *tugu*?" In *The Potent Dead: Ancestors, Saints and Heroes in Contemporary Indonesia*, edited by Henri Chambert-Loir and Anthony Reid, 88–102. Honolulu: University of Hawai'i Press, 2002.

Robinson, Geoffrey B. *The Killing Season: A History of the Indonesian Massacres, 1965–66*. Princeton, NJ: Princeton University Press, 2018. Kindle ebook.

Robinson, Greg. "The Great Unknown and the Unknown Great: The Incarceration of Indonesians in the United States: An Untold Story," *Nichi Bei Weekly*, January 8, 2015. Available at: https://www.nichibei.org/2015/01/the-great-unknown-and-the-unknown-great-the-incarceration-of-indonesians-in-the-united-states-an-untold-story/ (accessed January 4, 2018).

Rodenburg, Janet. *In the Shadow of Migration: Rural Women and Their Households in North Tapanuli, Indonesia*. Leiden: KITLV Press, 1997.

Rodgers, Susan, ed. and trans. *Telling Lives, Telling History: Autobiography and Historical Imagination in Modern Indonesia*. Berkeley: University of California Press, 2005.

Roosa, John. *Pretext for Mass Murder: The September 30th Movement and Suharto's Coup d'État in Indonesia*. Madison: The University of Wisconsin Press, 2006. Kindle ebook.

Rosenberg, Emily S. *A World Connecting: 1870–1945 (A History of the World)*. Cambridge, MA: Belknap Press, an Imprint of Harvard University Press, 2012.

Rowe, John Carlos. "Transpacific Studies and the Cultures of U.S. Imperialism." In *Transpacific Studies: Framing an Emerging Field*, edited by Janet Hoskins and Viet Thanh Nguyen, Chapter 5. Honolulu: University of Hawai'i Press, 2014. Kindle ebook.

Salman, Michael. "Toward a Performative Theory of Southeast Asian Studies: Reflections from UCLA on the Future of Southeast Asian Studies and the Reversibility of Comparisons." In *Southeast Asian Studies: Pacific Perspectives*, edited by Anthony Reid, 267–294. Tempe: Program for Southeast Asian Studies Monograph Series, Arizona State University, 2003.

Santikarma, Degung. "Monument, Document and Mass Grave: The Politics of Representing Violence in Bali." In *Beginning to Remember: The Past in Indonesian Present*, edited by Mary S. Zurbuchen, 312–323. Singapore: Singapore University Press, in association with the University of Washington Press, Seattle, 2005.

Schlund-Vials, Cathy J. *Flashpoints for Asian American Studies*. New York: Fordham University Press, 2018. Kindle ebook.

Schlund-Vials, Cathy J. *War, Genocide, and Justice: Cambodian American Memory Work*. Minneapolis: University of Minnesota Press, 2012.

Schlund-Vials, Cathy J. "Epilogue: Re-Sighting Southeast Asian American Studies." In *Southeast Asian Diaspora in the United States: Memories and Visions, Yesterday, Today, and Tomorrow*, edited by Jonathan H.X. Lee, 317–326. Newcastle upon Tyne: Cambridge Scholars Publishing, 2015.

Setiyawan, Dahlia Gratia. "Collective and Conflicting Memories in Narratives of Migration from Indonesia to the United States." In *Southeast Asian Diaspora in the United States: Memories and Visions, Yesterday, Today, and Tomorrow*, edited by Jonathan H.X. Lee, 14–30. Newcastle upon Tyne: Cambridge Scholars Publishing, 2015.

Shigematsu, Setsu, and Keith L. Camacho, eds. *Militarized Currents: Toward a Decolonized Future in Asia and the Pacific*. Minneapolis: University of Minnesota Press, 2010.

Simpson, Bradley R. *Economists with Guns: Authoritarian Development and U.S.-Indonesian Relations, 1960–1968*. Stanford, CA: Stanford University Press, 2008.

Singh, Nikhil Pal. *Race and America's Long War*. Berkeley: University of California Press, 2017. Kindle ebook.

Soja, Edward W. *Postmodern Geographies: The Reassertion of Space in Critical Social Theory*. London: Verso, 1989.

Steedly, Mary Margaret. *Hanging without a Rope: Narrative Experience in Colonial and Postcolonial Karoland*. Princeton, NJ: Princeton University Press, 1993.

Steedly, Mary Margaret. *Rifle Reports: A Story of Indonesian Independence*. Berkeley: University of California Press, 2013.

Stewart, Susan. *On Longing: Narratives of the Miniature, the Gigantic, the Souvenir, the Collection*. Durham, NC: Duke University Press, 1993. Kindle ebook.

Stoler, Ann Laura. *Duress: Imperial Durabilities in Our Times*. Durham, NC: Duke University Press, 2016. Kindle ebook.

Stoler, Ann Laura. "Intimidations of Empire: Predicaments of the Tactile and the Unseen." In *Haunted by Empire: Geographies of Intimacy in North American History*, edited by Ann Laura Stoler, 1–22. Durham, NC: Duke University Press, 2006.

Stoler, Ann Laura. *Along the Archival Grain: Epistemic Anxieties and Colonial Common Sense*, Princeton, NJ: Princeton University Press, 2009.

Stoler, Ann Laura. "Tense and Tender Ties: The Politics of Comparison in North American History and (Post) Colonial Studies." In *Haunted by Empire: Geographies of Intimacy in North American History*, edited by Ann Laura Stoler, 23–67. Durham, NC: Duke University Press, 2006.

Strassler, Karen. *Refracted Visions: Popular Photography and National Modernity in Java*. Durham, NC: Duke University Press, 2010.

Szanton, David L., ed. *The Politics of Knowledge: Area Studies and the Disciplines*. Berkeley: University of California Press, 2004.

Szanton, David L. "Introduction: The Origin, Nature, and Challenges of Area Studies in the United States." In *The Politics of Knowledge: Area Studies and the Disciplines*, edited by David L. Szanton, 1–33. Berkeley: University of California Press, 2004.

Tachiki, Amy. *Roots: An Asian American Reader*. Los Angeles: University of California, Los Angeles, Asian American Studies Center, 1971.

Tajuddin, Azlan, and Jamie Stern. "From Brown Dutchmen to Indo-Americans: Changing Identity of the Dutch-Indonesian (Indo) Diaspora in America," *International Journal of Politics, Culture, and Society*, 28/4 (2015): 349–376. DOI: 10.1007./s10767-015-9197-z.

Tanaka, Michiko, and Akemi Kikumura. *Through Harsh Winters: The Life of a Japanese Immigrant Woman*. Novato, CA: Chandler & Sharp, 1981.

Tang, Eric. *Unsettled: Cambodian Refugees in the NYC Hyperghetto*. Philadelphia, PA: Temple University Press, 2015.

Trouillot, Michel-Rolph. *Silencing the Past: Power and the Production of History*. Boston, MA: Beacon Press, 1995. Kindle ebook.

Tyner, James A. *America's Strategy in Southeast Asia: From the Cold War to the Terror War*. Lanham, MD: Rowman & Littlefield, 2007.

Um, Khatharya. "Exiled Memory: History, Identity, and Remembering in Southeast Asia and Southeast Asian Diaspora," *Positions*, 20/3 (2012): 831–850. DOI: 10.1215/10679847-1593564.

Um, Khatharya. *From the Land of Shadows: War, Revolution, and the Making of the Cambodian Diaspora*. New York: New York University Press, 2015. Kindle ebook.

Van Bemmelen, Sita T. *Christianity, Colonization, and Gender Relations in North Sumatra: A Patrilineal Society in Flux*. Leiden: Koninklijke Brill NV, 2017.

Vergouwen, J.C. *The Social Organisation and Customary Law of the Toba-Batak of Northern Sumatra*. Leiden: Martinus Nijhoff, 1964.

Westad, Odd Arne. *The Global Cold War: Third World Interventions and the Making of Our Times*. Cambridge: Cambridge University Press, 2007. Kindle ebook.

Williams, Raymond. *Marxism and Literature*. Oxford: Oxford University Press, 1978.

Woo, Susie. "Transpacific Adoption: The Korean War, US Missionaries, and Cold War Liberalism." In *Pacific America: Histories of Transoceanic Crossings*, edited by Lon Kurashige, 161–177. Honolulu: University of Hawai'i Press, 2017. Kindle ebook.

Ying, Wu Da, and Peilin Ngo. *Chinese-Indonesian: An Odyssey through Racism, Ethnicity, and Science*. Irvine, CA: Wu Da Ying and Peilin Ngo (self-published), 2013.

Yoneyama, Lisa. *Cold War Ruins: Transpacific Critique of American Justice and Japanese War Crimes*. Durham, NC: Duke University Press, 2016. Kindle ebook.

Yuh, Ji-Yeon. "Moving within Empires: Korean Women and Trans-Pacific Migrations." In *Gendering the Trans-Pacific World*, edited by Catherine Ceniza Choy and Judy Tzu-Chun Wu, 107–113. Leiden: Brill, 2017.

Zurbachen, Mary S., ed. *Beginning to Remember: The Past in Indonesian Present*. Singapore: Singapore University Press, in association with the University of Washington Press, Seattle, 2005.

Zurbachen, Mary S. "Historical Memory in Contemporary Indonesia." In *Beginning to Remember: The Past in Indonesian Present*, edited by Mary S. Zurbachen, 3–32. Singapore: Singapore University Press, in association with the University of Washington Press, Seattle, 2005.

Index

Archives
  Archiv- und Museumsstiftung der VEM
    (AMS der VEM)   1, 8, 132, 136–139, 148
  Leiden University, Special Collections   1,
    8, 112–114, 132, 133–136, 139, 148
  Women's personal collections   3, 5–6,
    116–118, 122–131, 139
Artifacts
  Biographical artifacts   124–126, 139
  Cultural practices artifacts   125, 129–131,
    139
  Recreated artifacts   125, 126–129, 139
  Reintegrated artifacts   125, 131–139

Empires
  Cultures of domesticity   65–72, 166, 168,
    222–224
  Interimperialism and   19–21
  Multilingualism and   39–44
  Sumatra and   23, 35–39
  Transformations under   21–22

Germany and Rhenish Mission   24, 29–33,
    157–158

Indonesian American History
  Archives and   95
  Comparison to other communities   56
  Field of study   8–13
  Dutch Indonesians   45–46
  Exchange programs   46
  Interimperialism and   55–56
  Knowledge workers and   49–55, 57–58
  Maritime laborers   45, 233–234
  Migration of students   46–47
  Migration of teachers   46–47
  U.S. Cold War migration   45–47, 56–58
  Diaspora and   12–13
Interimperialism
  Indonesia and   3–4, 21–39
  Multilingualism and   39–44, 57
  Temporality and   42–44

Japan and World War II
  Empire and World War II   34–35
  Language and   40–41

Occupation   34–35, 118–119, 182–187,
    209–210, 212

Loembantobing, Cornelia   28, 112–113
Loembantobing, Raja Apoel
  Assisting US scholars   50–51, 191, 230
  Birth   201
  Bengkalis   181, 185, 209, 210
  Bukit Batu   184–185, 213–214
  Early education   181–182
  Migration to US   51, 191, 232
  Pearaja   180, 202, 203, 215
  Return to Indonesia   54, 235
  Role in Minar T. Rony's migration to US
    53, 84–85, 191, 232–233
  Yale University, study at   51, 54, 191–192,
    232–234
Loembantobing, Raja Aris
  Images of   112–114
  Family of   112–113, 169
Lumbantobing, Raja Pontas
  History of   24, 62, 100, 151
Lyman, Henry
  Samuel Munson and   36, 41–42, 100,
    151

Mark, Demak Tobing
  Bukit Batu   214
  Kisaran   216–217
  Medan   229, 230
  Methodist English School   43–44, 53,
    230
  Migration to US   53, 191–192
  Studying in US   235–236
Munson, Samuel
  Henry Lyman and   36, 41–42, 100, 151

Netherlands
  Dutch colonial system   23–24, 27, 29,
    32–33, 163–164
Nommensen, Ludwig Ingwer   24, 28, 62, 100,
    151

Rony, A. Kohar
  Education   53–54
  Library of Congress   54, 237, 242

Migration to U.S.   53–54
Minar T. Rony and   235–238, 242
Rony, Minar T.
  Assisting US scholars   51–53, 110–111,
    230–232
  Bengkalis   185, 203–206, 208–212
  Birth   201
  Bukit Batu   77, 212–215
  Cultures of domesticity and   214,
    223–225, 229
  Economics, study of   228–229
  Family history   199–201
  Geographical knowledge   1–2
  Grandmother in Simorangkir   218–220
  Interest in becoming doctor   80, 109,
    204–206, 211–212, 222
  Japanese Occupation   34–35, 208–215
  Labor as young woman   77–78, 215, 230
  Library of Congress   239, 241–242
  Los Angeles   242
  Loss of father   79–80, 120–122, 216–218
  Mentoring by father   83–84, 105–107,
    204–206, 210–212
  Marriage to A. Kohar Rony   85, 235–237
  Migration to US   49–50, 84–85,
    232–234
  Multilingualism and education   39–40
  Nommensen University   229
  Opleiding School voor Vak
    Onderwijzeressen (OSVO)   71,
    222–226
  Pearaja   59, 199, 202–203, 215–222,
    244–245
  Retirement   242–243
  Siantar, as student   104–105, 181–182,
    207–208
  Siantar, as teacher   71–72, 226–228
  Simorangkir, family   108, 218–220
  Sekolah Guru Kepandaian Puteri (SGKP)
    72, 228
  SGKP Katolik   230
  SKP Kristen   71–72, 226–228
  Wartime   208–210, 214–215, 217–218
  Washington, D.C. and   238
  Yale University and   49–50, 234–238

Si Singamangaraja XII
  Leader of Toba Batak   27, 29, 169
  Memories of   101, 199

Toba Batak
  Dutch colonialism and   24, 27, 29, 32
  Marriage and family   63–65
  Patrilineality and   59–63
Tobing, Artauli R. M. Panggabean
  Marriage   237
  Researcher   133, 147–148
  Travel   243
Tobing, Bistok P.L.
  Boyhood   206, 229
  High School   193
  Infancy   217
  Marriage   237
  Researcher   133, 136, 147–148
  Travel   243
Tobing, H.L.
  Adat, discussion of   155–157
  Bengkalis   180–181, 203
  Birth and early childhood   153–154
  Bukit Batu   183–184
  Christianity and German missionaries
    30, 32–33, 157–159, 162, 164, 166
  Cultures of domesticity and   166, 168,
    171–173
  Dutch colonialism   101–104, 163–164,
    171–173, 177–178
  Education   32–33, 68–70, 164–169,
    200–201
  Japanese Occupation   182–187
  Josua Institut   189–190
  Magetan   175–177
  Marriage   170–171, 200
  Medan, work in   78–79, 81–83, 189–191,
    229–230
  Meisjeskweekschool voor Inlandsche
    onderwijzeressen (MKS)   22–23,
    69–71, 167–169, 201
  Midwifery   177, 201–202
  Migration to US   54–55, 85, 87, 192–193,
    238–239
  Parents and siblings   153–155, 161
  Pearaja   75–77, 87, 177–180, 196–197,
    202–203
  Persatuan Wanita Kristen Indonesia
    (PWKI)   82–83, 190–191, 229–230
  Sekolah Guru Taman Kanak-Kanak
    Persatuan Wanita Kristen Indonesia
    (SGTKPWI)   81–82, 190–191

Tobing, H.L. (cont.)
  Tarutung as young child   81, 159–161,
    200–201
  Widowhood   78–79, 120–122, 188–190,
    217–218
  Yale University and   54–55, 192–193, 195,
    238–239
Tobing, Raja Gerhard Lumban
  Amuntai   22, 171, 173
  Bengkalis   180–181, 182, 204–206
  Death of   78, 118–122, 187–188, 217–218
  Education   33, 40, 75, 170, 177–178, 202
  Family history   169–170, 199–200
  Japanese Occupation   41, 182, 185, 186,
    210
  Kisaran   187–188, 216–217
  Leiden University   40, 75, 177–178, 202
  Magetan   175
  Marriage   22, 170–171
  Medical doctor   83, 171, 173–175, 181,
    187–188, 204–206, 210, 211–212, 216
  School tot Opleiding van Inlandsche
    Artsen (STOVIA) [School for the
    Education of Native Doctors]   33, 40,
    164, 170, 178
  Semarang   173–174, 201

United States and Indonesia,
  Cold War interests   44–50, 53–54
  Economic investments   37–39
  Interimperial Context   35–39
  US Scholars   50–53, 191, 230–232
  Sumatra   35–39

Women's Memorykeeping
  Artifacts and   116–118, 122–124, 139–140
  Labor of   4–5, 95, 97–98
  Memory and silences   98–99, 107–111
  Political space and   91, 93–94
  Temporality and   7–8, 97–98

Zuster Frieda Lau
  Education and   32–33, 68–69, 166

www.ingramcontent.com/pod-product-compliance
Lightning Source LLC
Chambersburg PA
CBHW071734270326
41928CB00013B/2667